First Approaches
to the
NORTHWEST
COAST

Sebastian Cabot

Christopher Columbus

Ferdinand Magellan

Vitus Bering

Sir Francis Drake

*Wedgewood medallion of
Captain James Cook*

Captain James Cook

OPPOSITE

ABOVE

Near Icy Cape – August 18, 1778

"The Resolution *beating through the ice with the* Discovery *in danger in the distance."*

COPIED BY DANIEL I. BUSHNELL JR. FROM A BOOKLET CALLED "DRAWINGS BY
JOHN WEBBER OF NATIVES OF THE NORTHWEST COAST OF AMERICA" – 1778

BELOW

The Resolution *&* the Discovery *in Nootka Sound – 1778*

PORTION OF AN ORIGINAL SKETCH DRAWN ON THE SPOT BY JOHN WEBBER

Vancouver's Discovery *on the Rocks and* Chatham
From Vancouver Public Library
Collection

*Home of
Captain Cook
when he
was a boy*

*First monument
to Captain Cook
erected by
Captain Palliser
on his family
estate, The Vache,
Chalfont St
Giles, Bucks.*

INSCRIPTION
COVERS
FOUR SIDES.
PHOTO TAKEN BY
FRANCES WOODWARD,
PROVINCIAL
ARCHIVES, 1966

TO THE MEMORY OF
CAPTAIN JAMES COOK.
The ableſt and moſt renowned
Navigator this or any country
hath produced.

He raiſed himſelf, ſolely by his merit,
from a very obſcure birth, to the rank
of Poſt Captain in the royal navy, and
was, unfortunately, killed by the Savages
of the iſland Owhyhee, on the 14ᵗʰ of February
1779, which iſland he had, not long before,
diſcovered, when proſecuting his third
voyage round the globe.
He poſſeſſed, in an eminent degree, all the
qualifications requiſite for his profeſſion
and great undertakings; together with the
amiable and worthy qualities of the beſt men.
Cool and deliberate in judging; ſagacious
in determining; active in executing; ſteady
and perſevering in enterpriſing from
vigilance and unremitting caution; unſubdued
by labour, difficulties, and diſappointments
fertile in expedients; never wanting

TOP LEFT
Captain John Meares

TOP RIGHT
"Callicum & Maquilla –
Chiefs of Nootka Sound"
OPP. PAGE 109 – MEARES' VOYAGES

Captain John Meares's
long boat entering the
Strait of Juan de Fuca
FROM AN OLD ENGRAVING

Captain Nathaniel Portlock
&
Captain George Dixon
purchasing skins from Indians

In the Strait of Juan de Fuca
"Captain Gray obliged to fire upon the natives who disregarded his orders to keep off."
(S.S. Columbia)
BY E. G. PORTER

Friendly Cove – Nootka Sound
DRAWN BY W. ALEXANDER FROM A SKETCH ON THE SPOT
BY H. HUMPHRIES IN VANCOUVER'S JOURNAL

Launching of the North West America *at Nootka Sound*

The Spanish Insult to the British Flag
at Nootka Sound – 1789
The seizure of Captain Colnett of the
Argonaut *by Don Esteban Martinez*

First
Approaches
to the

NORTH-
WEST
COAST

BY

DEREK PETHICK

DOUGLAS & McINTYRE
VANCOUVER

Douglas & McIntyre Ltd.
1875 Welch Street, North Vancouver
British Columbia

Canadian Shared Cataloguing in
Publication Data

Pethick, Derek, 1920-
First approaches to the Northwest coast

Bibliography: p. 224

ISBN 0-88894-061-0

1.
Northwest coast of North America–
Discovery and exploration.
2.
Fur trade–Northwest, Pacific.

I. Title.

FC3821.P48   970.00964′3

F851.5.P

PRINTED AND BOUND IN CANADA BY
THE HUNTER ROSE COMPANY

Contents

*This book
is for
Alfred and Martha
Carlsen*

Foreword

One of the most notable developments of recent years has been the increased interest of Canadians in the earlier days of their history. The purpose of this book is to stimulate this trend, especially for British Columbians.

Material dealing with the first voyages to the Pacific northwest coast has appeared in a wide variety of publications over the years. I think, however, that this may be the first time that detailed accounts of these voyages have been collected in a single volume and placed in their larger historical setting.

My thanks are due to the Canada Council for giving me some financial assistance while this work was in preparation; also to the staff of the Provincial Archives, Victoria, for their cordial co-operation and assistance.

DEREK PETHICK
Saanich, 1976.

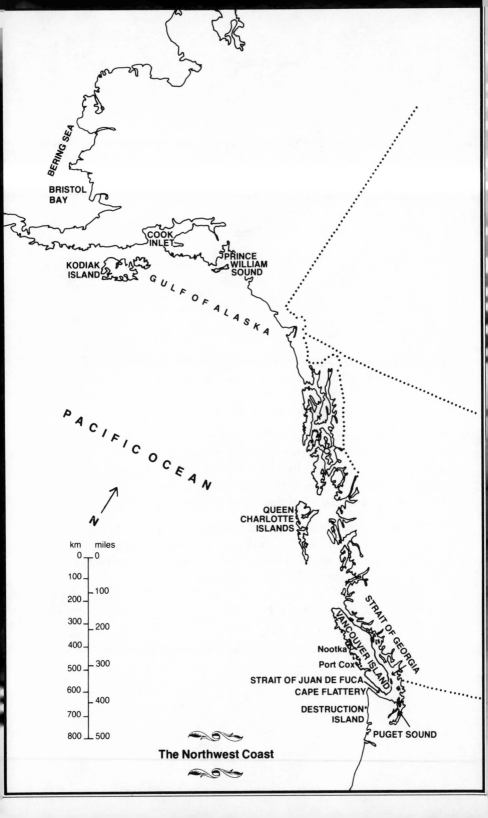

BERING SEA

BRISTOL
BAY

COOK
INLET

PRINCE
WILLIAM
SOUND

KODIAK
ISLAND

G U L F   O F   A L A S K A

P A C I F I C   O C E A N

N

km   miles
0   0

100   100

200   200

300

400   200

500   300

600   400

700

800   500

QUEEN
CHARLOTTE
ISLANDS

STRAIT OF GEORGIA

VANCOUVER ISLAND

Nootka

Port Cox

STRAIT OF JUAN DE FUCA

CAPE FLATTERY

DESTRUCTION
ISLAND

PUGET SOUND

The Northwest Coast

I pressed on, taking fresh trouble for granted.

—Juan Francisco de la Bodega y Quadra.

CHAPTER ONE

The Space Race Begins

Today man stands upon the moon;

tomorrow, perhaps, upon the distant planets. Yet this great journey into the unknown, advancing now with giant strides, began some centuries ago with tiny steps. The exploration of the Pacific northwest was but a logical stage along the way. In the eighteenth century the white man first set foot in what is now British Columbia, but to place this discovery in its proper perspective we must go back even earlier.

One thing we can say with certainty: the whole story would have been further advanced at every point if the Roman Empire had not been shipwrecked on the rocks of the Dark Ages. The Europeans' knowledge of the geographical outlines of the world was far more extensive and accurate in the second century of the Christian era than it was in the fifteenth, as may be seen by comparing the best maps of the two periods. Ptolemy of Alexandria, about 150 A.D., produced a geography in which the latitude and longitude of a very large number of places were listed. From this, maps could be easily constructed in which the vast area from Ireland to China, as well as the northern half of Africa, could be delineated with considerable accuracy. His work represented the accumulated knowledge of merchants who passed along the great trade routes, bringing silks and spices from Africa and the Orient to grace elegant dinner parties held in the sophisticated metropolis on the Tiber.[1]

Then night descended; western Europe was overrun by the Goths, who themselves were pushed westward by pressures from central Asia. The impetus of civilization was lost, science and scholarship dried up, and people retreated into fortified towns. Feudalism attempted to establish local law and order, but wider horizons, both geographical and intellectual, became clouded over with fear, ignorance, and legend. In the eighth century the rise of Islam interposed a hostile creed, backed by fanatical warriors, between Europe and Asia. Later, Vikings and Norsemen swept down from northern latitudes to harry the coasts of Europe. Survival, not progress, became the watchword, while life became "solitary, poor, nasty, brutish and short."

So long centuries passed. Then about the year 1100 the dark clouds began parting. The cities of northern Italy were the first to witness a revival of commerce, no doubt because they were the ports through which goods from the Moslem lands and beyond made their way into Europe. With commerce came wealth, with wealth came leisure, with leisure came learning, and gradually the western world moved upward from its nadir.

Several factors kept the process, once begun, in motion. The universal desire for a more comfortable existence was a constant stimulus to the acquisition of goods which might make possible an easier or more elegant mode of life. This desire helped to increase commerce, as many of the goods were not produced in Europe. There were always a few spirits eager to push beyond the horizons of either the physical or the intellectual world, and there was a small but steady improvement in the means by which such exploration might be furthered. The compass, apparently invented in China and later used by Arab traders in the Indian Ocean, had appeared in Europe by the end of the thirteenth century; aids to navigation such as the astrolabe were being developed from more primitive instruments; ships were being built capable of withstanding the buffets of the open sea; gunpowder gave its possessors an incalculable advantage over those without it; paper was replacing parchment, making the diffusion of knowledge and the production of maps more rapid; our modern system of numbers superseded the cumbersome Roman numerals; and the rivalry of nations, so prominent a feature of the modern world, embarked upon its long and stormy career.

Moreover, long before Columbus a few courageous travellers – some impelled by the commercial impulse, others by the wish to convert the heathen to Christianity, a few perhaps by mere curiosity – had travelled across the plains of Asia, seen the wonders and mysteries of the East, and returned to tell the tale. Marco Polo, at the end of the thirteenth century, is by far the best known, but throughout the Middle Ages there were nearly always a few hardy souls struggling across burning deserts and through snow-choked mountain passes, or standing lost in wonder before the splendors of golden Samarkand or the court of the Great Khan of Tartary.[2]

In addition, there is a respectable body of evidence to support the assertion that, long before the Middle Ages had ended, daring Scandinavian voyagers had discovered and colonized Iceland and Greenland, and possibly even touched the coast of North America. Cultural contact with Europe was later lost and the European settlements, either as a result of disease, intermarriage or warfare with the local natives, eventually disappeared. Thus this interesting series of events, recorded in the "Icelandic Sagas," does not seem to have embedded itself in the consciousness of continental Europe, or to have exerted any influence on the subsequent development of exploration.[3]

Such was the situation as the fifteenth century opened, and not many years of it had elapsed before it was evident that western Europe had entered a new phase. As it happened, the nation which had the honor of signalling the new era was one of the poorest in Europe and was reckoned to be unfavorably located. The Mediterranean was the great highway of commerce, crossed daily by scores of merchantmen; Portugal, by contrast, faced the inhospitable open Atlantic, and was thus thought to be at a permanent disadvantage. Yet her ships were to unlock the door to a world wider than even the most daring had suspected to exist.

The key to the door was the fortress of Ceuta on the southern shore of the Strait of Gibraltar. From this base, Moslem power not only menaced European ships, but was available to support Granada, a Moorish kingdom, in what is now southern

3

Spain, that was destined to prove the last outpost of Mohammedan power in Europe. In the summer of 1415 a great Portuguese armada, reported to have comprised a hundred ships and eighty thousand men, captured Ceuta. This battle is much less well known, at least in English-speaking countries, than the battle of Agincourt fought in the same year, but it was beyond doubt of greater historical significance.

This soon became apparent in the years that followed. Just as the defeat of the Spanish Armada in 1588 was to release a great flood of national energy in England and bring her at once into the front rank of powers, so now the local but decisive victory over the traditional Moslem foe marked the opening of Portugal's great age.

The ultimate commander of the Portuguese forces at Ceuta had been King John, but the men in the field had been led by his three sons. The youngest of these, Prince Henry, was now to gain undying fame as the leader of an even sterner, more important struggle: that against the proud Atlantic itself.

In 1415 no doubt his grand design was as yet unborn, and the moment of its conception is unknown. Perhaps one day while pacing the shore alone, watching the gray waves endlessly breaking, breaking endlessly against the western edge of Europe, it came to him that "Peace hath her victories no less renowned than war," and he resolved to win new laurels in another field. In any case, he established a scientific station (as we should call it today) at Sagres, on the extreme southwestern point of his country. From here, until his death in 1460, Prince Henry the Navigator, as he came to be called, although he never went to sea, directed his offensive against the almost unknown Atlantic.

His motto was "resolve to do greatly," and he spared no effort to live up to it. The really resounding triumphs of navigation were to come in the half-century after his death, but one can hardly doubt that they would have been long delayed if Prince Henry had not prepared the way for them.

Year by year he sent out fresh expeditions; each one crept a little farther down the western coast of Africa, then returned with an account of its discoveries. These were collated, incorporated into maps, and made available for other navigators, thus creating a body of authentic geographical knowledge. Meanwhile the writings of Ptolemy were translated from Greek into Latin, and these gave a powerful confirmation and impetus to the new current of affairs.

Moreover, these developments began dissipating an older body of legends – fears and fantasies which long had daunted even the bravest hearts. It soon became apparent that there were no fabulous monsters or boiling rivers waiting to engulf whole ships. Instead, the newly discovered areas seemed not only peaceful but warm and fertile, and soon their products were flowing back to Europe. The timorous were reassured, the merchants of Portugal grew richer, and the voyages of exploration became more daring.

Soon after 1470 the first ships crossed the equator; in 1482 or 1483 another reached the mouth of the Congo and the men set up inscribed stone pillars – possibly an early form of "taking possession";[4] in 1488 Bartholomew Diaz rounded the Cape of Good Hope and sailed into the Indian Ocean. He might well have continued on to India, but his weary crew insisted on turning back.

These were achievements remarkable enough, yet now the pace merely quickened. Like a thunderclap came news from an astonishing direction: a Genoese mariner, Christopher Columbus, sailing under the flag of Spain, had sailed westward across the Atlantic and found land, fertile and friendly, in the west!

He had actually reached Watling Island in the Bahamas, but it was assumed (by no one more firmly than himself) that this was merely an outlying part of Asia. The islands in the area were called, as they are to this day, the (West) Indies. At all events, there was no lack of volunteers for three subsequent voyages by Columbus to the Caribbean, and some of the characteristic features of European civilization, such as the Christian religion, were soon transplanted to the New World.

From this time on, nearly every year brought new discoveries. In 1497, Vasco da Gama was put in charge of a small Portuguese flotilla. Leaving Lisbon on July 7, he sailed down the coast of Africa, rounded the Cape of Good Hope, and in May 1498 anchored at Calicut on the coast of India, thus becoming the first European to reach that country by sea. When he returned to his native land, he displayed to King Manuel vessels of gold and silver, precious jewels, and "calico" cloth named from its place of origin.

Encouraged by the favors showered on da Gama, others of his countrymen were soon attempting to equal his success. At the turn of the century, Pedro Cabral, endeavoring to take the same route to Asia, was carried so far to the west in mid-Atlantic that he touched the coast of Brazil; then, sailing eastward, he rounded the Cape of Good Hope and was soon trading successfully with the natives of Ceylon. Within the next few years his countrymen were firmly established at Goa, Ormuz (at the mouth of the Persian Gulf), and Malacca. In 1513 the Portuguese reached Canton, and within a few decades they had formed a settlement at nearby Macao.

A Spanish captain, Vicente Pinzon, who had once sailed with Columbus as commander of the *Nina*, also touched the coast of South America at this time. Finding that the water in the area was not salt but fresh, he realized that a great river must have its mouth nearby, and he became the first European to enter the Amazon.

Other Spaniards were soon making major discoveries. Ponce de Leon, who had also once sailed with Columbus, explored Puerto Rico and the Bahamas, and then on Palm Sunday, 1513, landed in a beautiful region which he named Florida. Juan Bermudez was shipwrecked in 1515 on a previously unknown island, which was henceforth called Bermuda. In 1519 Alonso de Pineda sailed along the coast of what is now Texas until he reached Mexico.

Another Spaniard, Vasco Núñez de Balboa, had meanwhile achieved an even more spectacular distinction. With a band of his countrymen and numerous Indian followers, he crossed the Isthmus of Panama in September 1513, and from the top of a hill he became the first white man to behold the immeasurable prairie of the Pacific. Then, descending to its eastern shore, he waded out a little way into the water and, holding up his sword, took possession of the world's largest ocean, and any coasts that it might wash, in the name of Spain. As we shall see, this action was to be cited during the Nootka crisis of 1790 as evidence that the entire western coast of both North and South America belonged to Spain.

6

News of this soon reached the ears of a Portuguese navigator, Ferdinand Magellan. Although he had already proved his worth in voyages to the East Indies, when he asked King Manuel for a fleet to reach them by sailing west across the Atlantic, he was rebuffed and as a result entered the service of Spain. In 1519 he was given command of a fleet of five ships and he set sail for the South American coast. He then made his way southward along it, and in the spring of 1520 anchored in about 50° south latitude.

Here a mutiny broke out which Magellan put down with great severity, executing some of the rebels and marooning others. One ship which he sent southward to reconnoitre was lost, but some of its crew were eventually rescued. Moving ever farther down the coast, he discovered the passage into the Pacific, named the Strait of Magellan to this day. At this point, one ship secretly abandoned the expedition and sailed back across the Atlantic, reaching Seville in May 1521.

In November the three remaining ships made their way into the Pacific and began the long voyage across its endless expanses. After nearly dying of starvation, they eventually reached the Philippines, where they were once again in touch with European civilization. Magellan himself never lived to return to his native land, for he was killed in a skirmish with some natives.

The survivors sailed on, but were soon so short-handed that they had to abandon one of their three ships. Another, the *Trinidad*, was also soon left behind. The sole survivor, the *Victoria*, sailed on across the Indian Ocean, carrying by now a rich cargo of cloves. Eventually, in September 1522, eighteen men, almost at the end of their strength, staggered ashore at Seville. The first voyage around the world was over.

This was perhaps the greatest feat of this astonishing age; yet others were almost as striking. Another Spaniard, Hernando Cortes, landing on the western shore of the Caribbean in 1519, advancèd rapidly on Mexico City (then called Tenochtitlan), seized the local ruler, Montezuma, and maintained control of the country for some time, while looting it of vast sums of gold.

Other Spaniards in this period discovered and explored what is now called Lower (Baja) California, and one, Alvarez de Vaca, crossed the continent, partly by land and partly by sea, from Florida to the Gulf of California. This was the farthest north that such a passage had been made, and was possibly the first time that a white man had seen the mouth of the Mississippi.

Another of nature's wonders was also soon revealed to the eyes of white men. Francisco de Coronado explored what are now the southwestern United States and saw the great herds of buffalo, while in 1540 others acting under his orders gazed into the seemingly bottomless depths of the Grand Canyon. Meanwhile Hernando de Soto explored the region north and northwest of Florida, and then marched westward until he reached the Mississippi in 1541. De Soto himself died of fever the following spring, but in 1543 the survivors of his expedition made their way down the great river on rafts to its mouth, eventually reaching Spanish outposts in the Caribbean.

Another Spaniard, Francisco Pizarro, set out in 1531 from near the Isthmus of Panama, marched far down the western coast of South America, and discovered the highly sophisticated culture of the Incas. He proceeded to demonstrate his own variety of sophistication by capturing their king, Atahualpa, extracting an entire room full of gold as a ransom for him, and then killing him for not being a Christian.

One of the world's greatest mountain ranges and one of its greatest rivers now fell victim to European determination and audacity. Francisco de Orellana, leaving Guayaquil on the western coast of South America in February 1541, crossed the Andes and, in a primitive boat which he and his followers built, sailed down the Amazon to its mouth, which they reached in August 1542.

The wide reaches of the Pacific also saw Spanish ships in this period. As early as 1527 they began going from Mexico to the Moluccas, and in 1565 they made the first voyage eastward across the Pacific to Mexico. This route would be used by Manila traders for over two hundred years. In 1595 Mendana, who had earlier sailed westward from Callao to discover the Solomons, discovered the Marquesas, and a decade later Quiros may have touched at Tahiti.

Most exploration so far had been confined to tropical or semi-tropical areas, mainly because their products – spices and

8

precious metals – were those most valued by Europeans. More northerly climes were not, however, neglected, and during this period their outlines were also being steadily revealed.

English exploration in the north Atlantic began with John Cabot, an Italian who had made Bristol, England, his home port. In 1497 he sailed westward from there and was soon exploring the mouth of the St. Lawrence. The following year Sebastian Cabot was in the region of Greenland, Labrador, and Newfoundland. His reports of the extensive fishing grounds in the vicinity of Newfoundland led to the rapid exploitation of this natural resource by many European nations.

The King of France was soon taking an interest in this area. In 1524 he sent out Giovanni Verrazano, an Italian, who explored much of the New England coast, including the harbor of what is now New York, and returned safely to France. In 1534 Jacques Cartier explored the Gulf of St. Lawrence and the Bay of Chaleur, took possession of an undefined area for France, and then returned home. The following year he was back, sailing up the St. Lawrence, past what is now Quebec, as far as Montreal. It was apparent that the river continued westward for a great distance yet, perhaps to China, and hence the name Lachine. In 1541 Cartier returned to the area, but did not add much to geographical knowledge. He may, however, be considered the father of the present "French fact" in Quebec.

English explorers meanwhile continued active, especially in attempts to find a "northwest passage," or "Strait of Anian," through North America to the Pacific. In 1576 and again in 1578 Martin Frobisher explored the coast of Greenland; on the latter expedition he sailed some way into Hudson Strait. John Davis made three voyages to the same area between 1585 and 1587, on the third one reaching 72°N and exploring the strait which now bears his name. In later years, we might note, he wrote a treatise on navigation, discovered the Falkland Islands, and was finally killed by Japanese pirates near Sumatra in 1605. Such was the sort of career which an adventurous spirit might have in this period.

Others were having experiences almost as unusual. In 1577 Francis Drake set off around the world, following approximately the same route taken by Magellan. In one respect, however, he diverged considerably from it, coming well up the western coast of first South and then North America before striking west across the Pacific. Exactly how far north his *Golden Hind* sailed is still a matter of dispute, but it was at least as far as San Francisco Bay, and, some say, nearly as far as Vancouver Island. In any case, he has been given credit for good intentions, the highest mountain on the island being later named after his ship.[5]

A decade later Thomas Cavendish became the second Englishman to circumnavigate the globe. Sailing from Plymouth with three ships in July 1586, he captured so many Spanish ships in South American waters that when he finally got back to his home port in September 1588 (a few weeks after the defeat of the Armada), his sailors were clothed in silk, his sails were made of damask, and his top mast was covered with cloth of gold.[6]

Henry Hudson made several important voyages in the early seventeenth century, some for the Dutch East India Company of Amsterdam. On one of them he sailed up the river which now bears his name. Later, in the service of an English company, he sailed into Hudson Bay and later James Bay, where his party went into winter quarters. Discontent accumulated in their bleak surroundings, and, on June 22, 1611, mutineers put Hudson and some of his men into an open boat and set them adrift. The mutineers, after many adventures and several casualties, made their way back to England, where they were promptly imprisoned but eventually released.

Another Englishman of this period, William Baffin, also left his name on the map. Searching for the northwest passage, he reached 77°45′N, a mark that was to stand for two centuries. In 1616 he passed through Davis Strait and discovered Baffin Bay. On his voyage the route to the tropics eluded him, but he eventually reached them by more conventional means. In later years he surveyed the Red Sea and the Persian Gulf, dying in 1622 of wounds sustained in this area.

As the seventeenth century opened, and commercial rivalry between the major European nations became more marked, Holland began seeking a place in the sun. Soon the Dutch had established themselves in parts of the West Indies and Brazil, and had also gained control of the Moluccas, or Spice Islands, in the Far East, where their empire was to endure into our own time. During much of this period they were the only European power permitted to trade (though on a very restricted basis) with Japan.[7] They also founded a colony in South Africa, where their descendants live to this day, and settled the area around New York, which they called New Amsterdam. Such well-known names as Roosevelt are a testimony to the survival of their stock.[8]

Indeed, for a time there seemed no limit to what this small nation might achieve. In the first half of the seventeenth century Dutch mariners touched the shores of Australia, and in 1642 (the year that Galileo died and Newton was born) Abel Tasman discovered Tasmania and New Zealand. Yet another Hollander, Cornelis Schouten, became the first white man to round Cape Horn, naming it after the town of Hoorn in his native land.

The focus of our story, however, is North America, and here not merely exploration but settlement by Europeans continued. The colony founded in 1585 under the sponsorship of Sir Walter Raleigh on Roanoke Island off the coast of North Carolina vanished mysteriously, but that established in 1607 at Jamestown, Virgina, was to be continuously inhabited from that day to this, and was soon put on a sound economic basis by the production of tobacco for the European market.

All along the western coast of the Atlantic, indeed, there was now much activity. In 1608 Samuel de Champlain founded a French colony at Quebec, while Montreal came into being a few years later. In 1620 the "Pilgrim Fathers" began the settlement of Massachusetts, the Scots established a colony in Nova Scotia in 1627, while by the middle of the century the French had colonies on Martinique and Guadeloupe, both valuable sources of sugar.

Toward the end of the century, the star of Holland began to wane and that of England to rise. In 1664 New Amsterdam was taken by an English fleet and renamed New York, and soon there were English colonies, such as Connecticut, Rhode Island, New Hampshire, New Jersey, and Delaware, stretching along the Atlantic seaboard, as well as one, Pennsylvania, farther inland.

The French, however, had by no means abandoned hope of

11

eventually controlling the entire continent of North America. In 1682, from the region of the Great Lakes, La Salle descended the Mississippi all the way to its mouth, named the area Louisiana in honor of his king, and then once more ascended the river. From this time on, many of his countrymen were to envision it as an artery joining together a great inland empire.

As the decades passed, more of North America saw the coming of Europeans. Early in the seventeenth century Etienne Brulé became the first white man to see Lake Huron; about 1660 Pierre Radisson also carried out extensive explorations in the region of the Great Lakes; Daniel Du Lhut, a few years later, did the same, the modern city of Duluth being named in his honor. A few years later Europeans first saw Niagara Falls. In the closing years of the century Henry Kelsey, in the employ of the Hudson's Bay Company, travelled from the Churchill River toward "the barren grounds," and perhaps reached southern Manitoba.

As the new century dawned, the pace of exploration was maintained by both British and French explorers. Anthony Hendry, starting from Hudson Bay, reached the valley of the Saskatchewan, and traveled some way up it by canoe; La Vérendrye and his sons explored much of the prairie region, the sons reaching the foothills of the Rockies in early 1743. Far to the north, Samuel Hearne reached the Arctic Ocean at the mouth of the Coppermine River in 1771.

Clearly, then, the blank spaces on the map of both the world and North America were being rapidly filled in, and as the eighteenth century moved out into mid-channel, many no doubt took stock of what had been accomplished. The achievements of the previous three centuries had assuredly been tremendous.[9] Most of the general outline of the continents had been charted, with the exception of Antarctica; large parts of the interior of Africa, Australia, and South America were still unknown, but the interior of North America was being systematically penetrated, and its eastern half now held few mysteries.

All this had had a profound effect on the native populations of the world, as Europeans either overwhelmed or ·overawed them with their superior technology and their vitality. Some of the major preoccupations of the white man – the diffusion of Christianity, the establishment of his characteristic political institutions, and the desire for material possessions – had become dominant features of life in the lands where he now held sway. Ways once confined to a small area of the globe had now been diffused to all but the remotest parts of the planet. In other words, West European civilization had become a world civilization, and, backed as it was by the continuous discoveries of western science and technology, seemed likely to dissolve all others, a problem with which many cultures struggle to this day.

So far, however, one part of North America had remained immune to this great transformation. This was the area known today as the Pacific Northwest. The reasons for this were readily apparent. To the east stood the Rocky Mountains, and beyond them the almost uninhabited prairies; to the west was the world's largest ocean, whose Asiatic shores were, at best, the outposts of European civilization; to the north lay an unknown region of mist and fog which merged eventually into a barrier of perpetual ice. If these obstacles could be surmounted or evaded, however, and the rich resources of the area revealed, it was inevitable that the same process would continue here that was already well advanced elsewhere.

So matters stood, three centuries after the first tentative voyages by Portuguese sailors down the western coast of Africa. A number of powerful states were well established in western Europe, and the military, economic, and scientific power at their disposal was rapidly increasing. Now was the time to press onward, to fill in the remaining blank spaces of the map. Inevitably, attention turned to the northwestern coast of North America, and it is the exploration of this area which will now become and remain the central theme of our story.

CHAPTER TWO

Eastward
from
Asia

Nearly
everyone in
British Columbia

is aware of the great westward movement of exploration and settlement which, beginning at the eastern edge of North America some centuries ago, continued until the entire continent was inhabited by people whose forebears came originally from Europe. There is, however, a similar chapter in the history of the human race which is far less well known: this is the great eastward movement of exploration and settlement. Beginning in European Russia, the eastward movement continued until the entire land mass between the Baltic and Bering seas was brought under the control of the tsars, and Russian explorers began to direct their attention toward the shadowy area where Asia and North America either approached each other or were joined. Part of the interest which attaches to British Columbia's history lies in the fact that these two movements reached the Pacific Northwest at approximately the same time.

In what we should call the Middle Ages, Novgorod (near modern Leningrad) was the major center of Slavic power. In the fifteenth century, however, under the vigorous Tsar Ivan III, Moscow became the undisputed capital, and soon brought under its control a large area surrounding it. As time went on, lands farther and farther east were added to the Russian empire. This process continued under a succession of tsars until by the early eighteenth century Russia claimed control over an enormous area stretching from the Baltic to the western shore of the Pacific Ocean. Very little, however, was actually known about the easternmost parts of this vast realm.

Yet slowly the mists of ignorance were dissipated. In 1639 the port of Okhotsk was founded on the Pacific. In 1706 Russians from Europe reached the tip of the Kamchatka peninsula overland and ten years later made the first crossing of the Sea of Okhotsk. Much of the impetus behind this movement was undoubtedly supplied by the search for sables, which abounded throughout eastern Asia.[1] Thus even so early, fur was an important factor in the relations between Europe and the world beyond it. Indeed, this was already apparent in other parts of the planet, The Hudson's Bay Company having been founded in 1670 to exploit the fur trade of North America.

Toward the end of the seventeenth century the most remarkable of all the tsars, Peter the Great, came to the throne, and in the face of violent opposition from a variety of sources set about dragging his country into the modern world. He introduced European dress (though not European liberalism), reformed the calender (though only to the extent of adopting the Julian system, which other countries were abandoning in favor of the Gregorian, so that Russian dates would long be out of step with those elsewhere), encouraged education and industry, built a strong navy, and made plans for an Academy of Sciences. He also carefully maintained the continuity of Russian history in one respect – he ruthlessly exterminated those who opposed his policies.

It is a measure of his greatness that he did not hesitate to travel abroad in search of first-hand knowledge of western Europe. Leaving Moscow in 1697 under an assumed name, but with a large group of advisers who were also expected to learn all that they could, he first visited Germany and Holland. In the latter country this extraordinary man suddenly decided that the only way to understand fully the art of shipbuilding was personally to take part in the process. For four months, while still holding

15

unlimited power of life and death over even the greatest of his subjects, he toiled as a humble worker in the shipyard at Zaandam. Then, having decided that he had learned enough from the Dutch, he went on to England, where he studied watch-repairing and coffin-making before once more going to work in a shipyard, this time at Deptford. Finally, having engaged a wide variety of English experts to aid in his endeavors to modernize his country, Peter returned to Russia, where one of his first acts was to crush a rebellion against his new ideas by having eight hundred active dissenters put to death.[2]

The next few years were largely occupied by wars with Sweden, in which Russia was ultimately successful, and the construction of a grandiose new capital, St. Petersburg, on the shores of the Baltic. Yet all this time, the exploration and exploitation of the two Americas by the other great powers was steadily proceeding. Peter, observing the interest of Spain, France, Holland, and England in the new world, eventually began wondering whether Russia, approaching it from a quite different direction, that is, from eastern Siberia, might not participate in this new phase of European expansion.

One question had still not received a decisive answer: were Asia and North America completely separate continents, or were they joined together somewhere in the northern latitudes? There had long been many who held the first view, as was shown by various unsuccessful attempts to find a northeast passage from the Atlantic across the top of Asia and then south to the Pacific; it had not yet been proved that this was possible. As early as the mid-seventeenth century, however a Cossack named Semyon Deshnev had sent a report to the government offices in Yakutsk in northeastern Siberia. He told how, setting out on a fur-hunting expedition from the mouth of the river Kolyma, which flowed into the Arctic Ocean in 161°E longitude, he had sailed eastward around Cape Chukchi (now called East Cape) and had finally reached land again at the mouth of the river Anadyr on the Pacific. If this report had received the attention of the highest Russian authorities it might have had some effect on both their thought and their actions, but instead it gathered dust for many decades.[3]

Peter now resolved to settle this question once and for all.

Accordingly, in 1719, he sent out two men, Fedor Luzhin and Ivan Evreinov, on an expedition across Asia to discover answers to the questions surrounding the relationship of its easternmost tip to North America. The two men made the five-thousand-mile journey from St. Petersburg to the Kamchatka peninsula in two years, but apart from exploring the northern Kurile Islands, they did not, apparently, have much to tell the Tsar when they returned in 1723.

Yet Peter was not discouraged, and even as he lay on his deathbed in 1725, he was considering a more elaborate expedition to the eastern frontier of his vast domains. His successor and widow, Catherine, supported this project, and a few weeks after she ascended the throne, a group of thirty-three men under Vitus Bering, a Danish captain in the Russian naval service, began the long journey to the Pacific.

Slowly they advanced across the heartland of Asia. They had set out in the early spring of 1725, and by the end of the year the expedition, with seventy-five wagon loads of supplies and materials, had made its way, sometimes on foot, sometimes on horseback, sometimes by boat, by way of Vologda and Tobolsk, to the settlements of Ilimsk and Ust-Kut. One group under Bering spent the worst months of the winter at the former, and another group under one of his lieutenants named Spanberg, also a Dane, at the latter.

They were still only half-way to their destination, and in the spring of 1726 they set out in three groups down the river Lena to Yakutsk. From there they proceeded to the Pacific Ocean at Okhotsk. The advance party under Spanberg reached the port – only a small fishing village – early in 1727. In the spring the men built a boat, the *Fortune*, in which they ferried supplies across the Sea of Okhotsk to the Kamchatka peninsula, and then transferred them to Lower Kamchatka Post on its eastern coast, facing the open Pacific.

Bering himself soon arrived at Okhotsk, and under his direction another ship, the *St. Gabriel*, was completed at Lower Kamchatka Post in the summer of 1728. The men made tar to caulk the seams from the gum of larch trees, they boiled seawater to provide salt, made butter of a sort from fish oil, and the obliging local natives showed the strangers how to make a kind of liquor from grass. All contingencies thus being provided for, in mid-July the expedition set out in the *St. Gabriel* to explore the north Pacific and, hopefully, to find North America.

Keeping close to the Asian shore, and sailing in a northeasterly direction, the ship eventually reached 65°30′. By this time there was apparently no longer any land to the west (the East Cape, reckoned to be the tip of Asia, is 66°N), and it thus seemed to many on board that the separation of Asia and North America had been established. The men held a conference (a curiously democratic feature of life on Russian ships, but one which in emergencies was quite customary), and decided to continue the voyage a little longer before turning back. In mid-August at 67°14′ the *St. Gabriel* began its return to Kamchatka, discovering Diomede Island soon afterward. This island (65°47′N and 169°W) is almost in the center of what is now called Bering Strait, and the ship was thus within easy distance of the mainland of North America. However, bad luck or misty weather prevented those on board from sighting it.

Little else of note occurred on the voyage, though some other islands were sighted and named, and the ship safely reached Kamchatka in September. Bering remained there through the winter, returned to Okhotsk in the summer of 1729, and finally reached St. Petersburg in the spring of 1730.

He had not, perhaps, added greatly to geographical knowledge. In his own eyes he had merely confirmed what he already knew – that Asia was not joined to North America – but the Empress Catherine decided that a much more elaborate expedition should be sent under the same commander to the same region. Some experts took the occasion to suggest that the new expedition would save a great deal of time if it proceeded direct to Kamchatka by sea around Cape Horn; however, as this would mean that little knowledge of eastern Siberia would be gained, the laborious land route was once again chosen.

This time the preparations were on a remarkably large scale. The port of Okhotsk, only a small fishing village when Bering reached it late in 1726, was to be greatly enlarged. Land around it was to be broken and cultivated by convicts transported from prisons in Yakutsk, and sheep, horses, and cattle were to be introduced. Supplies of food would thus be available for the expedition when it reached the Pacific and sailed out into it. Carpenters and ironworkers were also to be imported from European Russia to aid in building ships. A new local governor was despatched to Okhotsk to ensure that all this was done.

The aims of the expedition were also to be much more ambitious than those of its predecessor. Not only was the question of a land bridge to North America to be settled once and for all, but the exact position of Japan was to be ascertained and the waters between it and Siberia were to be thoroughly explored. Scientists of various kinds were to accompany Bering and make detailed reports on all that they found. Also, a beginning was to be made in the industrial and agricultural development of eastern Siberia.

The staff of the expedition had by now been chosen. Among Bering's aides were his fellow Dane, Martin Spanberg, a Russian, Alexei Chirikov, and Sven Waxell, a Swede who was eventually to write an interesting account of the enterprise.

Preparations both at St. Petersburg and at the advance bases continued throughout 1732, and finally in the spring of 1733 the main body of the expedition set out. It was unusually large, consisting of about five hundred men, including a considerable detachment of soldiers; there were also surveyors, interpreters, painters, secretaries; as well there was a large collection of scientific books.

Slowly the party crawled across the plains of central Asia. The first major city that it reached was Tobolsk on the eastern side of the Urals. Here several more scholars and scientists sent from St. Petersburg caught up with the main party: these included Professor Muller, a historian, Dr. Gmelin, a botanist and chemist, and a French astronomer, Louis Delisle de la Croyère, who had at one time done some exploring in Canada.[4] Later George Steller, a German botanist who was to compile a valuable account of the flora and fauna of the Aleutian area, joined the others at Tobolsk.

Eventually the party reached Yakutsk. It remained there no less than three years, during which time some of the less intrepid scholars in the expedition returned to the more comfortable life of St. Petersburg. Convicts conscripted by the authorities into the service of the expedition who attempted to avail themselves of a similar privilege were, however, discouraged; as Waxell later recorded, "We set up a gallows every twenty versts along the river Lena, which had an exceptionally good effect, for after that had been done we had only very few runaways."

Finally in 1737 Bering arrived at Okhotsk. He was now on the shore of the Pacific, where Spanberg's advance party had arrived in 1735 and had begun building ships for the exploration of the north Pacific.

Curiously enough, between the time that Bering left St. Petersburg and the time that he arrived at Okhotsk, a Russian captain had become, as far as is known, the first of his countrymen to see the mainland of North America. Michael Gvozdev, sailing in the vicinity of the East Cape of Siberia in 1732, later reported having seen a "large country" (bolshaya zemlya) to the east; he did not, however, endeavor to explore it.[5]

Unaware of this encouraging development, in 1738 Spanberg, with three ships, the *Archangel Michael*, the *Hope*, and the *Gabriel*, made a voyage across the Sea of Okhotsk to the Kamchatka peninsula, and later explored the Kuriles. In 1739 a similar voyage was undertaken, in the course of which two Russian ships visited Japan and some Russian sailors went ashore. They made observations of the Japanese people, their clothing and customs, and established the exact geographical location of that country.

All this time fresh supplies were being laboriously transported across Asia to Okhotsk, and ships were being prepared and provisioned for the great expedition. Finally in September 1740 all was in readiness, and the *St. Peter*, under the command of Bering, and the *St. Paul*, in the charge of Alexei Chirikov, sailed from Okhotsk. Two provision ships accompanied them to the western shore of the Kamchatka peninsula. Then the *St. Paul* and the *St. Peter* sailed south around the tip of that long finger of land and up its eastern shore to a harbor in Avacha Bay, which in honor of the two ships was named Petropavlovsk. Here the expedition spent the winter under conditions of reasonable comfort, while more supplies were transported across the peninsula by the local natives.

Summer finally arrived (it was now eight years since the main party had left St. Petersburg), and in early June 1741 the two ships sailed bravely out into the open Pacific. Soon, because of heavy fog, they lost contact with one another, and each continued its explorations alone.

The *St. Peter* sailed approximately northeast, and one day in mid-July those on board sighted in the distance high snow-covered mountains (now called the St. Elias range) on the mainland of North America. A few days later the ship anchored near an island which was given the name St. Elias (it being the day dedicated to that saint), but which is now called Kayak Island (59°52′N, 144°30′W). Beyond doubt the ship had attained the purpose for which it had set out, but when Bering was congratulated on his success, the cautious Dane replied, "We think now we have accomplished everything, and may go about greatly inflated, but they do not consider where we have reached land, how far we are from home, and what may yet happen. Who knows but that perhaps trade winds may arise which may prevent us from returning? We do not know this country, nor are we provided with supplies for a wintering."[6]

It would be some time yet before Bering's fears would be seen to be justified, and in the meantime a party was sent ashore to explore the island. For Steller, the German botanist, this was the great moment – a chance to examine every detail of a totally unknown part of the world. To Steller's incredulous dismay, Bering allotted only one day to this project, and the botanist was forced to scramble about on the rocky islet and make what notes he could. It is remarkable that in so short a time he was able to observe so much.

For example, by examining trees which had been chopped down by the natives, all of whom had fled into the dense thickets which covered much of the island, he was able to deduce that they used rude stone axes. The remains of a fire were found, and Steller identified bones, which had clearly been part of a feast, as those of a reindeer. In a subterranean hiding place were found arrows, thongs made from sea-weed, and utensils filled with smoked fish. A wooden implement for making fire by friction was also discovered. The flora and fauna of the area received close attention in these few brief hours. Steller drew up a long list of plants and accurately described the wild life – black and red

21

foxes, ravens, magpies, and many previously unknown varieties of birds. Then, with infinite reluctance, he was forced to return on board and the ship sailed away.

It was soon apparent that the prevailing winds and currents would hinder a speedy return. Nevertheless the ship made what progress it could to the westward, and slowly made its way along the southern edge of the Aleutian chain. It passed Kodiak Island, later another island to which the party gave the name Tumannoi, Foggy Island, which is now called Chirikov Island (55°50′N, 155°35′W), and then another group of islands farther west.

On one of these they went ashore for water. Scurvy had by this time made its ominous appearance, and one of the crew, Nikita Shumagin, was the first to die of it. He was buried on the island (55°25′N, 159°55′W) which was then named after him.[7]

Soon afterward, when a party was sent ashore from the ship to another small island, the first contact was made with the local natives. A few gifts were exchanged, and as the Russians had a native from eastern Siberia with them as an interpreter, a certain amount of communication was possible. However, the inhabitants were plainly disconcerted by the strange appearance and huge (to them) craft of the strangers. They broke off contact and the ship sailed away.

September now arrived, and the *St. Peter* continued her laborious attempt to return to Kamchatka. It had long been apparent that this would prove far from easy. The prevailing winds were contrary, scurvy continued its attack, and provisions began to run short. Deaths were numerous, and every few days the crew had to watch as the corpse of one of their companions was thrown overboard.

As September gave way to October and then November, the condition of the crew became desperate. As Waxell, one of the fortunate survivors (as was his twelve-year-old son, who accompanied him on the voyage) later described the situation:

> By now so many of our people were ill that I had, so to speak, no one to steer the ship. Our sails, too, had worn so thin that I expected them to fly off at any moment. When it came to a man's turn at the helm, he was dragged to it by two other of the invalids who were still able to walk a little, and set down at the wheel. There he had to sit and steer as

well as he could, and when he could sit no more, he had to
be replaced by another in no better case than he. . . .

Our ship was like a piece of dead wood, with none to direct it. We had to drift hither and thither at the whim of the
winds and waves. I tried to instil courage into the men, ap-
pealing to them; for there was no question of exerting authority in such a situation, where desperation already held
sway.[8]

In this state of affairs, with the ship slowly drifting westward,
and Bering confined to his bed below deck, November arrived.
The situation was now critical, as the ship's log records:

We had few men to manage the ship; twelve of our number
were dead; 34 were totally disabled from scurvy; only about
ten were able with great difficulty to get about at all, and
they were not fit for all kinds of sea duty.[9]

One morning an island was sighted; after a conference in
which every member of the crew took part, it was decided that it
would be better to spend the winter on it than to endure further
the perils of the ocean. The ship was anchored, and the sick
members of the crew were with difficulty helped ashore by those
still in fair health. Some of them, perhaps unaccustomed to the
arctic air, died in the boat which was carrying them to the island
(today called Bering Island, 166°E, 55°N).

The ground was entirely covered with snow, and no trees of
any kind grew there, so that for shelter the men were dependent
on hollows in the sand, and for fires on what driftwood they could
find. To add to the unpleasantness of the situation, the numerous
blue foxes on the island often ate the hands and feet of the dead
before they could be buried.

This desperate state of affairs was now intensified by a violent storm which broke the ship's cables and drove it ashore,
where it soon filled with water and became imbedded in the
sand. As no land was visible from even the highest point of the island, it began to appear that the crew of the *St. Peter* would be
marooned there until they died.

Even so, they had enough spirit left to make some attempt to
cope with their situation. They agreed on a system of rationing,
in which all would equally share the remaining food supplies;

they would keep a reserve in case a return voyage to their home port became possible, and it was hoped that in the spring there would be enough plants and roots to support existence.

So the winter days dragged by. In Waxell's words,

> Men were continually dying. Our plight was so wretched that the dead had to lie for a considerable time among the living, for there was none able to drag corpses away, nor were those who still lived capable of moving away from the dead. They had to remain lying all mixed up together in a ring with a little fire in the centre.

Early in December, it became plain to all that the expedition's commander was beyond all hope of recovery, a fate in which he seemed to acquiesce. He was now sixty, worn out by age, responsibility, and disease, and one day his spirit yielded to the unequal struggle. The historian Bancroft described the sad but not inglorious scene:

> It was under such circumstances that Vitus Bering died – on this cold forbidding isle, under the sky of an arctic winter; the 8th of December 1741, in a miserable hut half-covered by the sand which came trickling down upon him through the boards that had been placed to bar its progress. Thus passed from earth, as nameless tens of thousands have done, the illustrious commander of the expeditions which had disclosed the separation of the two worlds and discovered north-westernmost America.[10]

Waxell now assumed command. It is an amazing sidelight on human nature, or perhaps on the tsarist system of government, that one of the first disputes which he had to settle was between those who wished to lighten their misery by playing cards and those who believed that this would be at variance with the Tsar's orders. Waxell, after pondering the matter, gave his decision:

> My answer to this was that the regulations or ukase against playing cards had been made without any thought of this desert island, because at that time it had not yet been discovered. If they had had any inkling then of our men's card-

24

playing and of our pitiable circumstances, I was sure that they would have introduced a special paragraph giving permission for all suitable pastimes.

It was now 1742, and the scurvy began showing some signs of abatement. The men were able to obtain some meat by killing foxes, sea-otters, and fur-seals, and when a dead whale was washed ashore, they cut off and boiled chunks of its blubber. As the snow began to disappear, Steller the botanist pointed out various herbs which the men found an aid to their recovery. He also took the opportunity to make detailed notes on the "sea cow," a bizarre form of life which within twenty-five years was to become extinct.

Yet this situation clearly could not continue forever, and in March the survivors, numbering about forty-five, conferred on what to do. Some wished to send a small group westward in the ship's boat until it found land and, hopefully, assistance; others believed that the ship itself could be refloated. The difficulties inherent in both suggestions were exposed in the debate, and it was finally decided to build a new ship from materials salvaged from the *St. Peter*. A document was drawn up, to which everyone put his name as a sign of agreement with the plan.

Only one man in the group had any knowledge of shipbuilding, but desperation lent hope, and in May the keel of the new craft was laid. Only part of the men could take part in this work, as the rest had to be constantly in search of food for all. By the end of July the new ship, forty feet long and also named the *St. Peter*, was completed, as was a small boat. The men placed all supplies on board, and one evening in August they got away from the island, sailing westward. Four days later they sighted Kamchatka peninsula, and in a few days more were safely back at Petropavlovsk, bringing with them the pelts of several hundred sea-otters which they had killed on Bering Island.

Meanwhile the *St. Peter's* sister ship, the *St. Paul*, had also had an eventful voyage. Chirikov had sailed in a northeasterly direction until in mid-July, only a day or two before Bering first saw land, he reached the islands lining the North American coast between what are now capes Addington and Bartholomew. Since he could not locate a good landing-place, he sailed north to about 57° and there sent ashore a party of eleven men. Although contact with this group was maintained for a few days, it was then lost; fearing that misfortune had come to the men, a second smaller party was sent in search of them. When this, too, did not return, after a period of anxious waiting, with heavy hearts the survivors of the expedition sailed away.[11]

After touching at Cape Elizabeth on the west side of the Gulf of Alaska early in August, the ship sailed westward along the southern side of the Aleutian chain. Along the way deaths from scurvy were numerous, but eventually the ship got back to Petropavlovsk. The last casualty of the expedition was the astronomer De la Croyère, who died as he was being taken ashore.[12]

The following summer Chirikov made a second brief voyage, but only got as far as Attu on the western tip of the Aleutian chain. As it happened, on his homeward voyage he passed near Bering Island, unaware of the fate of his fellow explorer, and that the survivors of the *St. Peter* were still marooned on it.

The survivors of the great expedition now made preparations for the long journey back to St. Petersburg. They travelled in several groups, and one of the very last to arrive was Waxell, in 1749, sixteen years after he had first set out.

So ended this remarkable attempt to reach North America from Asia. It had been on the whole a success. Many had lost their lives along the way, but two things were now firmly established: that Asia and North America were almost certainly separated by water, but that a sea journey from one to the other was feasible. Moreover, the exact position of both Japan and some of the Aleutian chain of islands had been established. It was apparent, too, that the newly examined areas were rich in furs, and that a profitable trade in them could likely be developed.

Although Bering was dead, the projects which he and Chirikov had initiated were soon carried forward by others, and the next fifty years saw great advances made in the direction which the two men had first marked out. Curiosity or the hope of glory may have influenced some of Bering's successors, but the main motivating force was undoubtedly the chance of deriving wealth from the fur trade.

At first Bering and Copper Islands, since they were nearest to Kamchatka, received the most attention; Copper Island, as its name implies, was also found to be rich in that useful metal. Thus as early as 1743 we find one Emilian Bassof, a soldier who had seen at first hand the furs brought back by the *St. Peter*, forming a partnership with a Moscow merchant and making a profitable voyage to Bering Island. In the next few years he made three others, on one of them bringing back no less than 1,600 sea-otters, 2,000 fur seals, and 2,000 blue arctic foxes.[13]

Others soon followed Bassof, and there was a tendency, as the islands closest to Russia began to become exhausted of their furs, for ships to go farther east along the Aleutian chain, which was, we may note, ice-free the year round. Moreover, though trade relations with the natives were sometimes amicable, rapacity often gave an edge to cruelty, and blood was frequently shed on both sides.

Meanwhile the government at St. Petersburg had realized that the fur trade might be a source of considerable income to the national treasury. Agreements began to be drawn up by which in return for a proportion of the furs secured, an expedition would be granted the sole right to trade in a particular area for a specified time.

Few of those taking part in this new field of economic enterprise can have objected, as the rewards for a successful voyage were very high. For example, in 1752 a single ship brought back to Kamchatka 1,772 sea-otters, 750 blue foxes, and 840 fur seals, while another expedition, wrecked like Bering on an unknown island, constructed a small craft from the salvage and returned safely to its home port with 820 sea-otters, 1,900 blue foxes, and 7,000 fur seals.[14]

A system of dividing the profits was by now in general operation. By this method, a certain proportion of the profits of a voyage went to the owners of the ships, and the rest was divided into equal parts among the crew, with an extra portion for the navigator and the chief hunter, and a small part set aside for the church.

Fur-gathering expeditions soon became remarkably numerous. Black foxes from the middle Aleutians were now being brought back in quantity, as were walrus tusks, no doubt obtained by the natives from the mainland of Alaska. In the 1760s, Kodiak, the most easterly of the Aleutian chain, became a regular source of furs. Perhaps a symbol that a new era – the age of commerce – was dawning is to be found in the fact that ships were no longer exclusively named after Biblical characters; one which set out in 1756, for example, was named after its commander and his wife.

The major market for the furs gathered by the Russians was China, and trade in them took place at the remote town of Kiakhta, on the border between the two countries, three hundred miles south of Irkutsk. Here merchants from both nations gathered to strike bargains, and the Chinese exchanged tea and silk for furs. So important did this center of commerce become that furs even made their way to it from North America by way of London and St. Petersburg.[15]

The Russian government once more began taking a more active part in the stimulation of geographical discovery, and the Empress Catherine set in motion an important expedition. In July 1768 two ships built at Okhotsk, the *St. Catherine* and the *St. Paul*, under Captain Krenitsin and Lieutenant Levashev, sailed from Kamchatka in the direction of North America. While wintering at Unalaska (54°N, 166°30′w) in the Fox Islands, however, losses from disease were so considerable that the following summer the ships returned to Okhotsk. The expedition was, nevertheless, not a total failure, as the members made valuable ethnological observations of the natives and their way of life.

In spite of government participation, private traders were still the major force in the fur trade, and for the next twenty years they made numerous voyages to the Aleutians. As the years went by some perceptible changes took place. The center of the fur-gathering process gradually shifted eastward, meaning longer voyages and therefore more capital. Consequently, there was a tendency for small enterprises to be combined into larger ones.[16] Moreover the traders evolved a methodical system of operation by which the natives of the area were steadily drawn, albeit somewhat forcibly, into the network of international trade. As a contemporary English scholar reported:

> The Russians have for some years past been accustomed to go to these islands in quest of furs, of which they have imposed a tax on the inhabitants. The manner of carrying on this trade is as follows: the Russians go in autumn to

Bering's and Copper Island, and there winter; they then employ themselves in catching the sea-cat [fur-seal] and afterwards the "scivutcha" or sea-lion. The flesh of the latter is prepared for food, and it is very delicate. They carry the skins of these sea animals to the eastern islands. Next summer they go eastward to the Fox Islands, and again lay their ships up for the winter. They then endeavor to procure, either by persuasion or force, the children of the inhabitants, particularly of the Tookoos [minor chiefs], as hostages. This being accomplished, they deliver to the inhabitants fox-traps, and also skins for their boats, for which they oblige them to bring furs and provisions during the winter.

After obtaining from them a certain quantity of furs, by way of tax, for which they give them quittances, the Russians pay for the rest in beads, false pearls, goat's wool, copper kettles, hatchets, &c. In the spring they get back their traps and deliver up their hostages. They dare not hunt alone, nor in small numbers, on account of the hatred of the natives.[17]

There was also by this time abundant evidence that the impact of the western way of life had seriously disrupted the social fabric of the native culture, a tragedy which would be repeated in many other parts of the world:

There are upwards of a thousand inhabitants on Unalaska, and they say that it was formerly much more populous. They have suffered greatly by their disputes with the Russians, and by a famine in the year 1762; but most of all from a change in their way of life. No longer contented with their original simplicity, they long for Russian luxuries; in order therefore to obtain a few delicacies, which are presently consumed, they dedicate the greatest part of their time to hunting, for the purpose of procuring furs for the Russians. By these means they neglect to lay up a provision of fish and roots, and suffer their children frequently to die of hunger.[18]

As the century reached the three-quarter mark, one name began to stand out among the swarm of traders endeavoring to enrich themselves from the fur trade. This was Gregory Shelikof, who was eventually to become responsible for the first permanent

Russian settlement in North America. Beginning in a small way by trading with the Kurile Islands, he soon acquired partners and expanded his operations to the Aleutian chain. He employed experienced pilots, and although it was frequently several years before the ships which he sent out returned, the cargoes that they brought back more than repaid the patience of their owners.

The supply of furs on some of the Aleutians was by this time showing signs of exhaustion, and Shelikof resolved to extend his operations to the mainland of North America. In the summer of 1783 three ships, the *St. Simeon*, the *St. Michael*, and the *Three Saints*, set out from Okhotsk with 192 men, an unusually large expedition. After losing contact with the *St. Michael*, the other two ships wintered on Bering Island, and the following year sailed eastward to Unalaska Island, where they took on fresh water and provisions. Then the ships proceeded to Kodiak, where Shelikof anchored in what he named Three Saints Bay. The natives attempted to drive the Russians away, but were repulsed after heavy casualties.

Shelikof now opened a momentous chapter in the history of the northwest coast: he began the construction of the first permanent settlement in the area by people of the white race. He had brought with him expert axe-men, and soon buildings and fortifications were rising. The natives, now in a somewhat better mood, watched these proceedings with the greatest curiosity, and even offered to assist in the work. Shelikof (whose wife accompanied him on all his voyages and was as shrewd in business matters as her husband) also established a school, in which an effort was made to teach the natives Russian and the basic doctrines of Christianity.

In 1786 the little settlement was joined by the *St. Michael*, which had suffered various misfortunes during the three years that it had taken to reach North America from Okhotsk. Shelikof now prepared to return to Okhotsk, but before doing so he put an experienced man named Samoilof, formerly a merchant in Siberia, in charge of the settlement. The instructions that he gave Samoilof were remarkably detailed, and as well as illustrating Shelikof's ambition, perception, and energy, they showed beyond doubt that the Russian occupation of the area was intended to be permanent. He drew up regulations to maintain discipline in the colony, to prevent scurvy, and to extend trade. Samoilof was to keep the school in operation, to drive out bad characters, and to exclude other trading companies ("by peaceable means if possible"); he was to construct more buildings, to collect samples of minerals for transmission to St. Petersburg, and to set up a system of informers among the natives.

Most remarkable of all, perhaps, Shelikof confidently envisioned a further considerable extension of Russian political and economic control over the north Pacific coast. He instructed Samoilof to establish various new posts extending over several hundred miles of coastline, each to be staffed by about a dozen men. As soon as reinforcements were available from mainland Russia, the active exploration of the more southerly parts of the Pacific coast was to be set in motion, and more posts set up "farther and farther along the coast of the American continent, and in a southerly direction to California, establishing everywhere marks of Russian possession."

Having thus disclosed (at least to his trusted countryman) the full extent of his visions – nothing less than the complete political and economic control of the Pacific coast from the permanent ice pack in the northern mists to the outposts of Spanish power in sunny California – Shelikof sailed away. Even his return voyage he was careful to turn to good account. He took with him forty natives, some of whom were to be shown the glories of the Russian way of life and then returned to their homeland, some to be taken as far as St. Petersburg for the edification of the Empress Catherine, and the remainder, mostly children, to be educated in Okhotsk and Irkutsk so that in due course they could return "to exercise a civilising influence among their countrymen."[19]

Only one thing was lacking to make Shelikof's cup run over: his company might do its best to discourage rivals, but it had as yet no legal authority to bar them from the hunting grounds. It was always possible that a more resourceful or fortunate rival might displace him from his promising new field of operations, and at this point monopoly, that vision so dear to the hearts of free enterprisers, began haunting his imagination. If the government could be induced to grant his company sole trading rights in Alaska, the prospect would indeed be rosy. Shelikof, no man to halt Hamlet-like between conception and execution, at once took steps to convert his dreams into reality. Hastening from Okhotsk to Irkutsk, the capital of eastern Siberia, he presented an outline of his plans to General Jacobi, the local governor, being careful to stress that they would "add to the glory of our wise empress." Jacobi was apparently converted, and recommended Shelikof to the authorities in St. Petersburg.

There, in due course, the enterprising merchant arrived, and with his partner Golikof presented his case. The empress appointed a committee to look into the matter, which, largely on the recommendations of Jacobi, urged that Shelikof and Golikof be granted the exclusive right to trade in Alaska, as well as a loan from the treasury to build up their business. Catherine, after considering this report, decided in the fall of 1788 that the company should have exclusive control over the area that it had already occupied, but that its competitors should be allowed to exert themselves in adjoining areas. The request for a loan was refused, on the grounds that the money was needed for the armed forces; however, the two businessmen were each given a sword and a gold medal "for services rendered to humanity," and with that they had to be content. Shelikof had not achieved all he sought – the total exclusion of all possible rivals from his chosen field of operation – but at least he had come a long way from his humble beginnings. There was always a chance that he might go further yet.

And with this imperial ukase of September 28, 1788,[20] we may pause for a moment in our story and take stock. It was now sixty-three years since Vitus Bering had set out on his first expedition to see what lay beyond Siberia, and forty-seven years since he breathed his last on the barren, wind-swept island that would henceforth bear his name. Much had been accomplished since then. The sea route from Asia to America, though still dangerous, was now well marked out, and there was seldom a moment when ships were not coming or going along it, bearing European goods for the dark-skinned natives of the new world, or carrying away fortunes in furs. Exploration, having yielded to trade, was passing over into settlement; the first Russian colony in North America had been established, and other outposts of Russia were rising throughout a wide area, especially in the region of what are now called Cook's Inlet and Prince William Sound. That all of northwestern America would, in the course of unfolding time, become part of the tsar's dominions – already the most extensive in the world – now seemed, at the very least, a possibility.

Yet time bears many surprises in its train, and the plans of men are not always brought to fruition. The extension of Russian power in this distant part of the globe had by no means gone unnoticed in other European capitals, and already their governments were drawing up plans to share in the unrolling of the map and the development of the North Pacific's newly discovered resources.

Spain, England, France: these too were imperial powers, these too felt an urge to extend their sway in distant seas. And indeed, well before Shelikof began hastening across half a planet, from Alaska to the foot of the throne at St. Petersburg, others had already laid the foundation of a political and commercial rivalry between the great powers, the outcome of which would not be decided for many decades to come. It is to these other probings of the northwest coast of North America, more especially those by Spain and Britain, that we now must turn our attention.

CHAPTER THREE

Northward
from
California

When
Shelikof
was about to leave

Kamchatka for his long journey to St. Petersburg, word was brought to him that an English vessel was anchored at Petropavlovsk. Scenting a chance for trade, he hastened to the port and found there the *Lark*, commanded by a Captain Peters and owned by the East India Company. Shelikof bought from the ship a considerable quantity of goods, which before long he resold to other merchants in the area. The *Lark*, whose large crew was drawn from many nations, then sailed eastward into the Pacific, while Shelikof began his lengthy trip westward across Asia.

Of the two traders, it was Shelikof that fortune would smile on, for the *Lark* was later wrecked on Copper Island, with the loss of all but two of its crew. Although Shelikof and Peters suffered different fates, both had set out on their journeys with a common aim: to profit from the fur trade of the North Pacific. Their chance encounter is thus a reminder that already eyes other than Russian ones had detected fortunes waiting for the enterprising in that distant corner of the world.

In 1786, the fur trade was still in its early stage; only a dozen years, for example, had elapsed since the first ship had appeared in the waters of Vancouver Island. Yet many more were to follow, and Shelikof and his compatriots would soon find that they were faced with formidable competitors. Indeed, before long a fierce struggle for the fur trade was well under way along the entire north Pacific coast. It continued for many decades, and did not die down until the resources of the area had been depleted and the attention of mankind turned to the possibilities of other economic resources in the area.

The first nation to challenge the Russian monopoly of the fur trade of the north Pacific was Spain, which had long had a convenient base from which to launch expeditions to that area. Her vast empire comprised much of South and Central America, and she had already established a civilization of considerable sophistication. Indeed, exploratory voyages up the western coast of North America had been made several times. As early as 1542, Juan Rodriguez Cabrillo, a Portuguese in the service of the Spanish crown, had sailed to a point somewhere between 41° and 43°N. The following year, Bartholomew Ferrelo had reached about the same latitude, as did Sebastian Vizcaino in 1602-03.[1] Yet, perhaps because the coastal area north of Mexico seemed lacking in either economic resources or good harbors, interest then lapsed. It was not revived until late in the eighteenth century, when reports began filtering into the foreign office in Madrid of the great harvest of furs being reaped by the Russians in the extreme northwest part of North America.

By this time, Spain's greatest days were behind her – perhaps the destruction of the Great Armada of 1588 had really marked the turning-point in her fortunes – and some were already born who would take part in the rebellions which, in the first part of the nineteenth century, would result in the overthrow of her empire in the New World. Yet between these two eras came a remarkable revival of national energies, much of its concentrated in the reign of Carlos III, who occupied the Spanish throne from 1759 to 1788.

This energetic monarch, aware that his country was not participating as it might in the eighteenth-century movement known as the "enlightenment," resolved to move it out into the broad mainstream of the age. In the face of hostility or apathy he not only attempted to reform and stimulate the machinery of government, but he encouraged the progress of the natural sciences. His dominions in the New World provided a vast and still largely unexplored field for the studies of botanists and anthropologists, and institutes for the training of scientists in a variety of fields were established in Spain and also in Mexico City. This was to bear abundant fruit when the time came to send expeditions up the western shore of North America.[2]

Nor was the development of sea power – so essential to empire-builders – neglected. There were already Spanish naval bases in the Caribbean at Havana and Vera Cruz, and it was now resolved to establish one on the Pacific coast in about the same latitude. The king in distant Madrid gave his strong approval, and accordingly, in the late 1760s, the naval department of San Blas was set up. In some ways this shallow harbor (21°32′N, 105°19′W) was unsatisfactory, as the high humidity in the area was often injurious to health. However, there was an abundance of good timber, including cedar, in the vicinity, and before long San Blas was the scene of a thriving shipbuilding industry. At one time it employed as many as 375 men, and even the local Indians proved helpful, as they collected materials for making pitch and tar. Some attempt was also made to develop other economic resources in the area, notably salt, tobacco, and pearl fishing.[3]

Expeditions to California by both land and sea were made in 1769 and 1770; the sites of Monterey, San Diego, and San Francisco were reached, and preparations made for establishing them as outposts of Spanish power. Since the area that is now the southwestern United States (areas now including Arizona and Nevada) had long been subject to the Spanish crown, its wearer controlled a considerable proportion of North America. Neither Britain nor France was as yet a factor in this region, the United States had not yet become a separate nation, and consequently King Carlos III seemed likely to extend his realms still farther.

The main threat to the realization of this ambition came from another great power. As we saw, Russia had already made striking advances in the exploration of northwestern North America and in the exploitation of its resources. The tsar's government, which felt no particular urge to share its new-found knowledge with the world, had maintained considerable secrecy in this matter. Yet then, as now, nations kept an eye on each other, and by 1770 it was well known in Madrid that St. Petersburg had brought under its effective control a sizable part of the northwest coast of North America, and was actively engaged in extending its power in that region.

To the Spanish king and government this was a challenge, and one which must be met. Accordingly, in the spring of 1773 a despatch arrived in Mexico City from Madrid, drawing the attention of Viceroy Antonio Bucareli to the Russian advances, and informing him that he was to make preparations for an expedition to the Pacific northwest.

Bucareli, the Spanish viceroy in New Spain from 1771 to 1779, was an unusually capable official. He had already supervised the exploration of parts of California, and was to be responsible for the establishment of a permanent settlement at San Francisco in 1776. He had also opened an overland route from Spanish-controlled areas in the interior to the Pacific coast, thus linking more closely the various parts of this remarkably vast empire, and had improved communication by sea along its Pacific coastline. He now ordered Juan Perez, the senior naval officer at San Blas (and the first Spanish captain to enter the harbors of both San Diego and Monterey from the sea) to submit plans for the proposed operation. This Perez did in the fall of 1773, and late in December he received detailed final instructions from the viceroy regarding the expedition. First, Bucareli firmly asserted its fundamental purpose:

> The kindness of the King, who entrusted this government of New Spain to my charge, not only imposes on me the obligations of preserving these vast territories to him but also of endeavoring to enlarge them, as much as I am able, through new discoveries in unknown areas, so that their numerous Indian inhabitants, attracted to the kind, mellow and desired vassalage of His Majesty, may receive by means of the spiritual conquest the light of the gospel which will free them from the darkness of idolatry in which they live, and will show them the road to eternal salvation. These are the true motives that move the pious royal heart of His Majesty in these undertakings.[4]

At this point, however, the "true motives" of the expedition fade discreetly into the background, and more mundane aspects of the expedition receive virtually exclusive attention:

> Its complement, besides the aforesaid captain, will consist of a second pilot, a chaplain from the Apostolic College of San Fernando in this capital, a surgeon, a boatswain, a first and second boatswain's mate, a first and second caulker, a first and second steward, a gunner, fourteen helmsmen, twenty seamen, thirty apprentice seamen, six cabin boys, and four cooks – all of which add up to eighty-eight [*sic*] enlistments.

Perez was given firm orders regarding any previously unknown areas that he might discover:

> He is not to make any settlement, no matter how advantageous and simple it may seem to him. However, he will conspicuously mark out the places which he considers suitable so that it may not be too difficult to find them if, in view of his reports, it should be decided to send an expedition to occupy them. . . .
>
> All places where possession is taken will be marked with a large wooden cross, making its pedestal from rocks and concealing in it a bottle or glass flask in which he will place a copy of the testimony of possession signed by him, the chaplain and the two pilots. And in order that in the days to come this document may better be preserved and may serve as an authentic testimony, the bottle will be sealed rightly with pitch.

All possible precautions were to be taken to conceal Spain's new venture from the prying eyes of foreigners:

> In the aforesaid event of discovering a settlement . . . he will endeavor to avoid intercourse with it; but from a distance he will observe whatever he can, noting its location, the landmarks they may have built, the number of inhabitants, and if they have or do not have vessels to depend upon.
>
> If another vessel is encountered, he must be very careful and must use all the means available to avoid communication. In the event that this should prove inevitable (which must be proved on his return here) he will endeavor to con-

ceal the purpose of his voyage. If the vessel encountered should be more powerful and should question him and oblige him to answer, he can state that he sailed from San Blas with provisions for the new settlements of San Diego and Monterey, provided he is within a reasonable latitude; but if he is beyond this, it will be necessary to add to the above-said that the weather has driven him further, etc. . . .

The natives which the expedition would undoubtedly encounter were clearly expected to play a key role. They would provide valuable data for the new sciences of man (anthropology and ethnology, as they would one day be called), furnish useful information regarding the activities of other white nations, and, if properly treated, would be likely to welcome any future Spanish expedition which came with a view to permanent settlement:

> If settlements of Indians are found in the locations where he lands, after he has treated them affectionately and given them some of the articles which he carried for this purpose, he will endeavor to learn about their customs, characteristics, their mode of life and their neighbors, the number of tribes, whether they live in peace or war among themselves, what religion they profess, what idols they worship, what sacrifices and religious rites, whether there exists among them some body of knowledge or manner of writing, and how they rule and govern themselves.
>
> He must not be satisfied solely with making the investigations indicated in the preceding articles, but he must also learn, by any means possible, if the Indians have ever seen other vessels before, if they have ever become acquainted with people different from their own, when, what were their aims and ambitions; if they penetrated into the interior or if they followed the coastline; if they gave them gifts and treated them well; if some of their gifts and tokens are still kept; if they promised to return – in all of these he will become thoroughly informed, by means of sign language or as best he can, recognizing the very great importance of this knowledge and information.
>
> He will not take anything from the Indians against their will, but only in barter or given by them through friendship.

All must be treated with kindness and gentleness, which is the most efficacious means of gaining and firmly establishing their esteem. Thus, those who may return to these places for the purpose of establishing settlements, if it be so decided, will be well received.

After informing Perez that he would be furnished with some Russian maps "published in St. Petersburg in the years 1758 and 1773,"[5] as well as 468 bundles of trade goods, Bucareli concluded with very detailed instructions regarding the exact formulas and ceremonies to be used in taking possession of any newly discovered territory.

A ship, especially built for the expedition, was launched at San Blas in October 1773 and christened the *Santiago*.[6] During the next few months final preparations were made, and after taking communion in the chapel at San Blas, the ship sailed north at midnight on January 24, 1774.

Late in March the *Santiago* stopped briefly at San Diego, where two priests disembarked to do missionary work among the natives, a leak in the ship was mended, and some spare masts were cut. After a stay of about three weeks, the ship set sail on April 5 and reached Monterey, about seventy-five miles south of San Francisco, on May 8. Here two other priests who were to accompany the expedition came on board: Father Tomas de la Peña y Saravia, born in Spain in 1743, and Father Juan Crespi, born in Mallorca in 1721. Both have left interesting accounts of all they saw on the voyage. Crespi was no stranger to such ventures, having taken part in the expedition which, in the summer of 1769, planted the banner of Spain at San Diego and Monterey and then moved north to explore the area around San Francisco Bay. He himself had covered this lengthy journey by land, while Juan Perez in the *San Antonio*, which was carrying some colonists for the new settlements, had met the expedition at San Diego. Crespi, we might note, was one of the first men to see the great California redwoods and to look out to sea through the Golden Gate. He was physically tireless and intellectually alert, and his accounts of his numerous journeys in this period help to bring them, even after a lapse of two centuries, vividly before our eyes.[7]

On June 6, after four young bulls and some pigs had been put on board at the last minute, the *Santiago* left Monterey, but was becalmed soon afterward. It also suffered its first casualty when the boatswain died (his body was taken ashore for burial). For the next few weeks the weather was remarkably poor, but steady progress northward, at some distance from the coast, was made. The ship reached 48°55' on July 13 and 50°24' the next day. Its supply of fresh water was, however, in danger of depletion, and after a conference with his officers, Perez decided to turn eastward and make a landfall.

On July 18 snow-covered peaks were sighted in the distance, and the next day at about 53°41' the *Santiago* anchored near the Queen Charlotte Islands. At first the natives (now known as the Haida Indians) were inclined to be timorous, only a single canoe with nine men in it approaching the ship. They were given some beads and in return presented the white men with some dried fish, but refused all invitations to come on board.[8] On the following day, however, no fewer than twenty-one canoes, one with an all-female crew, appeared and a lively scene ensued:

> All the afternoon these canoes, twenty-one in all, were about the ship, their occupants trading with the ship's people, for which purpose they had brought a great quantity of mats, skins of various kinds of animals, and fish, hats made of rushes and caps made of skins, bunches of feathers arranged in various shapes, and, above all, many coverlets, or pieces of woven woollen stuffs very elaborately embroidered and about a yard and a half square, with a fringe of the same wool about the edges and various figures embroidered in different colors. Our people bought several of all these articles, in return for clothing, knives and beads. It was apparent that what they liked most were things made of iron; but they wanted large pieces with a cutting edge, such as swords, wood-knives and the like – for on being shown ribands they intimated that these were of trifling value, and when offered barrel hoops they signified that these had no edge. Two of the pagans came aboard the ship, and were much pleased with the vessel and things on board of it.[9]

Father Crespi took the opportunity to set down a description of the natives:

> These Indians are well built; their faces are good and rather

41

fair and rosy; their hair is long and some of them were bearded. All appeared with the body completely covered, some with skins of otter and other animals, others with cloaks woven of wool, or hair which looked like fine wool, and a garment like a cape and covering them to the waist, the rest of the person being covered in dressed skins or the woven woollen cloths of different colors in handsome patterns. Some of these garments have sleeves; others have not.[10]

The females of the tribe did not, however, arouse much enthusiasm in the learned man of God. He described them as having

pendent from the lower lip, which is pierced, a disk painted in colors, which appeared to be of wood, slight and curved, which makes them seem very ugly, and at a little distance they appear as if the tongue were hanging out of the mouth.[11]

After a few more days spent in the vicinity, during which the ship reached a latitude somewhere between 54° and 55°,[12] the ship turned southward, and keeping well out from the mainland, soon came in sight of the west coast of Vancouver Island. Two days later, on August 8, at about 49°, Perez anchored in the vicinity of Nootka, though the exact location has long been in dispute.[13] It seems likely, however, that the *Santiago* did not enter the harbor, but anchored off the entrance to it, which Perez named "Rada [roadstead] de San Lorenzo de Nootka." He also took the occasion to give names to some other geographical features of the area, one of which, La Punta de San Esteban, survives as modern-day Estevan Point (though the location is slightly different from the original).[14]

During the voyage the ship's carpenters had made a cross fourteen feet long, inscribed with the letters I.N.R.I. (Jesus Nazarenus Rex Judaeorum), and the words "Carolus Tertius: Rex Hispaniarum; ano 1774." It was hoped that this could now be erected and formal possession taken of the area. The ship's launch was despatched with the cross and two priests to assist in the solemn ceremonies, but when a sudden wind sprang up and the *Santiago* appeared to be in danger, the launch was recalled and the cross was taken back to the ship.[15]

In this period the two scholarly priests made careful observations of the area. Father Peña, for example, noted that the lip-piece worn by the natives of the Queen Charlotte Islands was not in evidence at Nootka, and that

> The canoes of these pagans are not so large as those we saw at Point Santa Margarita in latitude 55°, nor of the same shape. The largest are about eight yards in length, with a long prow, hollowed out, and their sterns are blunter. The paddles are very handsome and are painted, and are shaped like a shovel with a point about a quarter of a yard long near the end.[16]

Trading between the two races was brisk during the *Santiago's* brief stay at Nootka, the whites exchanging abalone shells and knives for otter skins.[17] There is no mention, however, in the account of either priest of the famous silver spoons which the Spanish were later to claim were stolen from them at this time, and which were to figure prominently in international controversy, being put forward as evidence to support Spanish claims to having first discovered Nootka.

Scurvy had by this time made its ominous appearance among the crew, so all haste was made to complete the voyage. Moving swiftly south before a favorable wind, by August 26 the ship was off San Francisco Bay, and the next day entered Monterey. It rested there while the crew recovered their health, and then *Santiago* got back safely to San Blas in the autumn.

In two respects, Perez had not fulfilled his instructions. He had not reached 60°, nor had he taken formal possession for Spain of any region that he had visited. Moreover, he apparently failed to make any charts. Yet enough had been accomplished to encourage Viceroy Bucareli to organize a second expedition to the same area, which set sail a few months after the return of the first.

This time the commander was Don Bruno Hezeta, whose flagship was the refitted *Santiago*, with Juan Perez as its second-in-command. Don Juan Manuel de Ayala was put in charge of the thirty-six foot *Felicidad*, which was now renamed the *Sonora*. A third vessel, the *San Carlos*, was to accompany the other two ships as far as San Francisco Bay, which was now a small Spanish settlement. However, almost as soon as the three ships set sail, the captain of the *San Carlos* was stricken with mental illness and had to be removed from the ship and replaced by Ayala. Juan Francisco de la Bodega y Quadra was then given command of the *Sonora*, with Francisco Antonio Maurelle as his assistant. Two priests, Father Benito de la Sierra and Father Campa Cos, also accompanied the expedition.[18]

On March 16, 1775, the *Sonora* and *Santiago* left San Blas with orders to reach 65°. At first they sailed far to the west, then turned north, but in the face of contrary winds made almost no progress for some weeks. During this period the expedition suffered its first casualty, when one of the crew was found unconscious from drink: "The captain asked that when sober he should be punished mercifully, but at midnight the sailor died and went to be judged by the Supreme Arbiter."[19]

So little progress was being made that on May 21 a council of officers was held to consider whether to turn back to Monterey. Quadra was strongly opposed to losing an entire year in the race for control of the Pacific northwest; he declared that "the command of it has been delivered to me, and I must act according to the code of honor corresponding to my birth." He asserted that even "if fortune were so adverse that it gave me no assistance, then it is a glory for posterity when each man dies at his post for the King."[20] The officers decided that even though the *Sonora* was already in poor shape, the voyage would continue, and soon afterward, turning east, the two ships anchored at a point just below what is now the California-Oregon boundary, at 41°18′. The men named the harbor Puerta de la Trinidad (a name which survives to this day), and traded knives with the natives for deer and otter skins. The following day, Father Sierra tells us,

> a number of the inhabitants, women as well as men, all wearing crowns of flowers and foliage, came out to see us, coming alongside and receiving without hesitation whatever was presented to them, and inviting us to go to their settlements.

Since the local chief had ordered his men to remove the strings from their bows, there seemed no reason to expect trouble, and it was decided to erect the cross. Accordingly, on June 11 a party of men was sent ashore, together with the two priests. Before they made the arduous climb from the beach, the priests sang a Te Deum and Father Campa Cos celebrated mass. Then the men made their way to a prominent cliff, where, watched by the wondering natives, they erected the cross. On the way back to the ship some of the local inhabitants were found to be agreeable to taking a minor part in the ceremonies:

> On descending, near the beach we were met by four Indians, one of whom, the one whom the afternoon before we had considered the most intelligent of our visitors, was asked by the captain of the schooner to repeat "Long Live Charles III!" This he did very cheerfully in unison with our men at the salute with the guns, not being perturbed by the roar of the guns on board which were discharged when our men on shore fired volleys with the guns. . . .
>
> We pointed out the cross to them, charging them not to remove it; whereupon their chief harangued them, and they promised not to tear it down.[21]

The next day the Indians (unaware, perhaps, that they were now loyal subjects of the King of Spain) helped the whites to gather wood and water, and that evening a lively banquet was held on the beach. In the next few days the Spanish did some local exploring, and were much impressed by the giant trees of the area. They exchanged beads for sardines, and also questioned the natives closely as to whether they had ever seen other white men or comparable vessels. However, the difficulty of communication made it hard to obtain clear answers.

Quadra has left some interesting observations of the inhabitants of the area:

> They are extremely docile, of middle height, and seemed free from the notable ugliness of the Indians of the Americas. They live in square, well-constructed huts, built of large beams, the roofs of which were almost level with the ground. The doors are round and only one person can enter at a

time. The floor is perfectly flat and very clean. In the centre they have a square pit one yard deep to keep the fire, around which they warm themselves in the cold which they experience. . . .

The law they observe, as far as I perceived, is a perfect atheism, for it has never been possible to ascertain that they had any idol, nor even days or hours for sacrifices; it can only be conjectured that they keep some strange ceremony, for when an Indian died they wept and bewailed him and burned him in the chief's house, in which they would not allow any of our people to enter during the act, but upon entering nothing particular was found. . . .

Their arms are made with flint points, their knives of the same material, and some ill-finished ones of iron, cutlass-shaped, with wooden handles, and it is understood that they are provided with these arms from further north. . . .

What they most desired of all that was given them were steel knives and steel bows, though they liked beads, finger rings and hatchets. They despised food and drink, but one or two accepted it politely, pretended to eat it and then threw it away. . . .

They are exceedingly fond of tobacco and had many plantations of it.

Two sailors were so taken by the native way of life that they deserted; however they were soon apprehended, one of them being soundly whipped with musket-straps, "which would have taken his hide right off if the Indians, out of pity, had not pleaded for him."[22]

Finally it was decided that the expedition must push on northward, and this evidently cast a pall over the local populace:

They showed great grief at our departure, and told us by signs that they would mourn us for five days, begging us to return and assuring us that when we did we would find the cross as we had left it.[23]

On June 19 the ships set sail, but failed to make much progress for ten days. Then the winds became more favorable, and by July 9 the two vessels reached 47°30′, not far south of Cape Flattery, where they anchored. They named the local harbor (near modern Port Grenville, Washington) Rada de Bucareli, a name which has since disappeared from maps of this area.

At first all went well. At about 6 A.M. on July 14, according to Father Sierra,

> the commandant, I, the pilot and the surgeon and twenty armed men, went in the launch to take possession of the land, which was done without opposition but with the greatest possible haste and without mass being said, because the weather and the position of the frigate did not admit of any delay.[24]

A few hours later a local chief and his wife came on board and received presents. That afternoon, however, when a party of seven sailors from the *Sonora* went ashore, the natives hid in the bushes and then in a sudden assault murdered them all. Their boat was then demolished and the iron in it carried away in triumph.

Quadra had observed these events with horror ("how painful such a massacre was to me I leave it to the world to judge"). He decided, however, that it would be too dangerous to send another landing party in pursuit, and instead the whites awaited an opportunity for revenge. This was soon afforded when a group of nine Indians approached the now dangerously short-handed *Sonora*:

> A sailor who was at the masthead examining the shoals which the day before had not been seen because they had anchored at high tide, reported that the natives were putting on their skins and stringing their bows even as they approached with their deceitful signs of friendship and invitations to eat. But the men of the schooner, who already had seen what had happened ashore, also dissimulated, showing the Indians glass beads to induce them to come within range of their guns, and the latter, seeing how few men there were on deck, closed in to board the ship on the prow, whereupon our four men with a swivel gun and their muskets opened fire and killed seven of the nine, thus making them pay life for life for the seven Spaniards they had slain.[25]

Soon after these sobering events, the ships left the area and resumed their attempt to reach 65°. Progress was poor, and before long another conference was held to consider turning back to Mexico. Perez was all for doing so, "the wind being diametrically opposed to our reaching a higher latitude, the season far advanced, and the crew either sick or worn out." Quadra would not agree, being determined to disregard

> the labours, casualties, accidents, contingencies and the rest that I have suffered, and which I trust are inevitable to every navigator, and especially to explorers, and which must be borne with resignation and constancy, when it concerns the service of His Majesty, and the credit of the nation by whom we are entrusted with arduous undertakings.[26]

It was decided to persevere a little longer, and six men were transferred to the *Sonora* to replace invalids and casualties. Scant progress was made, however, and scurvy became more widespread. On July 24, some of Hezeta's officers again petitioned him to turn back, but once again he refused. Soon afterward, a great storm struck the ships, they lost sight of each other, and were unable to re-establish contact. Each captain was thus left to make his own decision as to what course to pursue.

As we shall see, Quadra in the *Sonora* elected to continue his voyage northward, and, in his own words, "pressed on, taking fresh trouble for granted"; Hezeta, however soon after sighting the northern end of Vancouver Island on August 11, decided that the *Santiago* should turn back to Mexico. Two days later he did a little trading with some natives who paddled out to his ship, while the next day saw the burial at sea of the master gunner. Favorable winds now carried his ship swiftly south; on August 17 the vessel passed the mouth of the Columbia, which the men recognized as a large river,[27] and on August 29 safely anchored at Monterey. The *Santiago* rested there for two months, during which time the *Sonora* reappeared and the two ships set sail together. The next day Perez died of typhus and was buried at sea, but finally, on November 20, both ships anchored at San Blas.

Before its return the *Sonora* had had an eventful voyage. It had parted company with the *Santiago* on the last day of July; on August 15 land was sighted in latitude 57°, and the next day a large mountain was given the name San Jacinto (later renamed Mt. Edgecumbe by Cook).

In about latitude 57°20′ the ship anchored at a location a little south of Salisbury Sound, which Quadra named Los Remedios, but which is now called Kalalina Bay. Here food and water were taken on board; a little trading was also done with the natives, but under the strictest precautions. The men took formal possession of the area, erecting a cross and carving another on a rock. Later, however, they saw the natives, for unknown motives, remove the cross and set it up again near their dwellings.

The inhabitants indeed seemed in two minds as to what attitude to adopt toward their unexpected visitors. The next day, when Quadra went ashore with a party of men, the Indians "went hurriedly to their house and, returning armed with extremely long lances with flint points, aimed them at us and made skirmishes with gestures of attack. . . ."

Quadra was able to defuse this potentially dangerous situation:

> I hastened forward and gave them to understand that if they came nearer I would fire upon them without further parley, and therefore they must lay down their arms and I would do the same with my men, for I only asked good treatment and friendship. To this argument they agreed, and retiring to their shelter gave me clear opportunity of obtaining all I required.

The voyage was then resumed and on August 22 the *Sonora* reached 58°. Yet even so daring a commander as Quadra knew that he had reached the limit of what was practicable. Accordingly,

> as the cold was excessive, owing to the many snow-covered ranges which lay all along the coast, and the rains were continuous, and the men were in a lamentable state and in rags, they resolved to turn back, examining the coast as they went.[28]

On August 24 Bucareli Sound or Bay (on the western side of the Prince of Wales archipelago in about 55°17′) was discovered,

and given the name which it retains to this day. Formal possession was taken, and the *Sonora* remained in the area for two days.
During this time her crew saw a remarkable natural phenome-
non – an active volcano, "the whole locality being illuminated at
night by the glare."

By this time the *Sonora* was beset by numerous misfortunes:

> Both the captain and the pilot were taken with fevers and
> scorbutic pains, a misfortune which demoralized the four
> sailors who were still fit for duty. Comprehending this, the
> officers made a supreme effort to dominate their maladies,
> and a few days later made their appearance on deck to reas-
> sure the men.[29]

The weather was also highly unfavorable, and the ship
nearly sank in a tremendous storm. As Quadra recorded, "We
thought we were foundering, for during the space of four minutes
there was nothing visible in the whole ship save foaming sea."
Yet, hugging the coast, the *Sonora* made steady progress southward, and in early October reached Monterey, where tended by
the kindly mission fathers, most of the men soon regained their
health. Resuming the voyage, the *Sonora*, in company with the
Santiago, arrived at San Blas on November 20 and, in the words of
Maurelle,

> thus ended our voyage of discovery; and I trust that the fa-
> tigues and distresses which we suffered will redound to the
> advantage and honor of our invincible sovereign, whom
> may God always keep under his holy protection!

There was to be one more Spanish expedition to the northwest coast in this period. In 1777 Viceroy Bucareli ordered Quadra to proceed to Peru and purchase a ship there, as well as anchors, cables, and guns. This he did, returning to San Blas in
February 1778 with the frigate *La Favorita*. During his absence a
second frigate had been constructed and named *Princesa*.

Don Ignacio Arteaga was put in command of this new
expediton, and elaborate maps were drawn up, collating all the
geographical knowledge of the Pacific coast available at that
time. The two ships, ordered to reach 70°, set sail from San Blas
on February 11, 1779, and, keeping close to the coast, by the end

of April had reached Bucareli Bay (55°18′N), which some of those on board were familiar with from the 1775 voyage. After exploring the region in the ship's launches, on May 13,

> mass was sung on shore with full solemnity, the cross was erected with due adoration, and the name "La Santissima Cruz" was given to the harbor, because it was discovered on the celebration day of the Holy Cross, and the festival was attended by several Indians, who remained throughout the mass with great respect and admirable silence.[30]

As on all these early Spanish expeditions, disease now made its appearance, and several men died. The ship's surgeon recommended that a shed be built on shore as a sort of hospital. This was done,

> and such was the care and watchfulness with which he looked after them, that although most of them were in the last stage, and the days at that season had proved very harsh, only two of them died, and he succeeded in a short time in rendering the rest of them sound and robust. . . .
>
> This recovery, like all our work on shore, was much assisted by the gentle behavior of the Indians since our occupation, for there never failed to come daily sundry canoes laden with fish, wolf-skins, bearskins, mats, and other trifling articles, which they bartered with the sailors for beads and pieces of iron, whereof they made particular account.

One transaction in this period was decidedly unusual, as the Spanish acquired four young native children, two boys and two girls, in return for trade goods. The chaplains approved of this, as did Quadra, who explained,

> I allowed this exchange, both because they offered them voluntarily and because the object was to make Christians of them, and free them from the wretched condition in which their unfortunate lot had placed them.

The Spaniards also invited on board a somewhat older Indian boy who they hoped would be useful as an interpreter. This proved a very wise move, for many more Indians began converging on the vicinity until they numbered, by Quadra's estimate, at least a thousand. The boy warned the Spanish that the Indians were planning to assault the two ships, and confirmation of their hostile intentions was given when they threw the cross on the ground. The ships' boats were sent ashore, the cross was rescued and before long set up again, but the atmosphere remained tense.

On June 13 two men were missed from a party which went ashore to wash clothes. It was feared that they had been kidnapped, so as a precaution the whites captured "a strong, stout and good-looking Indian" as a hostage. The two groups later held a parley regarding an exchange of prisoners but without result, and some of the Indians attempted to board one of the Spanish ships. They were fired on, and in the resulting confusion nineteen Indians were captured.

The whites now felt that they held the superior bargaining position, and sent a heavily armed party ashore. It seemed that open warfare might result, for

> directly they arrived, the shore was covered with armed men, wearing breast-plates, collars, helmets and in some cases large and handsome leather jackets covering them from head to foot, with long lances in their hands and letting fly many arrows though without effect.

The far-seeing Quadra had been careful to treat his hostages well, and a further parley resulted in the return of the two missing sailors. Good will all round appeared to have been restored, and friendly relations resumed. The only figures in this drama not to join in the general enthusiasm were the two sailors, who admitted that they had deserted with the intention of taking permanent residence among the Indians. Quadra was unsympathetic, and "ordered that they should receive a hundred lashes apiece, and be imprisoned according to their misdeed."

After making careful observations of the appearance and customs of the natives, and trying without success to find the source of their iron and copper rings, the Spaniards set sail, and moving northward reached Cape St. Elias (59°52′) on the south end of Kayak Island, with Mt. St. Elias looming up in the distance. This is the area that Bering had reached in 1741 from a totally different direction; thus the probing tentacles of two great empires had now, at least symbolically, made contact.

Shortly afterward, the Spanish went through the ceremony of taking formal possession at two localities: the "Port of Santiago," believed to be present-day Port Etches on Hinchinbrook Island, and "Regla Creek," at the entrance to what is now called Cook Inlet.

To reach 70°, however, seemed impossible, and in early August the ships turned back. In mid-September they anchored at San Francisco, where their crews were pleased to get "lots of vegetables and fresh meat." They left there on the last day of the same month and were back at San Blas on November 21.

This was to be the last Spanish expedition to the Pacific northwest for some years, but it had added, at least in theory, a large area to the already far-flung Spanish empire. This had now indeed reached the flood-tide of its glory, holding dominion over both palm and pine, and seemed likely to remain a powerful factor in the arena of international affairs for as far ahead as ordinary vision could foresee.

As it happened, however, there were forces at work which before long would upset such calculations. Despite the remarkable flowering of national energies in the decade that we have been examining, there had long been a fatal lethargy at the very heart of the Spanish empire which would lead, in due course, to paralysis of its limbs; the colonies of South and Central America (inspired to some degree by the American revolution) would soon be rejecting, by force or arms, control of their affairs from Madrid; and powers more vigorous than Spain would be reaching for the trident of power.

CHAPTER FOUR

Britain
at
Nootka

In
1728,
when Vitus Bering

was sailing from Kamchatka on his first expedition to the north
Pacific, half a world away in the small Yorkshire village of Mar-
ton another famous explorer was first seeing the light of day. One
day the name of James Cook would be even more renowned than
that of the intrepid Dane.

Cook's father, also named James, was a Scottish farm la-
borer, and the earliest working years of his son were spent tend-
ing livestock. Tiring of this, at seventeen the young James became apprenticed to a grocer and haberdasher in the village of
Staithes. Yet even these new horizons soon seemed too confining,
and after eighteen months he was apprenticed to John and
Henry Walker, shipowners of Whitby. For most of the period between 1746 and 1755 he sailed on colliers trading between New-
castle and London, although on occasion he took part in voyages
to Ireland and the Baltic. In his spare time he studied mathemat-
ics and navigation, and by 1752 he was the mate of the collier
Friendship. Three years later he was offered the command of the
ship, but surprisingly he declined the offer and instead, on June
17, 1755, enlisted in the navy as an ordinary seaman.

Considering the hard life on a man-of-war, this seems a remarkable decision. Two factors may have been at work: a desire

to see distant parts of the world, and an eagerness to participate in fighting the French, the traditional rival with whom war now threatened.

War indeed came in 1756, and Cook, still an AB, was assigned to H.M.S. *Eagle*. Within a month he was master's mate, and before long received further promotions. In 1758, now a warrant officer in charge of H.M.S. *Pembroke*, he was sent to North American waters, and was present when the great fortress of Louisburg at the mouth of the St. Lawrence capitulated during the summer.

The way to Quebec, center of French power in North America, was now open, but much remained to be done before it could be successfully attacked. The channel, especially upriver, was impassable because of hidden obstacles, and the exact location of these had to be determined. Several ships, among them Cook's, were assigned to this duty, and for many weeks, often under enemy fire, they charted the river. When this task was completed in June 1759, two hundred warships and transports sailed up the river, anchored before Quebec, and began the siege. In September, success crowned British arms at the battle of the Plains of Abraham, and, partly through Cook's tireless efforts, a large part of the world had been added to the empire of Britain.

Cook remained in North American waters for some time, charting the St. Lawrence as far west as Montreal, and also part of the coast of Newfoundland. At the end of 1762 he returned to England, and at the age of thirty-four married Elizabeth Batts, a girl of twenty-one. For the next few years he spent his summers charting North American waters and his winters at his home near London, where he soon had a small family. In this period he was, for the first time, in charge of his own ship, the *Grenville*, and though still not a commissioned officer, he was considered a rising man. In the fall of 1767 he left eastern Canadian waters for the last time, unaware that the most illustrious years of his career were still ahead of him, but determined to advance himself as far as he could in his chosen profession.

The stars themselves now came to his aid. Men of science had long known that the planet Venus would pass between the earth and the sun on June 3, 1769, and that observations made at that time would be useful in computing tables for navigators. The Royal Society decided that the "transit of Venus" should be observed from three widely separated points: the North Cape of Norway, Fort Churchill in Hudson Bay, and some island in the south Pacific. The king directed the Royal Navy to give the society its full co-operation, and the *Earl of Pembroke*, a Whitby-built bark of 368 tons, 105 feet long, was outfitted and rechristened the *Endeavour*.[1] It was decided that Cook was the best choice to command her, and in May 1768 he was commissioned a first lieutenant.

The exact south sea island from which observations were to be made had not yet been chosen, but as luck would have it, in the same month H.M.S. *Dolphin* returned to England from that area. This ship had been sent out to look for a large continent believed to be located somewhere in the southern hemisphere. Although the expedition had not succeeded in this, it had discovered a pleasant island which the commander of the *Dolphin*, Samuel Wallis, had named King George's Island, but which its natives called Tahiti. Wallis reported that this island had excellent anchorages and an abundance of food, water, and wood, and it was accordingly selected as the site for Cook's observations.

The scientific staff of the expedition was chosen with care. It included a rich young nobleman, and Fellow of the Royal Society, Joseph Banks, two Swedish scientists long domiciled in England, Daniel Solander and Herman Sporing, as well as several British draughtsmen and painters who were to make accurate pictures of the unusual varieties of bird, animal, and plant life known to abound in the Pacific. Some of the crew of H.M.S. *Dolphin* also signed on for the voyage.

Late in August 1768 the *Endeavour* left Plymouth, and two months later Cook crossed the Equator. By this time he had opened a sealed packet of additional instructions which informed him that he was not only to observe the transit of Venus, but was to search for the rumored large continent, believed to lie in about 40°s latitude. He was also to take possession for Britain of any new territories that he might discover, and to make detailed notes on the native races of the Pacific.

Moving down the coast of South America, the ship rounded Cape Horn early in 1769 and entered the Pacific. In April Cook reached Tahiti, and when those aboard went ashore after the long voyage they felt as if they were in paradise. The natives appeared to devote themselves to canoe racing, surfboard riding, dancing, and making love. Accounts brought back to Europe of this Arcadia fostered, to some extent, the myth of the "noble savage" which has proved so durable.

After several months of trading with the natives (sometimes for food, sometimes for the less official necessities of life), collecting botanical specimens, exploring nearby islands, and observing the transit of the planet to which the men seemed in some ways dedicated, with infinite reluctance the expedition left in search of the "Great South Land."

By latitude 39°s it became apparent that this continent was likely to prove permanently elusive, and accordingly the ship turned west. In early October Cook sighted New Zealand and anchored. During the winter the expedition accomplished much valuable scientific work, and established that the area consisted of two separate islands which were not in any way part of the Great South Land.[2]

Having taken possession of the north island on November 15, 1769, and of the south island on January 31, 1770,[3] in the spring of 1770 the *Endeavour* once more set sail. Before long the ship was moving along the eastern coast of Australia, where Cook took possession at Botany Bay (near modern Sydney) and apparently also near Cape York, the most northerly point of the continent.[4] During this period the ship was nearly lost on the Great Barrier Reef.[5] Then, passing through the Torres Strait (named after the Portuguese pilot who first sailed through it in 1606) Cook entered the Indian Ocean. From there the ship made its way to the Cape of Good Hope and so back to Plymouth, which it reached in July 1771.

A great deal had been accomplished. Hitherto unknown shores had been charted, botany and biology had had their fields greatly extended, and though the observations of Venus had not proved very useful due to the haze which surrounds that planet, astronomy and navigation had been provided with new data. Exotic forms of life such as the kangaroo would soon be familiar to European readers, and many new names such as New South Wales would soon be appearing on maps.[6] Medicine, too, had made advances, and though almost a third of the crew had died in tropical waters from malaria or dysentery, casualties from scurvy, thanks to the inclusion in the ship's stores of malt, pickled cabbage, and lime juice, had been minimal.

When he returned to England, Cook found himself a hero. The king listened eagerly to his account, while the Royal Society held meetings with the learned explorer. Yet the astronomical observations, like those in the other parts of the world, had not yielded the expected results, nor had the question of the great southern continent, in which many still believed, been settled once and for all. It was accordingly decided that a second expedition must be sent out under the same commander.

This time there were to be two ships. They were originally known as the *Marquis of Granby* and the *Marquis of Rockingham*, were renamed the *Drake* and *Raleigh*, and then, for fear of hurting the feelings of the Spanish (who did not regard these figures highly) were rechristened the *Resolution* and *Adventure*.

The scientific preparations were even more elaborate than before. Improved types of the sextant and chronometer were made available.[7] The wealthy amateur scientist Joseph Banks did not accompany the ships, but a variety of botanists, astronomers, and artists were assembled.

In July 1772, after visiting his aged father[8] and bidding farewell to his pregnant wife, Cook set sail with 110 men in the *Resolution*, accompanied by Capt. Tobias Furneaux with 80 men in the *Adventure*. The ships sailed south past Spain and Africa, called at Cape Town for additional supplies, and then moved farther and farther south into latitudes where no human being had yet ventured. In January, threading his way past huge icebergs, Cook became the first white man to cross the Antarctic Circle, but the pack ice was soon so thick that the ship turned north again. Soon afterward, in a thick fog, the two ships lost contact. It had previously been agreed that in such an eventuality they would rendezvous at Queen Charlotte Sound, New Zealand, which the *Resolution* entered in May 1773 to find the *Adventure* at anchor.

A little time was spent in resting and repairing the ships, and then the expedition sailed north to Tahiti, where old friendships were renewed and trading was brisk. Later, the exploration of the Pacific between Tahiti and the Great Barrier Reef was undertaken, during which, because of the affability of the natives, Cook gave their present name to the Friendly Islands.

In the fall of 1773 the ships again lost contact with each other in a storm. After several incidents, in one of which ten of the ship's crew were slaughtered and eaten by Maoris, the *Adventure* returned to England on her own. The *Resolution*, however, continued to explore the south seas alone.

Early in 1774 Cook once more sailed south, reaching the southerly latitude of 71°10's, at which point icebergs were too numerous to count. No great southern continent was visible, however, and Cook again turned north. In March he reached Easter Island (discovered by Jacob Roggeveen in 1722) where, like all subsequent visitors, he was astonished and puzzled by the array of great stone idols about whose origins he could learn nothing. Later the *Resolution* touched at the Marquesas Islands, discovered by the Spaniard Mendana in 1595; then it returned once more to Tahiti, where Cook (or "Tootee,"as the natives called him) was welcomed by old friends.

Leaving Tahiti in May, Cook explored other Pacific islands, giving their present name to the New Hebrides, and returned to New Zealand in the fall. Here he rested and refitted the ship, then he sailed east across several thousand miles of ocean to Cape Horn, which he passed without difficulty, and continued on to the Cape of Good Hope. After a rest, during which he learned that Furneaux in the *Adventure* had preceded him there,[9] he sailed north, reaching England at the end of July 1775. His second great voyage had taken three years and eighteen days; in that time he had lost only four men, a most remarkable achievement.

At last promoted to the rank of captain, as well as elected a member of the Royal Society, Cook was, at the age of forty-seven, more famous than ever, since Furneaux had already recounted some of the wonders which the two commanders had witnessed. Cook now had two young sons, but he was not allowed to relax for long with his family. Still a third expedition was prepared, and one of its purposes was to settle once and for all the existence of a passage between the Pacific Ocean and Hudson Bay. By this time, we might note, the reward of £20,000 voted by parliament in 1745 for the discovery of the northwest passage had been extended to include ships of the Royal Navy as well as private adventurers.

Cook was instructed to reach the North American coast at about 45°, but not to explore it in detail until he reached 65°, where he was "very carefully to search for, and to explore, such rivers or inlets as may appear to be of a considerable extent, and pointing towards Hudson's or Baffin's Bay." If he found the northwest passage, he was to sail through it. While in northern waters he was also to keep an eye out for a northeast passage, i.e., a channel across the top of Russia which led back to the Atlantic.[10]

There were doubtless several reasons for chosing 45° as the point at which to make a landfall. This was north of any point which, in British eyes, could be considered a part of the Spanish Empire. Britain had no wish to see the voyage cause an international incident, and Cook received explicit orders on this point:

> You are also, in your way thither, strictly enjoined not to touch upon any part of the Spanish dominions on the western continent of America, unless driven thither by some unavoidable accident, in which case you are to stay no longer there than shall be absolutely necessary, and to be very careful not to give umbrage or offence to any of the inhabitants or subjects of his Catholic Majesty.

There was also in Cook's instructions an unmistakable reference to the possibility that in his travels he might come upon Russian settlements:

> And if in your farther progress to the northward, as hereafter directed, you find any subjects of any European prince or state upon any part of the coast you may think proper to visit, you are not to disturb them or give them any just cause of offence but on the contrary to treat them with civility and friendship.[11]

That these orders were justified, at least in the case of Spain, is apparent from the fact that in Madrid some uneasiness was felt about the expedition even before it set out. No sooner had Spanish agents in England got wind of it than word was conveyed to the viceroy in Mexico, instructing him, if Cook's ships called there, to discover their real aims; the viceroy was also told to give Cook only very limited supplies. Indeed, once the ships had actually left the British Isles, even stronger instructions were issued. They were not only to be denied admittance to Spanish ports, but "if there should be force enough, owing to the diminished strength of Cook on arrival, or for other reasons, proceedings were to be taken to detain, imprison and try him and his men as the laws directed."[12]

Another reason, perhaps, for choosing 45° as the point of landfall was that if, by any chance, that fabled strait reported by Juan de Fuca actually existed, Cook would be able to locate it.[13]

His orders not to examine the coast very closely until he reached 65° were doubtless based on the strong conviction that the northwest passage could not lie south of this point. In 1771 Samuel Hearne, exploring the northern wastes of the continent, had reached the mouth of the Coppermine River at 67°48', and had reported that he had found no channel lying east and west across his path.

The scientific aspect of the expedition was also strongly stressed in Cook's instructions:

> You are also carefully to observe the nature of the soil and the produce thereof; the animals & fowls that inhabit or frequent it, the fishes that are to be found in the rivers or upon the coast, and in what plenty; and in case there are any peculiar to such places, to describe them as minutely, and to make as accurate drawings of them as you can.
>
> And if you find any metals, minerals, or valuable stones, or any extraneous fossils, you are to bring home specimens of each, as also of the seeds of such trees, shrubs, plants, fruits, and grains, peculiar to those places, as you may be able to collect, and to transmit them to our secretary, that proper examination and experiments may be made of them.

The expansion of the British empire was not, however, overlooked, and Cook was told

> to take possession, in the name of the King of Great Britain, of convenient situations in such countries as you may discover, that have not already been discovered or visited by

any other European power, and to distribute among the inhabitants such things as will remain as traces and testimonies of your having been there; but if you find the countries so discovered are uninhabited, you are to take possession of them for His Majesty by setting up proper marks and inscriptions as first discoverers & possessors.

As a sign that the British sense of humor was already well developed, it was made clear that new lands were only to be added to the empire "with the consent of the natives."

Two ships were outfitted for the voyage: the *Resolution* (462 tons) and a Whitby-built collier, the *Diligence* (298 tons), now renamed the *Discovery*. Cook commanded the former, while the latter was put in charge of Charles Clerke. Among those sailing with Cook were two men who would achieve fame independently: William Bligh, then only twenty-two, later to command the *Bounty*,[14] and a young midshipman, George Vancouver. Various scientists were also on board.

By the time the ships were ready to sail, two important events had taken place. One was the reporting by a British periodical of the Spanish discoveries of 1774 and 1775 on the northwest coast. Details of the voyages of these two years had been somewhat intermingled, and are far from accurate, but at least Cook knew (as he tells us in his account) that a rival power was active in the area which he would soon be visiting.[15]

Perhaps a more important development was the growing rebellion by the American colonies, which formally declared their independence a few days before Cook sailed. Fortunately, Benjamin Franklin, the United States minister to France, was an ardent scientist, and he provided a safe conduct so that the British ships would be in no way molested.

On July 12, 1776, Cook set sail, followed on August 1 by Clerke, and before long both ships reached the Cape of Good Hope. They then went on to New Zealand, which by now must have become a familiar place to those who had been on either or both the previous voyages.

It was now the spring of 1777, and for the remainder of the year the two ships explored the south seas, calling at Tahiti in August. Here Cook saw scenes of human sacrifice, but felt unable to intervene. The end of the year found the ships sailing north, and Christmas Island near the equator was discovered and named at that time.

January 1778 brought a remarkable discovery. Cook found a group of islands populated by Polynesians, and was amazed to discover that this race had spread so far north. He was much taken by the appearance and character of the natives, whose homeland he named the Sandwich Islands, in honor of the Earl of Sandwich, First Lord of the Admiralty; today they are called the Hawaiian Islands.[16]

No doubt the explorers would have liked to linger here, but there was little chance in this idyllic place of acquiring much information about the northwest passage. In early February the two ships set sail for the northwest coast of America, or, as Cook, using Sir Francis Drake's name, called it, "New Albion."

This they reached on March 7 at about latitude 44°, and began working their way northward under conditions which led Cook to name a nearby point Cape Foulweather. Another point was named Cape Gregory.[17] Later, at about 48°N, he gave Cape Flattery its present name (because it "flattered us with the hopes of finding a harbour")[18] but, surprisingly, he failed to find the strait whose entrance it guards. Indeed he went so far as to state: "It is in this very latitude where we now were, that geographers have placed the pretended strait of Juan de Fuca. But we saw nothing like it; nor is there the least probability that ever any such thing existed.."[19]

Cook sailed on up the coast, from time to time out of sight of land, until he reached 49°N. There he noted that the nearby mainland (as he thought it, though it was in fact Vancouver Island) was ". . .covered to a considerable breadth with high straight trees, that formed a beautiful prospect, as of one vast forest."[20]

On March 29 Cook entered a shallow bay, which he called Hope Bay. The northwest point of it he named Woody Point (now known as Cape Cook),[21] and the southwest point Point Breakers. The latter has been known since about 1850 as Estevan Point, and is believed by many to be the Punta San Esteban of Perez.[22]

Entering a narrow channel, Cook's ships passed through

into what he at first called King George's Sound (now called Nootka Sound), and anchored in Ship Cove (now Resolution Cove).[23] It was quickly discovered that the area was inhabited:

We no sooner drew near the inlet, than we found the coast to be inhabited; and at the place where we were first becalmed three canoes came off to the ship. In one of these were two men, in another six, and in the third, ten. Having come pretty near us, a person in one of the two last stood up, and made a long harangue, inviting us to land, as we guessed, by his gestures. At the same time, he kept strewing handfuls of feathers toward us; and some of his companions threw handfuls of a red dust or powder in the same manner.[24]

The next day a lively trade sprang up between the two races:

The articles which they offered to sale were skins of various animals, such as bears, wolves, foxes, deer, racoons, polecats, martins; and, in particular, of the sea otters, which are found at the islands east of Kamtschatka [sic].

Besides the skins in their native shape, they also brought garments made of them, and another sort of clothing made of the bark of a tree, or some plant like hemp; weapons, such as bows, arrows and spears; fish-hooks, and instruments of various kinds; wooden vizors of many different monstrous figures; a sort of woollen stuff or blanketing; bags filled with red ochre; pieces of carved work; beads; and several other little ornaments of thin brass or iron, shaped like a horseshoe, which they hang at their noses; and several chisels, or pieces of iron fixed to handles. From their possessing which metals, we could infer that they had either been visited before by some civilized nation, or had connexions with them. But the most extraordinary of all the articles which they brought to the ships for sale were human skulls, and hands not yet quite stripped of the flesh, which they made our people plainly understand they had eaten; and, indeed, some of them had evident marks that they had been upon the fire. We had but too much reason to suspect from this circumstance, that the horrid practice of feeding on their enemies is as prevalent here as we had found it to be at New Zealand and other South Sea islands.[25] For the various articles which they brought, they took in exchange knives, chisels, pieces of iron and tin, nails, looking-glasses, buttons, or any kind of metal. Glass beads they were not fond of; and cloth of every sort they rejected.[26]

From the familiarity of the Indians with iron and other metals, it seemed plain to Cook that they must have had contacts of some sort with Europeans. Now two objects were brought forward, acquired by the natives from a visiting tribe, which put this beyond doubt:

> But what was most singular, two silver table-spoons were purchased from them, which from their peculiar shape we supposed to be of Spanish manufacture. One of these strangers wore them round his neck by way of ornament. These visitors also appeared to be more plentifully supplied with iron than the inhabitants of the sound.[27]

All this time Cook and his scientific assistants had been making the most careful notes on the area. The climate, especially, struck them at once most favorably:

> The climate, as far as we had any experience of it, is infinitely milder than that on the east coast of America under the same parallel of latitude. The mercury in the thermometer never, even in the night, fell lower than 42°; and very often in the day it rose to 60°. No such thing as frost was perceived in any of the low ground; on the contrary, vegetation had made a considerable progress; for I met with grass that was already above a foot long.[28]

The natives also received close attention, and during the few weeks that the two ships were at Nootka, members of the expedition compiled a remarkably detailed account of their appearance and mode of life. It was apparent that physically they resembled Asiatics or Polynesians more than Europeans:

> The persons of the natives are in general under the common stature, but not slender in proportion, being commonly

pretty full or plump, though not muscular. Neither doth the soft fleshiness seem ever to swell into corpulence, and many of the older people are rather spare or lean. The visage of most of them is round and full, and sometimes also broad, with high prominent cheeks; and above these the face is frequently much depressed, or seems fallen in quite across the temples, the nose also flattening at its base, with pretty wide nostrils and a rounded point. The forehead rather low, the eyes small, black, and rather languishing than sparkling, the mouth round with large round thickish lips, the teeth tolerably equal and well set, but not remarkably white. . . . Their eyebrows are also scanty and always narrow, but the hair of the head is in great abundance, very coarse and strong, and without a single exception black, straight and lank, or hanging down over the shoulders. The neck is short; the arms and body have no particular mark of beauty or elegance in their formation, but are rather clumsy; and the limbs, in all, are very small in proportion to the other parts, and crooked, or ill made, with large feet badly shaped, and projecting angles. This last defect seems, in a great measure, to arise from their sitting so much on their hams or knees, both in their canoes and houses.

Upon the whole, a very remarkable sameness seems to characterize the countenances of the whole nation, a dull phlegmatic want of expression, with very little variation, being strongly marked in all of them. The women are nearly of the same size, colour, and form, with the men, from whom it is not easy to distinguish them, as they possess no natural delicacies sufficient to render their persons agreeable; and hardly any one was seen, even amongst those who are in the prime of life, who had the least pretensions to be called handsome.[29]

Psychologically, too, the Indians appeared to differ from Western Europeans of the day:

Their other passions, especially their curiosity, appear in some measure to lie dormant; for few expressed any desire to see or examine things wholly unknown to them; and which, to those truly possessed of that passion, would have appeared astonishing. They were always contented to procure the articles they knew and wanted, regarding everything else with great indifference; nor did our persons, apparel and manners, so different from their own, or even the extraordinary size and construction of our ships, seem to excite admiration or even engage attention. One cause of this may be their indolence, which seems considerable. But, on the other hand, they are certainly not wholly unsusceptible of the tender passions; if we may judge from their being so fond of music, which is mostly of the grave or serious, but truly pathetic sort. They keep the exactest concert in their songs, which are often sung by great numbers together, as those already mentioned with which they used to entertain us in their canoes.[30]

The native dwellings did not arouse much admiration in the visitors:

They are built of very long and broad planks, resting upon the edges of each other, fastened or tied with withes of pine bark here and there, and have only slender posts, or rather poles, at considerable distances on the outside, to which they are also tied; but within are some larger poles, placed aslant. The height of the sides and ends of these habitations is seven or eight feet, but the back part is a little higher, by which means the planks that compose the roof slant forward, and are laid on loose, so as to be moved about, either to be put close to exclude the rain, or in fair weather to be separated to let in the light and carry out the smoke. They are, however, upon the whole miserable dwellings, and constructed with little care or ingenuity. For though the side-planks be made to fit pretty closely in some places, in others they are quite open, and there are no regular doors into them, the only way of entrance being either by a hole where the unequal length of the planks has accidentally left an opening, or in some cases, planks are made to pass a little beyond each other, or overlap, about two feet asunder, and the entrance is in this space. There are also holes or windows in the sides of the houses to look out at; but without any regularity of

67

shape or disposition, and these have bits of mat hung before them to prevent the rain getting in. . . .

On the inside, one may frequently see from one end to the other of these ranges of buildings without interruption. For though in general there be the rudiments, or rather vestiges, of separations on each side, for the accommodation of different families, they are such as do not intercept the sight, and often consist of no more than pieces of plank, running from the side toward the middle of the house, so that if they were complete, the whole might be compared to a long stable with a double range of stalls, and a broad passage in the middle. Close to the sides in each of these parts is a little bench of boards, raised five or six inches higher than the rest of the floor, and covered with mats, on which the family sit and sleep. These benches are commonly seven or eight feet long and four or five broad. In the middle of the floor, between them, is the fire-place, which has neither hearth nor chimney. . . .

Their furniture consists chiefly of a great number of chests and boxes of all sizes, which are generally piled upon each other close to the sides or ends of the house, and contain their spare garments, skins, masks and other things which they set a value upon.[31]

The sea was clearly the main source of food for the community, and together with roots and berries provided a well-balanced and easily obtainable diet for the tribe:

The chief employment of the men seems to be that of fishing and killing land or sea animals for the sustenance of their families, for we saw few of them doing anything in the houses; whereas the women were occupied in manufacturing their flaxen or woollen garments, and in preparing the sardines for drying, which they also carry up from the beach in twig baskets, after the men have brought them in their canoes. The women are also sent in the small canoes to gather mussels and other shell-fish, and perhaps on some other occasions, for they manage these with as much dexterity as the men, who, when in the canoes with them, seem to pay little attention to their sex by offering to relieve them from the labour of the paddle; nor, indeed, do they treat them with any particular respect or tenderness in other situations.[32]

The work ethic was not, however, ineradicably entrenched at Nootka:

The young men appeared to be the most indolent or idle set in this community, for they were either sitting about in scattered companies to bask themselves in the sun, or lay wallowing in the sand upon the beach, like a number of hogs, for the same purpose, without any covering.[33]

The canoes of the Nootka, some forty feet long and seven feet broad, excited the admiration of the whites, as did the ingenious use of available materials, such as mussel shells and cedar bark, to make harpoons and ropes for hunting whales. This, Cook asserted, "shows a great reach of contrivance."[34]

As to the political or religious institutions of the tribe, Cook was unable in a few weeks to form a very clear picture. The carved "images" set up at the ends of the long-houses attracted his curiosity, but he found it impossible to decide whether they were "representations of their gods or symbols of some religious or superstitious object."[35]

Not all the contacts between the two races were set down in the official account of the expedition. Some must be derived from journals kept by those on board which have since found their way into print. Thus, for example, David Samwell, surgeon of the *Discovery*, recorded on April 6, 1778, some scenes on board the vessel:

Hitherto we had seen none of their young women though we had often given the men to understand how agreeable their company would be to us & how profitable to themselves, in consequence of which they about this time brought two or three girls to the ships; tho some of them had no bad faces yet as they were exceedingly dirty their persons at first sight were not very inviting; however our young gentlemen were not to be discouraged by such an obstacle as this which they found was to be removed with soap & warm water; this they called the Ceremony of Purification, and were themselves the officiators at it & it must be mentioned to their praise that they performed it with much piety & devotion.

Their fathers who generally accompanied them made the bargain & received the price of their prostitution of their daughters, which was commonly a pewter plate well scoured for one night. When they found that this was a profitable trade, they brought more young women to the ships, who in compliance with our preposterous humour spared themselves the trouble of laying on their paint & us of washing it off again by making themselves tolerable clean before they came to us, by which they found they were more welcome visitors and thus by falling in with our ridiculous notions (for such no doubt they deemed them) they found means at last to disburthen our young gentry of their kitchen furniture; many of us after leaving this harbour not being able to muster a plate to eat our salt beef from.[36]

Much of interest and value had been added to the stock of the world's knowledge in these few brief weeks, and two of Cook's observations were to cast a very long shadow indeed. One was his casual reference to "the largest pine-trees that I ever saw," which later visitors would confirm and future enterprisers one day make the basis of the most important industry of British Columbia. This development, however, did not come until the middle and later years of the succeeding century; more immediate in its influence was his enthusiastic description of the sea-otters which abounded in the area. Cook was a naval officer, not a businessman; but even he sensed that he should draw the attention of the world to these animals:

> The fur of these animals, as mentioned in the Russian accounts, is certainly softer and finer than that of any others we know of; and therefore the discovery of this part of the continent of North America, where so valuable an article of commerce may be met with, cannot be a matter of indifference.[37]

He added a prophecy which time would soon verify:

> I make no doubt, that whoever comes after me to this place, will find the natives prepared accordingly, with no inconsid-

erable supply of an article of trade, which they could observe we were eager to possess, and which we found could be purchased to great advantage.[38]

Within a decade the fur trade would have a drastic, dramatic, and irreversible effect on this remote corner of the globe. The great navigator, however, was to see none of these great changes or predictions come to pass. On Sunday, April 26, 1778, he said farewell to Nootka (which he still believed was part of the mainland of North America). The last scene was marked with regret on both sides:

> Our friends the natives attended us till we were almost out of the sound, some on board the ships, and others in their canoes. One of their chiefs, who had some time before attached himself to me, was amongst the last who left us. Having before he went bestowed upon him a small present, I received in return a beaver-skin of much greater value. This called upon me to make some addition to my present, which pleased him so much that he insisted upon my acceptance of the beaver-skin cloak which he then wore, and of which I knew he was particularly fond. Struck with this instance of generosity, and desirous that he should be no sufferer by his friendship to me, I presented to him a new broad-sword with a brass hilt, the possession of which made him completely happy. He, and also many others of his countrymen, importuned us much to pay them another visit, and, by way of encouragement, promised to lay in a good stock of skins.[39]

Quite a few of those on board the two ships had taken the opportunity of securing furs from the natives in exchange for trinkets, although more with a view of making clothes out of them than anything else. There is little indication in the various accounts of the voyage that their resale was envisioned.[40] When the ships left Nootka, they had with them, according to one estimate, "more than 300 beaver skins on board, besides other less valuable skins of foxes, racoons, wolves, bears, deer and several other wild animals."[41]

After leaving Nootka, Cook, as he had been instructed, paid little attention to the coast between 50° and 55°, and proceeded directly to more northern waters. Here he named Prince William Sound (after a son of George III), Cape Hinchinbrook, at the sound's entrance, as well as Mount Edgecumbe and Mount Fairweather. Early in May he sighted Mt. St. Elias and recognized it as the peak glimpsed nearly forty years before by Bering.

On May 11, Cook landed on what the intrepid Dane had called St. Elias Island, but which his British successor now named Kaye Island, after the king's chaplain. Here he "left a bottle in which was an inscription setting forth the ships' names, date &c and two silver two penny pieces (date 1772)." Although he does not say so explicitly, he evidently considered that he was taking possession of this remote spot for Britain – something which he had not done previously on the American coast, either at Nootka or anywhere else.[42] His judgment was that Russia had not yet contacted the natives of this area, since "if that had been the case, we should hardly have found them clothed in such valuable skins as those of the sea otter."

In late May Cook entered Prince William Sound and anchored in what he named Snug Corner Cove. The largest island in the sound he called Montagu Island. Yet the northwest passage was still nowhere to be found, and Cook soon proceeded farther west, entering the deep inlet to which he gave no name, but which was later called Cook's River and is today Cook's Inlet. Near the entrance to this inlet he named Mount St. Augustine and Cape Bede after two famous religious figures.

Later, on June 1, far up the inlet at a place which is still called Possession Point, the name that Cook gave it, the expedition did, beyond doubt, go through the formal procedure of taking possession.

Leaving the inlet after a stay of about ten days, Cook sailed westward along the southern side of the Aleutian chain, searching for a way through it into more northern waters. This he found at Unalga Pass, which he passed through and then anchored briefly at the harbor of Samgoonoodha (which the Russians later renamed English Bay, in his honor) on Unalaska Island. He then doubled back along the northern side of the Aleutians until he reached the mainland of Alaska again. At a point on its southwest shore, just north of Bristol Bay, at about $58°42'$N, he named and took possession of Cape Newenham.[43]

Moving north along the Alaska coast, in early August he saw the most western point of North America, as well as Diomede Island, the stepping-stone to Asia. Sailing boldly through Bering Strait into arctic waters, he eventually reached 70°44′N. Here a thick barrier of ice prevented further progress, and he made a quick trip to the corresponding shore of Asia and then back again. By now satisfied that there was no hope of discovering the northwest passage, he turned south, and eventually anchored once more at Unalaska. Here he made contact with Russian fur-traders; no interpreters were available, but Cook was shown some charts and was able to gain a fair picture of Russian activities in the Aleutian area:

> There are Russians settled upon all the principal islands between Oonalashka and Kamtschatka [*sic*], for the sole purpose of collecting furs. Their great object is the sea beaver or otter; I never heard them enquire after any other animal, not that they let any other furs slip through their fingers when they can get them. I never thought to ask how long it was since they got a footing upon Oonalashka and the neighboring isles, but to judge from the great subjection the natives are under, it must have been some time. All these furriers are relieved from time to time by others, tho those we met with came here from Okhotsk in 1776 and are to return in 1781 so that their stay at the island will be four years at least.[44]

On October 26 the two ships sailed for Hawaii, which they reached late in the year. Here they spent most of January 1779, and were received with great enthusiasm by the natives. Early in February Cook sailed away, but a storm soon forced him to return. This time, a series of unfortunate incidents caused increasingly tense relations between the natives and their visitors. Violence broke out, and in a brief but savage scuffle at the water's edge on February 14, 1779, Cook and four of his men were slain.[45]

That night the Hawaiians burnt his corpse on a funeral pyre, but a few days later Captain Clerke and Lieutenant King were able to recover his skull, arm and leg bones, and hands. These were solemnly committed to the deep, and then, with heavy hearts, the crew of the two ships sailed away to Kamchatka.

In the summer of 1779, a final search was made for the northwest passage in arctic waters, in the course of which Captain Clerke also reached 70°. Once again, however, the fabled strait eluded the expedition, and the two ships returned to Kamchatka. Near Petropavlovsk on August 22 Captain Clerke died, probably from the effect of the damp arctic air on his lungs. Capt. John Gore then took command of the *Resolution* and King of the *Discovery*.

At Petropavlovsk it was discovered that the business of the area was "entirely confined to furs, and carried on principally by a company of merchants, instituted by the present empress." Both the natives and the visitors were quickly able to profit from this situation:

> Our sailors brought a great number of furs with them from the coast of America, and were not less astonished than delighted with the quantity of silver the merchants paid down for them; but on finding neither gin-shops to resort to, nor tobacco, or anything else that they cared for, to be had for money, the roubles soon became troublesome companions, and I often observed them kicking about the deck. The merchant I have already had occasion to mention gave our men at first thirty roubles for a sea-otter's skin, and for others in proportion; but finding that they had considerable quantities to dispose of, and that he had men to deal with who did not know how to keep up the market, he afterward bought them for much less.[46]

King was able to ascertain some further particulars of the fur trade:

> The best sea-otter skins sell generally in Kamtschatka for about thirty roubles apiece. The Chinese merchant at Kiachta purchases them at more than double that price, and sells them again at Pekin at a great advance, where a farther profitable trade is made with some of them to Japan. If, therefore, a skin is worth thirty roubles at Kamtschatka, to be transported first to Okhotsk, thence to be conveyed by

land to Kiachta, a distance of one thousand three hundred and sixty-four miles, thence on to Pekin, seven hundred and sixty miles more, and after this to be transported to Japan, what a prodigiously advantageous trade might be carried on between this place and Japan, which is but a fortnight's, or at most three weeks, sail from it.[47]

It was now late in 1779, and the ships proceeded to Canton, where a bargain was struck between King and a Chinese merchant regarding twenty sea-otter skins "chiefly the property of the deceased commanders":

Having laid my goods before him, he examined them with great care over and over again, and at last he told me that he could not venture to offer more than three hundred dollars for them. As I knew from the price our skins had sold for in Kamtschatka that he had not offered me one half their value, I found myself under the necessity of driving a bargain. In my turn I therefore demanded one thousand; my Chinese then advanced to five hundred; then offered me a private present of tea and porcelain, amounting to one hundred more; then the same sum in money; and lastly rose to seven hundred dollars, on which I fell to nine hundred. Here, each side declaring he would not recede, we parted; but the Chinese soon returned with a list of India goods, which he now proposed I should take in exchange, and which, I was afterward told, would have amounted in value, if honestly delivered, to double the sum he had before offered. Finding I did not choose to deal in this mode, he proposed as his ultimatum, that we should divide the difference, which, being tired of the contest, I consented to, and received the eight hundred dollars.[48]

At Macao there were also willing purchasers for the products of Nootka:

One of our seamen sold his stock alone for eight hundred dollars; and a few prime skins, which were clean and had been well preserved, were sold for one hundred and twenty each. The whole amount of the value, in specie and goods, that was got for the furs in both ships, I am confident did not fall short of two thousand pounds sterling; and it was generally supposed that at least two-thirds of the quantity we had originally got from the Americans were spoiled and worn out, or had been given away, and otherwise disposed of, at Kamtschatka. When in addition to these facts it is remembered that the furs were at first collected without our having any idea of their real value; that the greatest part had been worn by the Indians from whom we purchased them; that they were afterward preserved with little care, and frequently used for bed-clothes and other purposes during our cruise to the north, and that probably we had never got the full value for them in China; the advantages that might be derived from a voyage to that part of the American coast, undertaken with commercial views, appear to me of a degree of importance sufficient to call for the attention of the public.[49]

By now the crews of the two ships were so anxious to return to Nootka for more skins that they were in a state "not far short of mutiny"; even King outlined in his journal a plan whereby at some future time a lively trade might be set in motion between China and North America. Discipline, however, prevailed, and in October 1779 the ships set their course for Europe. On October 6, 1780, four years and three months after setting out, the *Resolution* and *Discovery* were again in English waters.

So ended the last of these three great voyages of exploration. Hitherto uncharted lands had been added to the empire of Britain; even wider realms to the kingdom of knowledge.[50] Moreover, though none were aware of it yet, the world's commerce had received a sharp new stimulus; at least a few now knew that the entire northwest coast of America was rich in furs. As events were to show, once this fact became the common property of mankind, it would set in motion a general rush to the area, transforming it forever. Now that the *Discovery* and *Resolution* had left it, the sheltered harbor of Nootka was quiet again; yet within a decade it would be the busy marketplace of several nations.

CHAPTER FIVE

The First
of the
Fur-Traders

There is not the least doubt
that a very beneficial fur trade
might be carried on with
the inhabitants of this vast coast.

JAMES COOK

It was 1780 when the *Resolution* and *Discovery* returned to England, but it was to be several years before Nootka became part of the general consciousness of the world. Although John Rickman in 1781 and John Ledyard in 1783 had given many interesting details of Cook's last expedition, the official account, published under the authority of the British Admiralty, did not appear until 1784.[1] After this date, accurate knowledge of the northwest coast of America and of its rich resources in fur was readily available, and it was not long before those with an eye to profit-making began to converge on Nootka.

The first to consider such an enterprise was apparently one William Bolts, who, as early as 1781, was planning a voyage to Nootka from Trieste on the Adriatic Sea. A ship of 700 tons called the *Cobenzell*, accompanied by a tender of 45 tons, was to carry a large crew, including numerous scientists, to the northwest coast, circumventing the monopolistic rights of the East India Company and the South Sea Company by sailing under the Austrian flag.[2] It would appear, however, that high officials in Vienna were for some reason opposed to this venture, and succeeded in preventing it.[3]

The next to consider a fur-trading voyage to the northwest

77

coast was probably John Ledyard, who had sailed with Cook. In 1782 he tried to interest the Philadelphia financier Robert Morris in such a venture, but without success. Later Ledyard journeyed to France in hope of support there, but the government showed no interest. However, it is reported that Thomas Jefferson, the American minister to France, "approved most highly his design," and it is possible that the seed was sown in his mind which would result twenty years later in the famous journey of Lewis and Clark to the Pacific coast.[4]

The first actually to arrive at Nootka after the departure of Captain Cook was James Hanna, who, with a crew of thirty[5] in the 60-ton brig *Sea Otter*, made the long voyage from the Portuguese enclave of Macao on the coast of China in the summer of 1785. Cook had remarked of the natives around Cape Hinchinbrook that "these people were also desirous of iron, but they wanted pieces eight or ten inches long at least, and of the breadth of three or four fingers."[6] Taking his cue from this, Hanna loaded his ship with iron bars, which he planned to barter for furs.

His ship had been outfitted at Canton by John Henry Cox, a British trader in far eastern waters who had previously done well in that area out of toys, cotton, and opium,[7] and who had no doubt been aware for some time that Cook's expedition had disposed of furs from the northwest coast at good prices in Canton and Macao.

Friends of Cox connected with the East India Company provided additional financial backing, and on April 15, 1785, Hanna set sail in his small vessel from Macao. For a month he made little progress, and a shortage of water forced him to put into a small bay near Amoy on the Chinese mainland. Here he got "fresh fish and fowls, but at a very dear rate, the inhabitants being exorbitant and thievish." Then, leaving China behind, he sailed up the east coast of Japan, where he witnessed an active volcano, which

> made a horrible appearance, casting up repeated clouds of thick black smoak, [*sic*] which impregnated the air with a suffocating sulpherish smell; these clouds of smoak was always preceded by a clap of thunder or roaring like distant cannonading.

At daylight the decks was covered with a sort of stuff like lampblack that fell on us in the night from the vulcano [sic], the mouth of which is very wide & situated about the middle of the island.[8]

Moving across the Pacific at the rate of about fifty miles a day in a slightly northeasterly direction, by the end of July Hanna was approaching the mild but cloudy climes of the northwest coast of America. As he noted in his journal,

The weather for a long time has been as warm as Europeans can wish, the sea commonly smooth and winds moderate, but then it is so thick, wet & hazey or foggy that since the 14th May we have not had a clear sky or opportunity of observing for long. &c either by night or day. . . .

On August 3 Hanna "saw the stumps of two trees" and knew that land was close; three days later he "saw three beautiful white birds like tropick birds." At noon on August 8 he arrived at Nootka and noted that, "The land is remarkably high, and there appear to be several bays or rivers."

Unfortunately the remainder of Hanna's log was been lost, but other sources have provided some further details of the *Sea Otter's* historic voyage:

Soon after her arrival, the natives, whom Captain Cook had left unacquainted with the effects of fire-arms, tempted probably by the diminutive size of the vessel (scarce longer than some of their own canoes) and the small number of her people, attempted to board her in open day; but were repulsed with considerable slaughter. This was the introduction to a firm and lasting friendship. Capt. Hanna cured such of the Indians as were wounded; an unreserved confidence took place – they traded fairly and peaceably – a valuable cargo of furs was procured, and the bad weather setting in, he left the coast in the end of September, touched at the Sandwich Islands, and arrived at Macao the end of December of the same year.[9]

Captain Hanna had brought back 560 sea-otter pelts, and these he disposed of to Chinese merchants at Macao for 20,400

Spanish dollars. This first purely commercial voyage to Nootka had thus proved a considerable financial success.[10]

It evidently emboldened him to try his luck again the following year. Leaving Macao in May 1786 in a 120-ton vessel, also named the *Sea Otter*, Hanna got to Nootka in August, but found that "two ships had lately been there who had bought all the furs."[11] After staying in the area for two weeks, during which he secured only fifty pelts, he decided to try other places farther up the coast, including Queen Charlotte Sound (as yet unnamed). He also constructed a chart, and gave names to some points of interest.[12] The most easterly of what are now the Scott Islands, near the northern tip of Vancouver Island (which Hanna, like Cook, believed to be part of the mainland) he called Cox's Island, and the remainder of the group Lance's Islands.[13] He also named what is now San Josef Bay (50°30′N, 128°30′W) St. Patrick's Bay.

At Ahousat in Clayoquot Sound,[14] on the western coast of Vancouver Island, he struck up so close a friendship with the native chief, Cleaskinah, that the two men exchanged names. The chief, under his new name, was to become well known to later voyagers.[15]

Hanna did not have much luck, however, in securing additional pelts, and leaving American waters in early October, he was back at Macao on February 8, 1787, with a cargo which fetched only $8,000.[16] Even so, he resolved to try yet another voyage, but at this point fate intervened, and "before he could engage in a third, this active and able seaman was called to take that voyage from whence there is no return."[17]

Yet others were already following the path which Hanna had pioneered. The spring of 1785, when the *Sea Otter* first set sail for America, saw far-reaching projects being considered by the directors of the East India Company. These resulted in two expeditions which, starting from widely separated parts of the world, were to converge on Nootka in the summer of 1786.[18]

One of these expeditions had as its moving spirit James Charles Stuart Strange, born in Edinburgh in 1753, whose life was to touch history at widely different points. His godfather was Bonnie Prince Charlie, while his grandson, the Rev. Robert J. Dundas, would accompany Vancouver Island's first Anglican bishop, George Hills, when he arrived in Victoria on January 6, 1860, and would become the rector of St. John's church for the next five years.[19]

James Strange, the eldest son of Robert Strange, a Scottish artist and engraver (knighted in 1787), had entered the service of the East India Company in 1771. His health was somewhat erratic, yet the company evidently thought highly of him, for it granted him a long leave of absence from 1780 to 1785, which he spent in the British Isles. During this period the official account of Cook's voyages was published, and Strange gave it what he termed "an attentive perusal."

This immediately resulted in "an idea of the advantages which would result to the first adventurers who should undertake a voyage with commercial views to the North West Coast of America."[20] By this time, Strange was also familiar with Coxe's *Russian Discoveries*, which confirmed Cook's views as to the wealth in furs of the northwest American coast. Thus on his return to India in 1785, he at once set in motion his plan for following in the paths marked out by these British and Russian pioneers.

He was luckily able to enlist the enthusiastic support of David Scott (who later became chairman of the East India Company), and though the expedition was a private venture, financed by Scott and Strange, the company agreed to provide supplies, guns, ammunition, and trained personnel, including some soldiers in its employ. The two ships obtained for the expedition had highly appropriate names: the larger and older one, formerly the *Betsey*,[21] 350 tons, was rechristened *Captain Cook*, and the smaller one, 150 tons, was named the *Experiment*. The former, under Capt. Henry Laurie (or Lawrie), to whom Strange gave his copy of Coxe's *Russian Discoveries*, had a complement of sixty-one, including Strange, and the latter, under Capt. John Guise, about three dozen. Each ship was coppered and "amply provided with every store that either England or India could produce," while such essential trades as sail-makers, armourer, cooper, and caulker were well represented by skilled craftsmen. The *Captain Cook* also carried a young surgeon, John Mackay, who, as we shall see, was to have some remarkable experiences in the next two years. The *Experiment* had a surgeon's assistant.

Every care, indeed, was taken to make the expedition succeed.

Twice, elaborate instructions were given to the two captains. In early December 1785 on leaving Bombay, the general aims of the voyage were outlined to them:

> Although discovery is still in our wishes the primary object, we however request you will let no opportunity escape you of benefiting by trade. For this purpose you are supplied with a small investment composed of all such articles as appeared from Cook's voyages to be held most in esteem by the Americans.
>
> Should you find that the Spaniards have possessions so low as the latitude in which you make the coast of America, you will in such case proceed on to the northward and not explore until you have passed their most northern possessions. After this you will trade with the natives as you proceed to the northward, and as occasion may permit, picking up all the skins you can in exchange for your goods & whatever other articles you see a prospect of advantage from.
>
> We would wish you to range along the whole American coast up through Bering's Straits and from thence to proceed on towards the Pole, keeping the eastern shore on board, until the ice impedes your nearer approach to it, and then steering to the westward to keep as far north as the ice will permit, until you make the coast of Asia, which you will in like manner survey & afterwards direct your course to Kamtskatka [sic]. . . .On your leaving Kamtskatka, we direct you steer along the Asiatic shore for China, surveying as well as the time will permit all the islands in your way and particularly those of Japan.[22]

If the expedition had poor luck on the American coast, it might do a little trading in Chinese waters on its return; if, however, a large catch of furs had been secured, the ships might sell them and return at once to the Pacific northwest for more.

A rather daring suggestion was also made which, in due course, was to bear fruit:

> If you could in your range along the coast of America land any of your crews who chuse [sic] to turn out volunteers on the occasion in some centrical situation, with a promise of

82

returning to them again, we conceive it might be attended with singular advantage, as by their attaining the language thus, might in future prove very useful. We have therefore to desire that you will offer a proper pecuniary reward to any such volunteers, and as a further inducement assure them of our rewarding them amply ourselves, as also of our recommending them in the manner such a public-spirited service merits.

Another minor point was drawn to the attention of Laurie and Guise:

In your approach to the North Pole, we conceive sea horse teeth might be an object worthy of your notice, for as we understand they are valuable ivory & you are well provided with powder & shot.[23]

Finally, the example of the Great Navigator was held up before his successors:

As the health of the people is of the first importance, we flatter ourselves you will spare neither trouble or expense to secure it to them. We cannot on this head hold up to you a brighter example to copy from than you will find in attending to the advice of that humane & celebrated navigator, Cook.

On December 8, 1785, the two ships left Bombay, and by New Year's Day 1786 were off the coast of China. Here Strange issued a second detailed set of instructions to the two captains:

1. You are strictly to keep up the worship of God on board your ship; whenever the weather will permit. You are likewise to maintain good order among your men, taking care of their health during the voyage.

2. You are to take special care to have & keep your guns and fire arms always in readiness; to station your men at their several quarters; to put your ship in a good posture of defence; to have a sufficient number of cartridges filled with powder, and a proportionable quantity of shot to be at hand, in case of any sudden attack.

3. That you are frequently to exercise all the ship's company at the great guns and small arms & keep up a strict discipline in order to make them expert on all necessary occasions, inserting in the log book the times when they are so exercised.

4. That you are most peremptorily forbid to do or suffer any injury to be done to the natives in any part of the globe where your ship may touch. . . .

5. That to prevent the great dangers & frequent loss of ships by opening casks of arrack rum and other spirituous liquors at sea, I hereby strictly direct and require that during the whole voyage you do not at any time open or on any pretence whatsoever suffer to be opened, any cask of arrack or other strong liquor in the lazaretto, or elsewhere under any of the decks, but that whenever any of the casks great or small are to be opened, you do first bring them upon the upper deck & there draw them off. . . .

7. That you are on no account whatever to suffer either the officers or seamen to use tobacco with fire between decks. If the former transgress your orders on this head they are to be dismissed the service; if in like manner the seamen offend, they are to be corporally punished and their allowance of liquor stopped for the space of one month. . . .

10. That the between decks are carefully to be watched [*sic*] and scrubbed at least twice a week and to be clean swept every day. In wet or damp weather after washing the decks they are to be smoked, and the smoke is to be confined between decks at least half an hour. . . .

15. That as an encouragement to every seaman in the ship to be attentive to his duty while on deck, an additional month's pay shall be given to him for discovering and pointing out any rock or rocks so that they may be distinctly seen by the officer of the watch and recognized by him as such.

16. That any seaman discovering an island unknown before shall receive a gratuity of two months pay.[24]

It had originally been planned to buy sandalwood on the Malabar coast and sell it in China, thus partly defraying the cost of the voyage. As British ships were not allowed into Chinese ports at certain seasons of the year, Strange was to sail under Portuguese colors.[25] However, the sandalwood proved unavailable, and the ships proceeded directly to the port of Batavia in the Dutch East Indies, long considered a very unhealthy part of the world for white men. Here Strange put up at the only inn in town, and enjoyed a good night's sleep. On communicating his good fortune to a fellow lodger in the morning, however, he was somewhat disconcerted to be informed that

> during a residence of five weeks in the house he had in that space seen no less than seven bodies carried to their graves out of the very bed on which I had last night reposed, and that it had not, he believed, been aired once in all that period.

At once Strange, not suprisingly, "felt a thousand pains and aches" and for the rest of his stay "accordingly took up my lodging on a good billiard table, and which I continued in possession of until my departure."

The Dutch authorities were suspicious of Strange, clearly doubting his story about his eventual destination (or perhaps merely feeling uneasy about anyone who would sleep on a billiard table), but when his ships were finally provisioned for the next stage of his voyage, they let him go peacefully. In early February, the ships went aground off the coast of Borneo, in an area known to be infested by pirates. They were eventually refloated, though the *Experiment* was badly holed and later had to be beached and patched. All this under a blazing tropical sun somewhat dismayed the crews:

> Many of them on this occasion shewed symptoms of alarm and despondency and others of mutiny – however I found by humoring one, promising another and threatening a third, they were alike manageable.

As the ships made their way out into the open Pacific, scurvy began taking its toll, and in some ways the voyage became a race for time. By late June, however, the coast of North America was known to be close:

> Every mind was now occupied with the pleasing thought of going on shore. The sick were languishing for a mouthful of grass, and the promise of liquor excited many of the crew to go the masthead, who hitherto had never been there during the voyage. A gallon of arrack was the reward to be given to the fortunate he who first saw the land.

Finally on June 24, near the entrance to Nootka Sound,

> At seven o'clock this morning we made the coast of America, being then about twenty leagues off. On our nearer approach to the shore, we observed the tops of the hills still covered with snow, which as the sun shone on them had a most beautiful and majestic appearance.

A few natives immediately paddled out to the ships, bringing fish and vegetables which were given to the sick. The next day at least fifty canoes were swarming around the ships, and a few furs were traded. A few days later, following the example set by Cook, the ships moved to Friendly Cove,[26] where Strange bought a house as a hospital for his sick sailors. However, as "it was impossible to move a single step without being up to the ancles [sic] in mud, fish, guts and maggots," he soon had a tent erected for the invalids some distance from the village. While they recovered, he set about purchasing and cleaning furs, which were not so numerous as he had hoped.

He also found time to observe the customs of the natives, not all of which met with his approval. For example, he was brought three hands and a head in a basket, and when he professed ignorance of their purpose,

> My hero now gave me ocular demonstration, & very composedly put one of the hands in his mouth & stripping it through his teeth, tore off a considerable piece of the flesh, which he immediately devoured with much apparent relish. However prepared I was for this exhibition, yet I could not help expressing horror & detestation at the act. He immediately comprehended my meaning & endeavoured to recon-

cile me to the deed by assuring me that if I died, or if my friend or his friend died, he would not eat us; but the hand he had then eaten was the hand of his enemy whom he had killed in war & that the eating of it was a deed acceptable in the eyes of heaven, to which he at the same time pointed.[27]

The natives in this area seemed somewhat scornful of the knives and chisels of their white visitors, but when Strange tried them with cymbals, of which he had brought a great stock, he received an immediate response:

> The expression of rapture and delight which the first clash of them excited in the breasts of all present is not to be described. In displaying the effects of my musick, I composed for the occasion a sort of ring ting tune, and which had the merit of drawing from my polite audience such bursts of applause as was sufficiently satisfactory to me that I did not sing in vain; my song was encored again and again, nor did I give over whilst I was able to articulate. . . .The consequence of this exhibition was that I stripped my gentlemen to the buff in an hour's time, each contending with the other who should be first served. I got from some three & from others four skins for every pair of cymbals. My visitors now took their leave of me and went to Maquilla's house, by whom they were all entertained. They spent the evening (as I was informed by such of the gentlemen as slept on shore) in high glee and harmony; dancing, singing and making good use of their cymbals all night long. . . .I seldom after this period bought a skin without first being called upon to sing.[28]

Having so vividly demonstrated that "music hath charms to soothe the savage breast," Strange did a brisk business. Late in July, however, "having by this time got possession of every rag of furr [*sic*] within the sound & for a degree to the northward and southward of it,"[29] his expedition left Nootka, but not before saying goodbye to "a young man named Mackay, who acted as surgeon on board the *Experiment*." This adventurous spirit had volunteered to spend a year with the natives of Nootka, and was given paper, pens, and ink with which to record "every occurrence, however trivial, which might serve to throw any light on our hitherto confined knowledge of the manners, customs, religion & government of these people."³⁰

His guardian was to be the famous chief whom Strange referred to as Maquilla, but who is more generally known today as Maquinna. Mackay already stood in well with him, as he had cured the chief's child "who was much indisposed with scabby hands and legs." Maquinna assured Strange that he would find Mackay on his return "as fat as a whale," and, perhaps as an earnest of this, assigned him a native girl as a wife.³¹ From the ships' stores Strange provided him with the other necessities of life, such as beef, biscuits, salt, tea, sugar, and tobacco, as well as garden seeds, grain, and tools, and a male and female goat. Strange also left a musket and pistols for his use, first giving a demonstration of their power by firing a ball through a large native canoe 300 feet away. He told Maquinna that if natives attempted to use these weapons they would be badly hurt. When the chief seemed to doubt this, Strange gave him a pistol loaded with

> such a charge of powder as I well knew could not fail in its effects to give a very rude shock to the person who was to fire it. My gentleman very composedly received the piece, took his aim & fired; and had not some of his attendants been standing near him, he could not have failed measuring his length on the ground. . . .I now again offered the piece to any that chose to fire it. All however declined the honour and promised me never again to think of touching it.

Leaving Mackay to console himself with his new bride, in late July Strange sailed northward from Nootka, renaming Lance's Islands, near the northern tip of Vancouver Island, the Scott Islands, after his patron.³² By the middle of August he entered a large body of water which he named Queen Charlotte Sound, and while there did a little trading with the natives.³³ Furs were not plentiful, however, and Strange again sailed northward, anchoring this time in Prince William Sound on the southern coast of Alaska.

His voyage had not so far been a financial success, and now a further blow fell upon his hopes. About noon on September 5, while engaged in the unpleasant task of removing vermin from some furs that he had purchased, an alarming piece of news was brought to him: "that a vessel had hove in sight."

This almost certainly meant, he quickly realized, that another ship was also scouring the northwest coast for furs. The most that could be hoped was that he might gain some useful information from this rival adventurer, and with this in mind he despatched the ship's boat "not indeed to greet their arrival, but to try & find out from whence they came, where they had been, and where they were going."

Not every question which arose in Strange's mind received an answer, but at least he discovered that the intruder was the *Sea Otter*,[34] commanded by Capt. William Tipping. His ship, with her consort the *Nootka*, had left Bengal in March 1786, but the two vessels had taken somewhat different routes to the northwest coast. The *Sea Otter* surveyed the west coast of Japan before making for Nootka, while the *Nootka* proceeded directly to the port from which she derived her name. Captain Tipping told Strange that he had lately visited many of the islands in the Aleutian chain, but (although Strange treated him to a dinner on board the *Captain Cook*) was not inclined to be unduly communicative, for reasons evident to both commanders:

> The situation in which I was placed precluded me from asking Captain Tipping any questions whatever that referred in the most distant manner to his past or future plan of operations with respect to the object of his voyage; and indeed if I had waived the delicacy of this necessary reserve, he doubtless had too much sense to have gratified my impertinent curiosity. Our intercourse was mutually reserved, and considering indeed our clashing interests, we could not fail to view each other with a very jealous eye. . . .[35]

This slightly tense situation was not made easier by the natives who paddled out to the three vessels:

> The size and appearance of the *Captain Cook* attracted their notice in preference either to the *Experiment* or *Sea Otter*, for they all came alongside of us, nor did I suffer one of them to depart until I had disencumbered them of every rag of furr [*sic*] the size of my hand. This could not fail to be an

unpleasant sight to my rival, and so powerfully did it operate on his mind that in the evening of the same day he got
under way.

Nor did even the departure of Captain Tipping set his com-
petitor's mind at rest. Hardly had he disappeared from ordinary
view than Strange sent an oficer "to the summit of an exceeding
high mountain" to discover in which direction the *Sea Otter's*
prow was pointed. Cook's River seemed her likely destination, so
Strange, who had planned to go there himself, desisted.

It was still early in September, but as his voyage so far had
not been unduly successful, and provisions were running low,
Strange decided to return home. In a final attempt to make his
venture more profitable, he instructed Captain Laurie to investi-
gate Copper Island (near Bering Island) on his way back across
the Pacific, and if he decided that the island was rightly named,
to secure some copper ore and take it to Macao. He himself in
the *Experiment* would travel home by the most direct route.

With these plans in view, the two ships left Prince William
Sound on September 14. By early November the *Experiment* had
reached Formosa, and a few days later was off the coast of China,
where Strange was able to purchase, just in time, some oranges
for his scurvy-stricken crew:

> These I immediately gave to two of the sick, whose death I
> expected each minute. The good effects of this fruit were al-
> most instantaneous. Their speech (which was before almost
> extinct) returned; and their spirits which were totally sunk
> revived. They were in short saved by means of a dozen or-
> anges, without which (nothwithstanding we were within
> eight & forty hours sail of Macao) they must inevitably have
> perished.

On November 15 the *Experiment* anchored at Macao. A few
weeks later it was joined by the *Captain Cook*, which had been prevented by storms and scurvy from investigating the resources of
Copper Island. The expedition had also been disappointing in
that the number of furs had been well below expectations. Nevertheless, the two ships had secured about 600 pelts, which sold for
24,000 Spanish dollars in China,[36] and had somewhat increased

the knowledge of the northwest coast. Strange was by no means downhearted and he drew up proposals for making future voyages more successful. He suggested that only the East India Company itself had the resources to develop the fur trade properly, and that it should maintain a fleet of three ships for this purpose, establishing a triangular trade between China, Europe, and the northwest coast. He still hoped to see a trading post at Nootka, and threw out the suggestion that the fish and lumber resources might also be made profitable. If all else failed, the area would be a convenient place for dumping criminals.[37]

Strange himself, however, took no further part in such projects, but continued to serve the East India Company in more prosaic ways, in time becoming a paymaster and later a judge in India. On his retirement, he went home to Britain. Maintaining his interest in the exotic and the remote to the last, he stopped off en route at St. Helena to visit Napoleon.[38] He died in Scotland in 1840, prosperous and much respected. Perhaps, as he dozed by the fireside in his old age, his thoughts went back to the savage coast where half a century before he had serenaded the attentive Nootkas in the hopes of "every rag of furr."

Our story, however, has been left with two loose ends: John Mackay, waiting patiently at Friendly Cove for Strange to return, and Captain Tipping, hastening in the *Sea Otter* toward Cook's River. The former we may leave for the moment to the consolations of his dusky bride and his stipulated ration of "seven dried herrings heads a day,"[39] while we pursue the story of the *Sea Otter* and its consort the *Nootka*.

As we saw, awareness of the rich fur resources of the northwest coast had been steadily filtering into the world "east of Suez" for some time. In January 1786 a group of merchants, headed by J.H. Cox, with the approval of the East India Company and of Sir John Macpherson, Governor-General of India, formed the Bengal Fur Company, with the purpose of trying their fortunes in this promising new field of trade. They purchased two vessels, the *Nootka* of 200 tons and the *Sea Otter* of 100 tons. The former was put in the charge of Capt. John Meares, and the latter was under the command of William Tipping, both former lieutenants in the Royal Navy.

By the middle of February 1786 the two vessels were ready

to sail together from Calcutta to America. At this point, however, it was decided that the *Sea Otter* should be sent first to Malacca with a cargo of opium, from which a profit of 3,000 rupees could be expected. Captain Tipping thereupon set out on this errand, with instructions to go on from the Dutch East Indies to the northwest coast.

The *Nootka*, leaving Calcutta on March 2, got to Madras on March 27, where ten lascar seamen were added to its crew of forty Europeans. The ship was not so well equipped as those of the Strange expedition; for example, it had no carpenter. Sanitary precautions may also have been somewhat casual, for by the time the *Nootka* got to Malacca on May 23, scurvy had already made its appearance.[40] However, when Meares learned that the *Sea Otter* had already left that port for America, he set out in Tipping's wake across the north Pacific.

By August he was making his way cautiously through the misty Fox Islands of the Aleutian chain. Here he found the Russians busily gathering a rich harvest of furs from the natives, who, Meares noted, "in return . . . received small quantities of snuff, of which they are immoderately fond; and, obtaining their favourite article, they are content with their wretched condition, from whence, as respects any exertion of their own, they will never emerge." (*p.* vii)

Leaving Unalaska on August 20, Meares passed the Shumagin islands and then came to Kodiak. These areas were well within the Russian sphere of influence, but farther east, near Cape Douglas (about 59°N), it became apparent from the attitude of the natives with whom Meares traded pieces of unwrought iron for otter skins that the tsar's subjects had not yet penetrated this area:

> These people by refusing tobacco plainly proved that they had no connection with the Russians, and by frequently pronouncing the word English, English, it appeared also that the Nootka was not the first vessel of our country which had been seen by them – indeed it afterwards appeared that the *King George* and *Queen Charlotte* from London had been there before us. (*p.* xi)

With the voyages of these two last-mentioned ships – further evidence that traders were now beginning to converge from many quarters on the northwest coast – we shall soon be concerned. For the present, though, we must press on with Captain Meares, who in September guided the *Nootka* into Prince William Sound. When the adjoining coast seemed devoid of inhabitants, he considered wintering in Hawaii. He soon decided, however, that this would mean the end of all chance of a successful trading voyage, as "it would have been a matter of great difficulty, if not wholly impracticable, to persuade the seamen to return to the coast of America."

After a few days some natives made their appearance, bringing not only the hope of trade but also, perhaps, news of the *Nootka's* consort:

> They mentioned several English names, which appeared to be those of the crew of the *Sea Otter*. They also made us understand that a vessel with two masts had sailed from thence but a few days before, and that they had plenty of skins, which they explained to us by pointing to the number of the hairs of their heads. They also informed us, after their manner, that if we would stay, they would kill plenty of otters for us during the winter. (*p.* xii)

This sounded encouraging, and Meares was soon building a log house on shore. The natives were sometimes a problem, being given to pulling nails out of the ship with their teeth, but a volley of grape shot and a cannon ball "threw them into such a panic that one half of them overset their canoes from fright." Having demonstrated the stick, Meares now offered the carrot – in the shape of trade goods:

> These articles were then offered to their attention, when after repeated shouts of joy, such as were dressed in furs instantly stripped themselves, and in return for a moderate quantity of large spike nails we received sixty fine sea-otter skins. (*p.* xv)

In other respects, too, mutually agreeable arrangements were established. For some time the ship had been the recipient of visits from the local "king," one Sheenoway, who now demonstrated his good will in a practical manner:

Some time in October 1786 His Majesty brought us a young woman and offered her for sale; and she was accordingly bought for an axe and a small quantity of beads. We at first thought that she was one of his own women, but she soon made us understand that she was a captive and had been taken with a party of her tribe, who had been killed and eaten, which was the general lot of all prisoners taken in war. She alone had been preserved to wait upon the royal ladies, who were now tired, or perhaps jealous, of her services. She remained with us near four months, and appeared to be very contented with her condition.[41]

Winter was now fast closing in, and ice began forming round the *Nootka*. Meares resolved to stay where he was; whether the new recruit to the ship's company was a factor in his decision does not appear from his account. The men caught and salted down large quantities of salmon, and in their spare time went skating on the nearby ice.

By the time 1787 dawned, Meares must sometimes have regretted his decision, for with no sure word of the *Sea Otter*, the *Nootka* was now fast in the ice at this desolate edge of the world.

While tremendous mountains forbade almost a sight of the sky, and cast their nocturnal shadows over us in the midst of day, the land was impenetrable from the depth of snow, so that we were excluded from all hopes of any recreation, support or comfort during the winter, but what could be found in the ship and in ourselves. This however was only the beginning of our troubles. (*p.* xvii)

The truth of these words was soon apparent. Four men died early in the new year, four more in February, and by March thirty of the crew were sick with scurvy. Some resorted to desperate if sometimes effective remedies:

The first officer, on finding himself slightly affected in the breast, a symptom which generally foreboded a fatal determination in a very few days, got rid of it by continually chewing the young pine branches and swallowing the juice; but from the unpleasant taste of this medicine, few of the sick could be prevailed upon to persist in taking it. . . . These

melancholy circumstances were rendered more afflicting by
the hopeless minds of the crew; for such was the general dis-
couragement among them that they considered the slightest
symptom of the disorder to be a certain prelude to death. (*p.*
xviii)

The surgeon and pilot, those two essential figures, died and
were buried on shore:

The sledge on which we fetched the wood was their hearse,
and the chasms in the ice their graves; but these imperfect
rites were attended with that sincerity of grief which does
not always follow the gorgeous array of funeral pride to se-
pulchral domes. (*p.* xx)

There were more deaths in April. The men killed the ship's
two goats and made them into broth, while under the stress of
circumstance pine juice had now gained in palatability. Over
twenty men died during the winter, but as milder weather arrived in May, most of the survivors improved in health.

The situation, however, was still very serious, for there remained the problem of sailing the ship back to China with a
greatly depleted crew. Nevertheless Meares had hopes that, after
a fashion, his voyage might yet be crowned with success, for even
in these desperate circumstances trade was continued with the
natives:

They could not bury their own dead; they were only
dragged a short distance from the ship and left upon the ice.
They had muskets fixed upon the capstans, and man-ropes
that went down the cabin, that when any of the natives attempted to come on board, they might fire them off to scare
them. They had a large Newfoundland dog, whose name
was Towser, who alone kept the ship clear of Indians. He
lay day and night upon the ice before the cabin window,
and would not allow the Indians to go into the ship. When
the natives came to barter, they would cry "Lally Towser"
and make him a present of a skin before they began to trade
with Captain Mairs [*sic*], who lowered from the window his
barter and in the same way received their furs.[42]

Such were the circumstances under which, on May 17, the

natives informed Meares that they had seen two ships. Two days later a boat arrived from one of them, the *Queen Charlotte*, commanded by Capt. George Dixon, and before long the worst of the *Nootka's* troubles were over. However, this encounter also marked the beginning of a long acrimonious controversy between Meares and his rescuer. Over the next few years it would wend its acidulous way through a series of books and pamphlets, and as late as 1929 an entire book would be devoted to this complex dispute.[43]

At first, all seemed to go well. Meares visited Port Etches, where the *Queen Charlotte's* consort, the *King George*, commanded by Capt. Nathaniel Portlock, lay at anchor, and gave him some rum and rice, receiving in exchange much needed supplies. A few days later, however, there was a sharp change in relations. Portlock was Dixon's superior, and it quickly became apparent that although he was prepared to give Meares some assistance on grounds of humanity, he did not regard with any enthusiasm at all a potential rival in the fur trade, especially one who was doing business without licences from the East India Company and the South Sea Company.[44] We shall see presently how Portlock and Dixon were to combine these attitudes in a single course of action; first, however, we must explain how the *King George* and *Queen Charlotte* came to be, at the same moment, in the same remote corner of the globe as the *Nootka*.

The ultimate cause, as with all the vessels which made their way to the northwest coast in this period, was the search for fur. In this case, as in that of James Strange and his two ships, the East India Company was also concerned. The company had in 1785 concluded agreements not only with Strange but with a group of London merchants headed by Richard Cadman Etches. This group, calling itself the King George's Sound Company, was granted permission to send two ships to the northwest coast. In return, it had to post a bond of £20,000 and agree to some very stringent regulations, with provisions for heavy fines if they were contravened. It was not to send any ships to the south or west of Canton, nor to sell any European goods in China or the Indian Ocean. On completion of the voyage, all logs and journals were to be turned over to the East India Company.[45]

The promoters of this venture hoped, among other things, to establish "small factories for the purpose of purchasing and procuring furs" on the American coast, open up trade with Japan, and perhaps even find the northwest passage. They secured two ships, the *King George* of 320 tons and the *Queen Charlotte* of 200 tons, and chose as their commanders Nathaniel Portlock and George Dixon, both mariners of considerable experience, who had sailed with Cook. A licence from the South Sea Company and the approval of the British government were also obtained, and in September 1785 the vessels left England with a crew of fifty-nine on the larger ship and thirty-three on the smaller.[46] Sailing southward, they went ashore briefly in the Falkland Islands; then, rounding Cape Horn, they moved northwestward until they reached Hawaii. Here the crew, who were suffering from scurvy, recuperated.

In June 1786 the two ships left for Cook's River (actually a deep inlet on the southern coast of Alaska). They obtained very few furs in this area, and so decided to proceed to Prince William Sound, farther east. Here they were again aware of the activities of rival traders, as Russians came aboard the two ships, bringing salmon in exchange for salt. Some trading was also done with the natives, who demanded above all else pieces of iron.

As winter approached, it was decided to remain at Nootka. However, stormy weather and the poor health of the crew caused the abandonment of this plan, and instead the ships retreated to Hawaii.

When warmer weather returned in the spring, they set sail again for the northwest coast. It was in Prince William Sound in May 1787 that they found the *Nootka*, at a moment when Captain Meares and his mate were, in Portlock's words, "the only two persons capable of dragging the dead bodies from the ship over the ice and burying them in the snow on the shore."

Help was immediately given to the stricken ship and its crew, and Portlock lent Meares two crewmen to aid in sailing the *Nootka* back to China. The men each demanded £4 a month, a considerable advance over their previous wages of 30s, but Meares felt in no position to refuse.

Soon afterward, Portlock decided that this rival fur-trader must repay his help by quitting the vicinity. Accordingly, he handed Meares a letter in which he put his own position with complete candor. He had, he declared, originally planned to leave Prince William Sound, but had since changed his mind, having formed

> another plan, a part of which is to remain in the sound, and purchase every skin of every kind, that came in my way; and as your remaining in the sound and trading must, of course, stop a considerable part of the trade that I might get, I find myself in duty bound, on account of my employers' interests, to propose the following conditions which, if you would wish to keep the assistance I have already lent you, you will find it necessary to comply with.
>
> The conditions are these: that you bind yourself in a bond of five hundred pounds that no trade be carried on for skins of any kind by yourself or any of your crew, during your stay in the Sound this season, and that you let me have twenty bars of iron and some beads.[47]

An agreement was drawn up, dated at Port Etches, June 18, 1787, and in it Meares agreed to proceed directly to Canton and not to

> continue to trade or barter with the natives of any part of said coast &c for otter-skins or any other furs, the produce of the said coasts, on pain of forfeiting the sum of 1000 1. of good and lawful money of Great Britain to the said N. Portlock, his heirs, executors and assigns, for the use of the proprietors of the said ship *King George*.[48]

Soon after signing this document Meares left the area. Some idea of the ordeal that he had passed through may be gathered from the fact that his crew numbered only twenty-four, while the corpses left behind totalled twenty-three. Nevertheless with only half his normal crew he got back to Hawaii, stayed there a month, and then went on to Macao, which he reached on October 20, 1787. His furs, which numbered about 350, sold early in 1788 at Canton for $14,242.[49]

Portlock and Dixon remained in the area of Prince William Sound for some time, each gathering a good harvest of furs. It was then decided that the *Queen Charlotte* should proceed to Nootka in search of further trade, and that both ships should rendezvous later at Hawaii. In late August the *King George* left the northwest coast, arriving at Hawaii a month later. Here Portlock received news of both the *Nootka* and the *Queen Charlotte*. The former had left that port in early September en route for the far east; the latter, having secured 1,500 skins on the northwest coast, was also headed in the same direction.[50] While in the vicinity, Dixon had named the Queen Charlotte Islands as well as Dixon's Entrance or Dixon's Straits, as it was at first called. In a letter to his fellow commander, Dixon informed Portlock that at Nootka he had found signs of considerable interest by other fur-traders. Two ships were anchored there: the *Prince of Wales*, commanded by a Captain Colnett, and another ship, her consort, commanded by a Captain Duncan.[51]

Dixon had also learned from Colnett that yet a third ship, under a Captain Barkley, had visited Nootka earlier in 1787. Surprisingly enough, Colnett apparently did not mention what to us is perhaps the most interesting aspect of this voyage: that Captain Barkley had brought with him from Europe his teenage bride, the first white woman to visit what would one day be called British Columbia.

Portlock left Hawaii and went on to Formosa and then Macao, which he reached on November 21, 1787. Here a second letter from Dixon awaited him, informing him that the *Queen Charlotte* was now at Whampoa, as were the *Nootka* and Captain Barkley's ship *The Imperial Eagle*. There was also news of a more sombre nature. Two ships which had sailed eastward into the Pacific in 1786 had not returned, "the one commanded by a Captain Peters and the other by a Captain Tipping."

From a financial point of view, the voyage of the *King George* and the *Queen Charlotte* had been a mixed success. The men had secured 2,000 good skins and many others of lesser quality. On arriving at Canton they found that sea-otter pelts had recently been selling there at from $80 to $90 each, and they had visions of a rich return. However, the number of pelts thus suddenly thrown on the market – the greatest number secured by any trading voyage to date – depressed prices sharply. Moreover, all sales had to be effected by agents of the East India Company, who were, on this occasion at least, poor hands at driving a bargain, and in the end, the pelts averaged only about $20 each.[52]

Even so, the organizers of the expedition were "the gainers

to the amount of some thousands of pounds." In his account of the voyage, published in 1789, Portlock had no hesitation in declaring that "this branch of commerce, so far from being a losing one, is perhaps the most profitable and lucrative employ that the enterprising merchant can possibly engage in." He recommended that in order to exploit the fur trade more fully, a permanent settlement should be established somewhere on the northwest coast.[53] This would aid the development of a three-way trade, in which furs would be traded to the Chinese for tea, which would then be carried home to England. He also suggested that the post might, in time, draw traders from the central parts of North America, and in the process the elusive northwest passage might finally come to light.[54]

The remainder of the voyage of the *King George* and *Queen Charlotte* back to England was comparatively uneventful. Sailing sometimes in company and sometimes separately, they made their way through the Dutch East Indies, round the Cape of Good Hope to St. Helena, where they went ashore while the ships were put in good shape. Then they sailed northward, arriving at the Isle of Wight on August 22, 1788.

Clearly, the fur trade was fast becoming known to traders in many lands, and in the years to come more and more vessels, some from Europe, some from the Far East, some from New England, would be finding their way to Nootka and other parts of the northwest coast. Financial rewards would sometimes be substantial, yet the human cost would often be high. We have seen how the *Nootka* lost half her crew, and in the case of some other vessels the toll would be even higher. In fact, in this period four ships, which had played some part in the drama of the fur trade, were to be lost with virtually no survivors.

One of these, doubtless the victim of a winter storm, was the *Nootka's* consort, the *Sea Otter*. An officer of James Strange espied it from "an exceeding high mountain," as it was being sailed by Captain Tipping out of Prince William Sound in the direction of Cook's River. But this was the last glimpse anyone had of it; somewhere in the stormy seas of the north Pacific it foundered with all hands.

Another vessel, the *Lark*, was also lost in this period. This ship, built entirely of mahogany, sheathed in copper and mounting twelve guns,[55] had left Bengal in the spring of 1786 with a crew of seventy drawn from many nations. It reached Malacca a few weeks later, and arrived in early summer at Canton. Captain Peters stayed there several weeks and then went on to Petropavlovsk on the Kamchatka peninsula, which he reached in August.

Here, as we saw in an earlier chapter, he met the enterprising Russian merchant Gregory Shelikov, and some business was transacted between them. Then Captain Peters sailed boldly out into the open Pacific, but here all his plans came to naught. The *Lark* was wrecked on Bering's Island, and only two members of the crew, a Portuguese and a lascar, were saved. They eventually managed to make their way back across Russia to St. Petersburg, which they reached in the fall of 1788.[56]

Two more vessels which had earlier traded with the natives of the western coast of America were lost in this period. These were *L'Astrolabe* and *La Boussole*, which, under Capt. J.F. de La Pérouse and Capt. de Langle, conducted the most elaborately planned voyage of exploration yet made under Franch auspices. La Pérouse, born in 1741, was an experienced mariner, having taken part in an expedition into Hudson Bay in 1782 which captured two British posts. With the ending of hostilities between France and England, he was no doubt in some uncertainty as to his future, and glad to receive this important peacetime appointment.

Setting out from Brest on August 1, 1785, and sailing down the Atlantic, the two ships rounded Cape Horn early in 1786 and rested briefly at a port in Chile. Here La Pérouse informed his Spanish hosts that, according to the best of his information, the Russians already had four posts in northwest America. This piece of news was destined to have some effect on future Spanish actions.[57] Later the ships went on to Easter Island and then Hawaii. After resting there, they turned in the direction of the northwest coast. They planned to survey those parts of the coastline which Captain Cook had been unable to examine because of poor weather, with a view to expanding not only the empire of knowledge but perhaps that of France as well. As La Pérouse hopefully declared, in one of the numerous despatches which he sent back to the authorities in Paris from various parts of the world,

Though the Russians are established in the north and the Spaniards to the south, many centuries will unquestionably elapse before these two nations will meet; and there will long remain between them intermediary points, which might be occupied by other nations.[58]

Although the expedition was primarily scientific, it is apparent from the instructions given to La Pérouse that the information which he might acquire during the voyage was envisioned as laying the foundation for the latter extension of trade. For example, he was to find out what settlements, if any, the Spanish had north of San Diego and Monterey:

> The Sieur de la Pérouse will endeavour to learn the condition, strength and object of these establishments, and to satisfy himself whether they be the only ones formed by Spain on this coast. He will likewise enquire in what latitude furs may begin to be procured; what quantity the Americans can furnish; what commodities are best adapted for the trade; what conveniences may be found for making a settlement on this coast, if this new trade should offer the French merchant sufficient advantages to induce him to engage in it, with the view of exporting the furs to China, which is said to be a ready market for them.
>
> He will take care to bring home to France samples of all the different furs he can procure; and as he will have occasion, in the course of his voyage, to stop at China, and perhaps to touch at Japan, he will inform himself what kind of fur has the most ready, certain and profitable sale in each of the two empires, and what advantage France may hope from this new branch of trade. Lastly, he will endeavour, during his stay on the coast of America, to discover whether the Hudson's Bay settlements, the forts or factories in the interior part of the country, or any province of the United States, have opened any communication, any intercourse of trade and barter with the people on the western coast, through the medium of wandering savages. (I, 35-36)

Sailing in a northeasterly direction from Hawaii, on June 23, 1786, at about 59°, as the mist cleared away, a long chain of mountains covered with snow burst at once upon our sight which we might have discerned thirty leagues farther off had the weather been clear. We distinguished in these the Mount St. Elias of Behring [*sic*], with its summit rising above the clouds.

The sight of land, after a long voyage, usually excited feelings of delight; but on us it had not this effect. The eye wandered with pain over masses of snow, covering a barren soil, unembellished by a single tree. (II, 62-63)

Here, in a sheltered bay not far from Cape Fairweather (so named by Cook), the men anchored, naming the harbor Port des Français. (It is now called Ltua Bay, and is about 58°N.) They were not alone in this remote spot for long, as natives came paddling out to the ships with furs:

To our great surprise they appeared well accustomed to traffic, and bargained with as much skill as any tradesman of Europe. Of all our articles of trade, they appeared to have no great desire for anything but iron; they accepted indeed a few beads; but these served rather to conclude a bargain than to form the basis of it. (II, p. 78)

Many of the natives had daggers made of copper or iron hanging around their necks, which made La Pérouse speculate as to their origin:

Everything, therefore, leads us to presume that the metals we saw came either from the Russians, from the servants of the Hudson's Bay Company, from American merchants travelling into the interior parts of the country; or from the Spaniards; but I shall hereafter show that it most probably came from the Russians. (II, 80)

Trade was brisk, as the French bartered hatchets, adzes, and nails for otter skins and fish. Science, however was by no means neglected. An observatory was set up on a small off-shore island where the men presumed that they would be unmolested by the natives. This was to prove the least accurate of their calculations, as the Indians

landed upon it in the night, on the side next the offing;

crossed a very thick wood which it was impossible for us to penetrate in the day; and creeping on their bellies like snakes, almost without stirring a leaf, they continued to steal some of our effects, in spite of our sentries. They had even the address to enter by night into the tent where Messrs. de Lauriston and Darbaud, who were on guard at the observatory, slept; and took away a silver-mounted musket, and the clothes of the two officers, which they had taken the precaution to place under their pillows, without being perceived by a guard of twelve men, or even awaking the officers. (II, 84)

This was discouraging, and an attempt was made to compensate for the setback by discovering the northwest passage. However some hours of scrambling about on the great glaciers which came down to the water's edge suggested that this venture was unlikely to be crowned with much success.

The French still had a final card to play, and La Pérouse solemnly took possession of the island for King Louis XVI, giving that monarch's local counterpart "several yards of red cloth, hatchets, adzes, bar iron and nails." He also "buried at the foot of a rock several bronze medals, which had been struck before our departure from France, with a bottle containing an inscription recording our claim."

In the next few days the French made detailed observations of their new compatriots:

The men of this country bore holes through the cartileges of the nose and ears; and append to them different little ornaments. They make scars on the arms and breast with a very keen iron instrument which they sharpen by rubbing it on their teeth as on a whetstone. Their teeth are filed down to the gums, by means of a rounded piece of sandstone in the shape of a tongue. Ochre, lamp-black and plumbago mixed with seal oil are employed by them to paint the face and the rest of the body, which has a frightful appearance. (II, 126)

The arts of this area, though, were in some respects well advanced:

The Americans at Port des Français know how to forge iron, fashion copper, spin the hair of diverse animals, and form with the needle, of the thread thus procured, a stuff not unlike French tapestry. They intermingle with this slips of otter-skin, which gives their cloaks a resemblance of the finest silk plush. Hats and baskets of rushes are nowhere woven with more skill; and they ornament them with pleasing figures. (II, 135)

The "Puritan ethic" was not yet firmly established in this part of the world:

Exposed to perish with hunger in the winter, when the chase cannot be very productive, they live in the summer in the greatest abundance, as they can catch more fish in an hour than is sufficient for their family. The rest of the day they remain idle, spending it in gaming, of which they are as passionately fond as some of the inhabitants of our large cities. This is the grand source of their quarrels; and I do not hesitate to pronounce that this tribe would be completely exterminated if the use of any intoxicating liquor were added to these destructive vices.

Philosophers may exclaim against this picture if they please. . . . (II, 121)

The women of the tribe failed to arouse any enthusiasm in La Pérouse. Unable to summon up the traditional gallantry of his nation, he declared that their huge lip-pieces made them "the most disgusting beings in the universe."

So far, the two ships had not suffered a single case of scurvy, but now a serious calamity was to strike them. On July 13, two of their boats were overturned in a rough swell and twenty-one men were lost. A monument was erected to their memory, and on July 30 with heavy hearts the survivors sailed away.

The ships spent the rest of the summer surveying the Pacific coast from Mt. St. Elias in the north to Monterey in the south, reaching this port in mid-September. Then they set out on the long journey across the Pacific, arriving at Macao at the end of the year. The pelts which they had brought did not fetch a high price, for they were of poor quality, and the market was by now flooded with pelts from America. Only about $10,000 was realized from somewhere between 600 and 1,000 skins.[59]

Yet the commanders and scientists were not unduly dismayed. The purpose of the expedition had not been primarily commercial, and indeed one of the learned men on board, a M. de Lamanon, now deemed it an appropriate moment to launch into one of those flights of rhetoric in which the French seem to excel:

> I have formed collections of fishes, shells and insects, written descriptions of animals, and hope to make considerable additions to the number of known and organized beings. The natural history of the earth, sea and atmosphere engage my attention by turns. Though we are not the first circumnavigators who have had in view the progress of science, the English, at any rate, will no longer be the only ones.
>
> But what will always distinguish this voyage, what will render the French nation truly glorious in the eyes of all philosophers, of our contemporaries and of posterity, will be our having frequented nations, reputed barbarous, without shedding a drop of blood. . . .Our voyage will prove to the universe that the French are a mild people, and that in a state of nature man is not inclined to be mischievous.[60]

Early in 1787 *L'Astrolabe* and *La Boussole*, whose commanders planned to reach Europe again in June 1789, left Macao, and after considerable exploration of the north Pacific arrived at Kamchatka in September. The following year the southern part of the world's greatest ocean engaged their attention; but somewhere in that vast waste of waters a disaster must have struck them, for neither ships nor men were ever seen again.[61]

In some ways their voyage had been symbolic, for the state which had sent them forth was destined not long after to suffer a like fate. Royal France had fostered science, purified manners, presided, if somewhat reluctantly, over the emancipation of man from superstition; but in 1789 it was to strike upon a hidden reef and quickly disintegrate. This major historical convulsion would divert the energies of the French people from exploration and colonization; in the race for the unclaimed parts of the coast of northwestern America, France would no longer be a serious contender.

CHAPTER SIX

The
Young Honeymooners
and Others

We
have earlier
traced the varying fortunes

of the Bengal Fur Company, formed in 1786 by John Henry Cox and a group of merchants trading in the Far East. Of the two ships which the company had purchased early in that year, one of them, the *Sea Otter*, had been lost with all hands; the other, the *Nootka*, after losing half its crew from disease, had finally reached its home port of Macao with a modest harvest of furs.

Chinese authorities, acting under pressure from the East India Company, had meanwhile expelled Cox from Canton for engaging in private trade. However his firm continued to operate under other managers, chief of whom were John Reid and Daniel Beale. Beale secured papers which enabled him to pose as the local Prussian Consul, thus evading the inflexible monopoly, which applied only to British subjects. Reid and Beale persuaded Charles William Barkley, a young sea-captain in the the service of the East India Company, to resign from its employ and to join them in a private fur-trading venture. He was to invest £3,000 of his own money in outfitting a ship, sail it from England to Nootka, and then bring what furs he secured there on to the Far East, where he would be suitably recompensed. Three voyages in all were envisioned, which, it was expected, might well occupy an entire decade.

To Barkley, the prospect of adventure and reward seemed attractive, and in the British Isles he secured and outfitted a ship named the *Loudoun*.[1] Leaving those waters on September 6, 1786, Barkley arrived at Ostend (now in Belgium, but at that time part of the Austrian empire) a few days later.

Here final preparations for the long voyage were made, and the ship received a new name, the *Imperial Eagle*, and a new flag, the Austrian. This was to circumvent the East India Company's monopoly of British trade in far eastern waters.

Then, showing his willingness to venture into more than one kind of uncharted waters, Barkley embarked on a whirlwind courtship, meeting, wooing, and marrying Miss Frances Hornby Trevor. She had been born at Bridgewater in Somersetshire about 1770, at which time her father was rector of Otterhampton. In 1786 he was a Protestant chaplain at Ostend, and conducted the wedding service on October 27 of that year. The young couple (he was 25, she only 16)[2] then embarked on the *Imperial Eagle* and set sail for the northwest coast, a part of the world on which no white woman had as yet set eyes.

The ship, 400 tons and carrying 20 guns (and thus larger than any vessel that had as yet visited what is now the B.C. coast), left Ostend on November 24, 1786. Not long afterward the young bridegroom took ill, and as Mrs. Barkley later recorded in her reminiscences,

> my situation was very critical at that time from the unprincipled attentions of the Chief Mate supported by the Second Mate, who being a lieutenant in His Majesty's service ought to have had more honor.

Early in 1787 it was decided to call at Bahia in Brazil for medical attention and recuperation. The local authorities were at first uneasy at the sight of so much armament, but they eventually decided that the *Imperial Eagle* had no designs on them, and hospitality was extended and returned.[3] Barkley revived, his villainous adjutants apparently mended their ways, and the voyage was resumed.

Rounding the Horn, the vessel arrived at Hawaii in May 1787 – the same month, one recalls, that the *Nootka* was discovered by the *Queen Charlotte* in the less hospitable waters of Prince

William Sound. At Hawaii, Mrs. Barkley, as befitted a lady going travelling, acquired a lady's maid, a native girl named Winee.

On May 25 the ship set sail for Nootka, arriving there the following month,[4] and Mrs. Barkley became the first white woman to set eyes on Vancouver Island. Here trade went briskly forward. Indeed, it went even better than expected, as an unforeseen ally now came to the assistance of the Barkleys: John Mackay, the young surgeon of the *Captain Cook*, who had now been living with the Indians for a whole year. During this time he had learned the local language, gained the confidence of the natives, and adapted himself to their ways – too completely, in fact, in the eyes of Mrs. B.:

> Shortly after the ship had moored in Friendly Cove, a canoe was paddled alongside and a man in every respect like an Indian and a very dirty one at that, clothed in a greasy sea-otter skin, came on board, and to the utter astonishment of Capt. and Mrs. Barkley introduced himself as Dr. John Mackay, late surgeon of the trading brig Captain Cook. The visitor informed them that he had been living at Nootka among the Indians for the previous twelve months, during which time he had completely conformed himself to their habits and customs, which Mrs. Barkley in her diary emphatically states were disgusting.[5]

Yet soap and water soon worked wonders, and the young bride quickly reconciled herself to her new acquaintance. This process was no doubt hastened by his usefulness in aiding her husband reap a rich harvest of sea-otter skins.

It was under these circumstances that in July 1787 the *Imperial Eagle* was joined in this corner of the world by two unexpected visitors: the *Prince of Wales* and the *Princess Royal*, commanded by James Colnett and Charles Duncan. The background and circumstances of their voyage to Nootka will be recounted later, but for the moment suffice it to say that they were properly licensed, which the *Imperial Eagle* was not. However, the *Imperial Eagle* had secured all the furs likely to be offered at Nootka for some time, and the newcomers recognized the fact. Thus an apparently friendly atmosphere prevailed, and there was some exchange of provisions. Then the two young honey-mooners, as satisfied with their harvest of furs as they were with each other, sailed southward along the outer coast of Vancouver Island.[6]

About latitude 49°20′, they discovered a large sound to which they gave the name Wickananish's Sound after the leading chief of that area, but which is now called Clayoquot Sound. Here they secured more furs. Later they explored another large bay which uncomplainingly received the name Barkley Sound. Not forgetting his bride, the young captain named Frances Island and Hornby Peak after her, while as a tribute to the purser, John Beale, Cape Beale received its present name.[7]

Then, still proceeding southward, one July day the ship's company witnessed a surprising sight which Mrs. Barkley hastened to record in her diary:

> In the afternoon, to our great astonishment, we arrived off a large opening extending to the eastward, the entrance of which appeared to be about four leagues wide, and remained about that width as far as the eye could see, with a clear westerly horizon, which my husband immediately recognized as the long lost strait of Juan de Fuca, and to which he gave the name of the original discoverer, my husband placing it on his chart.[8]

Whether it had been glimpsed by this Greek sailor (whose real name was Apostolos Valerianos) in the late sixteenth century may never be known; certainly he had given its approximate location.[9] The immortal Cook, most meticulous of navigators, and explorers, had missed it completely. Yet now at last its existence was proved beyond a doubt. The passage into the interior of the continent was revealed, which might lead – who could tell? – as far as Hudson Bay!

Surprisingly, Barkley made no effort to explore it; perhaps he was reserving this for a later date. Instead, he sent six men, including the purser John Beale, ashore on an island near the mouth of the strait. When they did not return, a second party was sent in search of them, but found only their mangled bodies. The natives had evidently reacted violently to the presence of strangers in their midst. With sorrowing heart, Barkley named the tragic spot Destruction Island,[10] and not long afterward set sail for Macao.

He arrived in the closing days of 1787 with 800 pelts, valued at $30,000. Then, taking aboard another cargo, he set sail for Mauritius in February 1788. He was seen at sea by Captain Portlock of the *King George*, who noted that the ship was now flying Portuguese colors.[11] Finally, the *Imperial Eagle* arrived at Calcutta where, considering the success of his voyage, Barkley expected to receive a warm welcome from his associates in the venture.

To his astonishment, almost the reverse proved the case. The deceptions regarding the nationality of the ship had become common knowledge, and it seemed possible that those involved might find themselves in severe trouble. The promoters of the enterprise had therefore resolved to get rid of the vessel and cancel their contract with its captain. The terms on which they did so were grossly unfair, as they took over Barkley's investment in stores and fittings as well as his nautical instruments and charts, which before long found their way into the possession of the wily John Meares.

Barkley took steps to gain redress at law, and eventually a committee of merchants awarded him an out-of-court settlement of £5,000.[12] Nevertheless he had lost rather than gained by his endeavors, though his awareness that he had made a permanent contribution to geographical knowledge may have been some compensation.

The Barkleys, leaving Winee behind, now returned to Europe. They were to have further adventures in Pacific waters in 1791-92 when they were on the northwest coast in the brig *Halcyon*. The captain died in his bed in 1832, and his wife survived him by thirteen years.[13]

Mention should be made here of the two ships which the Barkleys met at Nootka in the summer of 1787 – the *Prince of Wales* and the *Princess Royal*. These two small vessels (the *Princess Royal* was only fifty tons and carried fifteen men)[14] were owned by the same group of merchants, headed by Richard Cadman Etches, that had sent out the *King George* and *Queen Charlotte*. It is an indication of the merchants' confidence in the future of the fur trade that the *Prince of Wales* and the *Princess Royal* left England even before the larger vessels had returned.

The ships sailed from London in September 1786, with Capt. James Colnett commanding the *Prince of Wales* (with John Etches, brother of the principal director of the company, on board) and Charles Duncan in charge of the *Princess Royal*. They passed through the Strait of Magellan, where they "settled a factory at Staten's Land for the purpose of collecting seal skins and oil."[15] Then they went on to Nootka, which they reached in July 1787 with many of the crew suffering from scurvy. As we saw, this was not the only setback to the hopes of Captain Colnett; he had arrived at Friendly Cove just after the *Imperial Eagle* had collected every fur which the Indians there had to offer. Nevertheless the newcomers remained in the area for a month, while the naturalist Archibald Menzies happily explored the surrounding woods, guarded by a relative of Chief Maquinna.

In early August the two ships set sail for Prince William Sound, but on meeting Captains Portlock and Dixon near Nootka, the captains of the two smaller vessels were persuaded to visit the Queen Charlotte Islands instead. This they did, staying in the vicinity some time, and gathering 1,800 sea-otter skins.[16] Later they did go north to Prince William Sound, anchoring in Snug Corner Cove. During this period Menzies, in honor of Sir Joseph Banks, president of the Royal Society, named Banks Island, and the ships explored Douglas Channel. On their return southward they touched briefly the west coast of Vancouver Island, but Colnett and Duncan did not think it worth their while to visit Nootka.[17]

They spent the winter of 1787-88 at Hawaii, but when spring returned the two ships once more set sail for the northwest coast. The *Prince of Wales* set its course toward Prince William Sound, while the *Princess Royal* sailed directly to Nootka, where a replacement for a damaged rudder was made from a convenient tree. Leaving Nootka on May 10, the latter ship spent much of the summer in the vicinity of the Queen Charlotte Islands. When Duncan returned to Nootka in early August, he soon encountered John Meares, whom Portlock and Dixon had rescued in the previous year, and who had since returned from the Far East to the northwest coast. Meares' ship, the *Felice*, was flying the Portuguese flag, and Meares claimed that it was commanded by "Don Antonio Pedro Manella or some such stuff."[18] Duncan was by no means deceived by this, but decided to go elsewhere, trading at Ahousat and then, returning south again, anchoring on the southern side of the Strait of Juan de Fuca.

On August 17 the *Princess Royal* left via Hawaii for Macao. In due course it met the *Prince of Wales*, which had, in the meantime, been as far north as Snug Corner Cove and had also discovered Bird Island, a small outpost of the Hawaiian group.[19] The two ships had had highly successful voyages, having gathered between them 1,689 pelts valued at $72,083.[20] The *Prince of Wales*, with Captain Duncan on board but commanded by James Johnstone (who later became the first to examine Johnstone Strait), soon sailed for the British Isles with a cargo of tea. It reached London on July 14, 1789, the day which coincidentally marked the beginning of the French Revolution.

Captain Colnett, however, remained in the Far East with the *Princess Royal*. Before long the ship was sold for $3,600 to Daniel Beale, acting for "The associated merchants trading to the North West Coast of America." The price suggests that the vessel was not highly valued, but as we shall see later, this would not prevent it from being involved in events which would reverberate in some of the major chancellories of Europe.[21]

Before detailing events in that year of destiny – so memorable not only for Nootka but for the whole western civilization of which it was rapidly becoming an outpost – we must turn back to the second voyage of John Meares to the northwest coast.

This enterprising if not always admirable adventurer, now well recovered from both his vicissitudes in Prince William Sound and any gratitude that he may have felt in being rescued from them, had, in conjunction with some other British merchants in the Far East, bought and fitted out two ships. These were the *Felice*, of 230 tons and a crew of 50, and the *Iphigenia* (more accurately known as the *Iphigenia Nubiana*) of 200 tons and a crew of 40. Meares himself planned to command the *Felice*, and a Captain Douglas, who was described as "well acquainted with the coast of America," would command the *Iphigenia*. Douglas would also receive one per cent of the value of the furs brought back by the two ships.

Detailed instructions were given to Meares by the "Merchant Proprietors." He was to bring back not only furs but whale-oil and whale-bone, ginseng and "snake root." He was to secure samples of the minerals used by the natives to make paint, and the ships were to carry back to China as many spars as possible. Moreover, Meares was told, "you will endeavour to propagate at Nootka and at the Sandwich Islands the breed of your poultry of every kind; also of hogs, goats and sheep."

Meares was no believer in wasting money, and in this category he included the obtaining of proper licenses from the East India Company and the South Sea Company. Accordingly, he took into partnership a Portuguese merchant of Macao, Juan Cavalho, who was able to obtain from the Portuguese governor of that enclave permission to fly the flag and carry the papers of that nation. Meares also took with him some Portuguese officers. Thus, if his expedition met with British ships, it could pass as Portuguese, whereas if Russians or Spaniards attempted to interfere with it, Meares could make a lightning change and stand resolutely beneath the billowing folds of the banner of St. George.

The ships were well equipped with remedies for scurvy, and carried cattle as well as "turkies," goats, rabbits, and pigeons. The ships also had some unusual human freight, including a Polynesian named Tianna, who, at his own request, had been brought by Meares to Macao from Hawaii in 1787. Having seen the marvels of China, he was now anxious to go home again. Aged about thirty-two, he wore European dress, but was still somewhat surprised that the white men prized gold and silver more highly than iron. Mrs. Barkley's former maid, Winee, now in declining health, was also returning to Hawaii, and the ships carried as well two natives from "Mowee" (no doubt Maui in the Hawaiian group). A native of Nootka named Comekela, brother of the celebrated Maquinna, was also, as it were, hitching a ride.

On January 22, 1788, the two ships left Macao, but misfortune was soon their companion. The *Iphigenia* sprang a leak and some of her rigging collapsed, while before long scurvy made its appearance. A mutiny took place on the *Felice*, but was "fortunately quelled by gentle means."[22] In early February it was apparent that Winee was failing, and on the fifth of that month she died and was committed to the deep. Meares recorded his opinion that she had "possessed virtues that are seldom to be found in the class of her countrywomen to which she belonged; and a portion of understanding that was not to be expected in a rude and uncultivated mind." (*p.* 28)

The ships sailed on, and soon anchored in the Philippines Here the Spanish authorities gave them a friendly reception, and permitted them to cut and fashion new spars and masts. The observant Meares noted that the fortifications of the islands appeared in weak shape, and that the natives were by no means reconciled to Spanish rule. Moreover, the clergy, judging by their behavior at the banquets which Meares attended, "did not appear to be of opinion that they were thrown into that corner of the globe to pass their time in penitence and prayer."

However, the stay of the two ships passed pleasantly, and there was even a ball at which, in honor of the visitors, a native band played not only English country dances but "some of the select pieces of Handel." (*p.* 44) Moreover, the local belles, Meares recorded, had attired themselves in such a way as "to make one fancy beauty even where nature had denied it." (*p.* 45)

Yet all good things must come to an end, and the ships resumed their voyage, parting company soon after emerging from the Dutch East Indies into the open Pacific. The *Felice* was soon at the Joseph Freewill (now Mapia) Islands (so named by Carteret of the *Swallow* who had discovered them in 1767), where it was found that pieces of iron produced an immediate response in the local inhabitants:

> When the piece of iron was held up to their attention, they were all seized with a kind of silent but impressive joy, that cannot be described; but the man who procured it immediately began to caper and dance round the deck, and laying down on his back, tumbled and rolled about in such an extraordinary manner that we really imagined he was suddenly affected by some very singular disorder, till he rose up and kissed the bit or iron with those emotions of extravagant joy, which manifested the extreme delight he felt in being in the possession of what he esteemed so great a treasure. (*p.* 79)

Passing through the Carolines and Ladrones, the *Felice* set a northeast course for Nootka. The ship was a scene of activity, as Chinese workmen on board made metal goods to be exchanged later for furs and carpenters prepared molds for a fifty-ton sloop to be built at Nootka. No lumber had been brought for this purpose, however, as "our timber was standing in the forests of America." (*p.* 89)

Emerging shaken but relatively unscathed from a typhoon, the *Felice* finally reached the coast of America on May 11, though strong winds prevented her from anchoring at Friendly Cove until two days later. During this period the *Princess Royal*, under Captain Duncan, left the harbor on her homeward voyage. In a shrewd move, Meares sent Comekela ashore

> dressed in a scarlet regimental coat, decorated with brass buttons, a military hat set off with a flaunting cockade, decent linens and other appendages of European dress, which was far more than sufficient to excite the extreme admiration of his countrymen. (*p.* 109)

Maquinna (or Maquilla, as Meares, like most early writers, termed him)[23] was away, as was his kinsman Callicum, so the visitors were received by one Hannapa, and invited to a great feast. Comekela this time surpassed himself, as he not only brandished a large spit stolen from the cook of the *Felice*, but

> contrived to hang from his hair. . .so many handles of copper saucepans that his head was kept back by the weight of them in such a stiff and upright position as very much to heighten the singularity of his appearance. (*p.* 110)

News of all this evidently reached the ears of Maquinna and Callicum, for they ended their visit to Wickananish, the mighty chief to the south, and returned to Nootka. The scene as their party arrived was an impressive one:

> There were twelve of these canoes, each of which contained about eighteen men, the greater part of whom were cloathed in dresses of the most beautiful skins of the sea otter, which covered them from their necks to their ancles. Their hair was powdered with the white down of birds, and their faces bedaubed with red and black ochre in the form of a shark's jaw, and a kind of spiral line, which rendered their appearance extremely savage. (*p.* 112)

Gifts were promptly exchanged between the two sides:

> A present, consisting of copper, iron, and other gratifying articles, was made to Maquilla and Callicum, who, on receiving it, took off their sea-otter garments, threw them, in the most graceful manner, at our feet, and remained in the unattired garb of nature on the deck. They were each of them in turn presented with a blanket – when with every mark of the highest satisfaction, they descended into their canoes which were paddled hastily to shore. (*p.* 114)

While trade went briskly forward, Meares made preparations for building a ship. First, however, he had to provide shelter for the workmen assigned to this task. Maquinna, according to Meares, granted the whites "a spot of ground,"[24] and the natives joined in the work, being paid in beads or iron; by May 28 a fairsized house was standing just east of the Indian village of Friendly Cove.[25]

> The house was sufficiently spacious to contain all the party intended to be left in the sound. On the ground floor there was ample room for the coopers, sail makers and other artizans to work in bad weather. A large room was also set apart for the stores and provisions, and the armourer's shop was attached to one end of the building and communicated with it. The upper story was divided into an eating room and chambers for the party. (*p.* 115)

A wall of earth was built around the house, a cannon was mounted and work began on the ship. Not all was toil, however, as the marriage of Comekela was celebrated by a feast at which three hundred people consumed half a whale. Maquinna outdid himself in magnificence, appearing "dressed in an European suit of cloathes with a ruffled shirt and his hair queued and powdered." He and his nobles also enacted a good-natured parody of their guests:

> The manner of taking off their hats, the curious gestures they fell into, in scraping and bowing to each other, with a few English words they had acquired and now repeated aloud, without connection or understanding, composed a

scene with which they were delighted and we could not be displeased. (*p.* 122)

Soon afterward, however, a darker note was struck, as natives brought to the ship "an human hand, dried and shrivelled up, the fingers of which were compleat and the nails long." It was realized that this had almost certainly belonged to one of Captain Barkley's lost men, and considerable ill-will ensued. Maquinna, grasping the situation, explained that his tribe had merely got this grisly relic in trade from another at some distance away, and the incident was smoothed over.[26] It did, however, provide Meares with some material for reflection:

> There is, indeed, too much reason to apprehend that the horrible traffic for human flesh extends, more or less, along this part of the continent of America. Even our friend Callicum reposed his head at night upon a large bag filled with human skulls which he showed as the trophies of his superior courage; and it is more than probable that the bodies of the victims to which they belonged had furnished a banquet of victory for him and the warriors that shared his savage glory. (*p.* 125)

Finally it was time for the *Felice* to leave Nootka, where a good number of skins had been collected and work on the new ship was well advanced. Presents were given and received; Maquinna got a suit covered with metal buttons and his womenfolk were also suitably rewarded. One of them was given a pair of shoe-buckles,

> which immediately on her receiving them, were hung in her ears with the same pride that European beauty feels in decorating its charms with the gems of India. (*p.* 131)

Meares now told Maquinna that another ship (by which he meant the *Iphigenia*) would soon be visiting Nootka, whereupon the great chief, showing an astonishing degree of sophistication, suggested leaving a letter for its captain.[27] Meares did so, and early in June the *Felice* left Nootka, sailing to Port Cox (which he named after his patron) in Clayoquot Sound, where Maquinna's great rival, Wickananish, held sway. After the ship had anchored, two lesser chiefs, Detootche and Hanna, came aboard, and later the mighty Wickananish himself.[28] A great feast was held on shore in the chief's longhouse; eight hundred male guests ate boiled whale, using mussel-shells for spoons, while their womenfolk looked on.[29]

Meares was astonished at the size of the longhouse, as "the trees that supported the roof were of a size which would render the mast of a first-rate man of war diminutive." He may also have regarded with some uneasiness the skulls with which the hall was festooned.

All, however, went well; the whites gave their hosts "several blankets and two copper tea-kettles," and were rewarded in their turn:

> About fifty men now advanced into the middle of the area, each of them holding up before us a sea-otter skin of near six feet in length and the most jetty blackness. As they remained in this posture, the chief made a speech, and giving his hand in token of friendship informed us that these skins were the return he proposed to make for our present, and accordingly ordered them to be sent to the ship. (*p.* 140)

In June, having secured at least 150 fine otter skins and having decided that the local females were "very superior in personal charms to the ladies of Nootka," Meares sailed away southward. Soon he arrived at the entrance to the Strait of Juan de Fuca, where he was much struck by "a very remarkable rock, that wore the form of an obelisk." This confirmed his belief in the old tale about the Greek sailor reputed to have seen it two centuries before. Had not the Elizabethan chronicler said that "at the entrance of this said strait there is on the northwest coast thereof a great Hedland or Iland, with an exceeding high pinacle, or spired rocke, like a pillar thereupon"?[30]

Meares did not, however, explore the strait at this time, but sailed down the coast of what is now the state of Washington as far as 45°30'. He found no important openings in the coast and saw few natives, so he decided to return to Nootka and see how his shipbuilding enterprise was faring. On July 10 he passed a headland which, he later declared, "obtained from us the name of Cape Beale."[31] This was but one example of his persistent tendency to distort facts to his own advantage. He was evidently hoping to curry favor with Daniel Beale, one of the promoters of his voyage, but he must have been well aware that the cape had been named by Captain Barkley in honor of John Beale, the unfortunate purser of the *Imperial Eagle* killed by the Indians on Destruction Island.[32]

If facts were no deterrent to Meares, neither were popular superstitions. On July 13 he sent thirteen men in the ship's longboat, under Robert Duffin, to explore and take possession of the Strait of Juan de Fuca. They returned on July 30 with most of the men wounded, but none dead, after a furious battle with the natives.[33]

Meares was later to make a number of remarkable statements about this expedition. Although he was well aware that the famous waterway had been discovered by Barkley in the previous year, he not only refrained from mentioning the fact, but even went so far as to say that "the boat's crew, however, was despatched, and discovered the extraordinary straits of John De Fuca, and also the coast as far as Queenhythe."[34] He also claimed that the boat had sailed "near thirty leagues up the strait" and that it was about "fifteen leagues broad."[35]

The first of these statements seems quite unlikely; the second is demonstrably untrue.[36] However, as he still had hopes that it led into Hudson Bay, he was no doubt anxious that it should not contract too rapidly.

Meares had instructed Duffin in writing to "take possession of this strait, and the lands adjoining, in the name of the king and crown of Britain,"[37] and he later claimed that Duffin had done so.[38] Yet in the journal carefully kept by Duffin throughout the expedition, there is no mention of this. Meares also asserted in his "Memorial" that in this period he had bought land from the natives at Tatoosh, but in his *Voyages* this transaction unaccountably escaped his recollection. Although it is difficult at this late date to establish the exact facts of all these matters, we may safely say that though Meares had many virtues, a fanatical devotion to the truth was not among them.

On July 26 the *Felice* was once more at Nootka, and though work on the new ship was well advanced, Meares soon had other troubles. A mutiny broke out on the *Felice* while most of the crew were on shore, but the eight troublemakers were quickly over-powered. Meares gave them the choice of being put in irons or living with the natives, and in a rash moment they chose the latter. Soon Maquinna was helpfully offering to kill them all; this assistance was declined, but an offer by Callicum to make them slaves of his tribe was accepted, and soon the luckless eight were toiling at the most menial tasks for their hard-hearted new master.

On August 6 the *Princess Royal* appeared off shore but did not anchor. Two days later the *Felice* set sail for nearby Port Cox, and soon afterward Meares exchanged necessities with Captain Duncan. The *Princess Royal* then sailed for Hawaii, en route to China, where, as we have seen, she joined the *Prince of Wales* later in the year.

Late in August the *Iphigenia*, sister ship of the *Felice*, arrived at Nootka. She had recently been searching for furs at Prince William Sound and Cook's River, much to the disgust of the Hawaiian passenger Tianna, who was used to warmer climes. A good harvest of furs had been collected, and Meares decided that he should take them to China in the *Felice* as soon as possible. All but the leader of the mutineers were now allowed to return to duty, with the loss of nine months wages, a penalty which was later remitted by the owners.

Nootka, unknown a decade earlier, was becoming a busy place. On September 17 another ship was seen off shore, and it was assumed that the *Princess Royal* had for some reason returned. To Meares' surprise the vessel turned out to be the sloop *Washington*, commanded by Captain Gray, from Boston. Gray, whose ship was the first to fly the Stars and Stripes in this part of the world, told Meares that the *Washington* and a sister ship, the 300-ton *Columbia*, had left Boston in August 1787, "under the protection of Congress, to examine the coast of America, and to open a fur trade between New England and this part of the American continent, in order to provide funds for their China ships, to enable them to return home teas and China goods."[39]

We shall hear more of these two ships later. In the meantime, however, a notable event occurred – the launching of the *North West America*, "the first bottom ever built and launched in this part of the globe."[40] This went off with great success on September 20, 1788, in the presence of Maquinna, Callicum, some Americans, and a vast throng of awe-struck natives. Robert Funter was selected as its captain, and crewmen were chosen from the other two ships.[41] Meares felt that he could now safely leave the scene of his endeavors, and he took aboard the *Felice* a large quantity of spars suitable for masts, which he knew that he could sell at a good price in China. "Indeed," he wrote, "the woods of this part of America are capable of supplying with these valuable materials all the navies of Europe."[42]

All this time Meares had been observing the Indian way of life with close attention, and his careful account of this, as well as of the local fauna and flora, ranks with that of Cook.[43] As it covers the same ground in much the same way, we need not repeat it in any detail here. We might note, however, that Meares estimated that Maquinna had perhaps 10,000 souls under his sway and Wickananish about 13,000. He also suggested that Nootka was not really on the mainland of North America, and showed shrewd historical insight when he declared that the political arrangements of the area were

> not very unlike to the general system of government in Europe at an early period of its civilization, and which is well known under the appellation of the feudal system. (*p.* 229)

Not all the institutions of Nootka, however, were reflections of those of medieval Europe. For example, the great chief was in the habit of eating one of his slaves for dinner every month. By way of choosing the menu, the slaves were all assembled in the banqueting hall, whereupon,

> A bandage is then tied over the eyes of Maquilla, who in the blindfold state is to seize a slave. His activity in the pursuit, with the alarms and exertions of these unhappy wretches in avoiding it, form another part of this inhuman business. But it is seldom a work of delay – some one of these slaves is soon caught – death instantly follows – the devoted carcase is immediately cut in pieces, and its reeking portions distributed to the guests, when an universal shout of those who have escaped declares the joy of their deliverance. (*p.* 256)[44]

Meares was also interested in the religion of the Indians. He

122

learned, for example, that their enthusiasm for copper was derived from an old man who had appeared in their midst many generations back in a copper canoe with copper paddles. He had told the natives that he had come from the sky, whereupon they had inconsiderately killed him and taken the copper. However the event had made a profound impression, and the squat totem poles in their houses, Meares was informed, "were intended to represent the form, and perpetuate the mission of the old man who came from the sky. (*p.* 290)

Fortified with this information regarding the chariots (or in this case the canoes) of the gods, Meares set sail in the *Felice* in September. Before leaving, he told Maquinna and Callicum that he would return in 1789 "and build more houses."[45] On October 17 he arrived at Hawaii, where he secured hogs, vegetables and coconuts, and then went on to China, anchoring at Macao on December 5, 1788, with a good harvest of furs.[46]

We may now conveniently round out the story of Meares' other two ships. The *Iphigenia*, as we saw, had come to Nootka by way of northern waters. Leaving the Philippines late in February 1788 (after having been forced by the Spanish authorities to give up nearly half her cargo of iron bars), the vessel, under the command of Captain Douglas, reached Cook's River in June 1788, later anchoring in Snug Corner Cove in Prince William Sound. Here a party was sent ashore and found signs of a visit by others to the area only a few weeks before; to a tree was affixed a notice, "J. Etches of the *Prince of Wales*, May 9th, 1788, and John Hutchins."[47] Through contacts with the natives, it became plain that Russian traders and hunters from Kodiak dominated the upper reaches of Cook's River, and for this reason Captain Douglas was unable to secure many furs.

Late in August the *Iphigenia* arrived at Nootka, remaining there for two months. It was apparently during this period that Douglas dismantled the fort built by Meares, taking some of the material aboard his ship and giving the rest to Captain Kendrick, who used it for firewood.[48] Then on October 27, in company with the newly launched *North West America* under Captain Funter, Douglas sailed for Hawaii. The two ships arrived in early December, and Tianna was restored to his people.

They spent the remainder of the winter in the pleasant

surroundings of the Hawaiian group, where relations with the natives were amicable, though realistic. For example, when two anchors were stolen, they were soon recovered.

> on presenting the king with a pistol, a musquet, and a small quantity of ammunition; accompanied also with some very necessary menaces, that if he did not restore the articles he had taken, his town should be laid in ashes.

In March 1789 the ships left once more for Nootka, where, as we shall see, they were to have some unexpected and remarkable adventures. Before long they would find themselves at the center of an international controversy involving some of the major powers of Europe. This, however, belongs to a latter stage of our story, and first we must say something of two minor players in the "Nootka crisis." These, as it happens, we have already met: the first American ships to anchor at Nootka, the *Columbia Rediviva* and the *Lady Washington*.

CHAPTER SEVEN

Stars and Stripes
on the
Northwest Coast

It
was now
more than a decade

since the thirteen American colonies had declared their independence of Great Britain, and somewhat less since they had up-
held it in battle and gone on to establish their own constitution
and federal government. Yet so far no ships flying the new nation's flag had appeared on the northwest coast. The year 1788,
however, would see it proudly flying at Nootka, while American
traders began taking an increasing part in the development of
the fur trade of the north Pacific.

It is not surprising that the principal movers in this new field
of investment and endeavor should be the merchants of Boston.
Often in the forefront of the revolution, they did not retreat to
the background when it came to reaping some of its rewards. For
the next forty years they would play a leading role in this promising new area of economic enterprise. They would also break decisively and permanently the monopoly of the far eastern trade
that had hitherto been enjoyed by the East India Company, and
give American ships and American free enterprise a dominant
position in the northwest fur trade which would not be regained
by Britain for some forty years.[1]

As it happened, at the close of the revolutionary war there
was an unusually pressing reason for the men of Boston to search

125

for new sources of profit. Victory might have crowned their brows, but it was attended by the disruption of traditional economic relationships. No longer did they have free access to the markets of Britain and her colonies; nor did New England as yet possess an economic hinterland. The decline of the slave traffic from the West Indies, and its abolition in 1788, also resulted in the loss of a lucrative field of investment. As one student of the period has put it:

> Then came the worst economic depression Massachusetts has ever known. The double readjustment from a war to a peace basis, and from a colonial to an independent basis, caused hardship throughout the colonies. It worked havoc with the delicate adjustment of fishing, seafaring and shipbuilding by which Massachusetts was accustomed to gain her living.[2]

All, however, was not lost. During the war New England had built up a large merchant navy (often employed as privateers), and had no shortage of trained seamen. Moreover, because of the easy availability of timber, its shipbuilding costs were comparatively low. What it needed was a market with which to exchange goods profitably.

China, the source of silk, tea, and porcelain, quickly suggested itself, and the war was hardly over when ships from New England began appearing in its ports. The first to set out was apparently a Captain Hallet, who, in the 55-ton *Harriet*, sailed from Boston for China in December 1783. He carried a large cargo of ginseng, much esteemed in the Far East as a "wonder drug." Putting in at the Cape of Good Hope, he met up with a British merchantman who bought his entire cargo for its equivalent value in tea, whereupon the *Harriet* returned to New England without those on board having set eyes on the busy harbors of Cathay.[3]

The first American ship actually to arrive in·the Far East was the *Empress of China*, commanded by John Green. This 360-ton vessel was provisioned with a cargo of ginseng, wine, brandy, tar, and turpentine at a cost of $120,000. With forty-six on board it set sail from New York on February 22, 1784, and travelling by way of the Cape of Good Hope and the East Indies, arrived at

Macao on August 23 of the same year. The venture resulted in a profit of $30,000, and the ship's supercargo, Major Samuel Shaw, was emboldened to return in the *Hope* to far eastern waters in 1786.[4]

The first ship from Massachusetts to reach the Far East was the *Grand Turk* of Salem. Under Capt. Ebenezer West, it returned to its home port on May 22, 1787.[5]

The perils of the sea were clearly no deterrent to Yankee daring, but there still remained an economic problem. New England had as yet few goods that were in demand in China, and was forced to export considerable amounts of specie to balance its trading account. This was not always easy for the young republic setting out on its journey through history, and inevitably a search was made for some article which, if not produced in New England, could be carried to China by its ships. The voyages of Captain Cook had provided much factual detail of the north Pacific coast and its rich resources in otter and beaver,[6] and it was now general knowledge that the Chinese were eagerly buying furs brought to their markets by the Russians from northwest America. So came the idea of trading trinkets produced in New England for furs, then carrying the latter to the ports of China, whence cargoes of silk or tea could be taken on board for Boston, or even, perhaps, for Europe.

Joseph Barrell, a leading Boston merchant, had read with attention accounts of Cook's last voyage, and before long he had induced five friends to join him in financing a trading voyage to the opposite side of the continent. Two other Boston men, Samuel Brown and Charles Bulfinch, invested money, as did Crowell Hatch, a New England sea captain, John Derby, a wealthy shipowner of Salem, and John Pintard, a merchant from the rising young town of New York.[7]

For $50,000 they were able to outfit two ships, the *Columbia Rediviva* of 212 tons and the tender *Lady Washington* of 90 tons.[8] The former was put under the command of John Kendrick, born in Massachusetts about 1740, who decided to take with him his two sons, John and Solomon.[9] In charge of the *Lady Washington* was Robert Gray, born in Rhode Island in 1755.

Among those on board the ships were John B. Treat, a furrier; also a Mr. Nutting, an astronomer, who died while the ships were in the south Pacific. Kendrick's eldest son, John, was fifth mate of the *Columbia* when it sailed, and R.D. Coolidge was first mate of the *Washington*. Both men were to have some unexpected adventures before many months had passed, and find themselves under a different flag from the one under which they had left Boston.

The Americans carried with them a letter from the French consul in Boston, explaining the purpose of their voyage, and (according to some historians) letters from the Spanish ambassador to the United States, saying that their vessels were not to be molested.[10] This, however, seems unlikely, as the governor of California in fact issued orders that the two ships were to be seized if they appeared in Spanish ports on the Pacific coast. The Spanish commandant at San Francisco, for example, had been given explicit instructions by his superiors on this point:

> Should there arrive at the port of San Francisco a ship named *Columbia*, which they say belongs to General Washington of the American states, and which under the command of John Kendrick sailed from Boston in September 1787 with the design of making discoveries and inspecting the establishments which the Russians have on the northern coasts of this peninsula, you will take measures to secure this vessel and all the people on board with discretion, tact, cleverness and caution, doing the same with a small craft which she has with her as a tender, and every other suspicious foreign vessel. . . .[11]

On September 30, 1787, the two ships left Boston, proceeding first to the Cape Verde Islands. Here they unaccountably remained for forty-one days before leaving for the south Atlantic, where they anchored for some time at the Falkland Islands. Near Cape Horn in the spring of 1788 the two ships parted company, and each entered the Pacific on her own.

In May 1788 the *Columbia* entered a harbor at Juan Fernandez Island and obtained some supplies. No difficulties occurred at the time, but later, when the local commander informed his superiors of the incident, he was arrested and dismissed. A ship was even sent from Callao to trace down the intruder into the Spanish Ocean, and posts in Chile, Peru, and Mexico were urged to capture the ship if they could. These actions were based on a Spanish royal ordinance of 1692, which asserted that any foreign vessels could be seized in the eastern Pacific, "seeing that no other nation had, or ought to have, any territories to reach which its vessels should pass around Cape Horn or through Magellan's Straits."[12]

No further contacts with outposts of Spanish power took place, however, and the two ships proceeded independently northward. On August 2 the *Washington* touched the Pacific coast at about 41°. Here a little trading was done with the natives, who, it was noticed, were frequently pitted with smallpox – a sign that they had already made contact with western civilization.[13]

In August at about 45° some further trading took place. As Robert Haswell, who had begun the voyage as third mate of the *Columbia*, but later transferred to the *Washington*, recorded in his journal (as his "log" should really be called):

> Traffic on a very friendly footing being thus established before evening we had purchased a number of good sea otter skins for knives axes adzes etca. but had we had copper a pece [sic] two or three inches square would have been far more valuable to them, they would hand there [sic] skins on board without scruple and take with satisfaction whatever was given in return. . . .[14]

A little farther up the coast the first serious setback to the voyage took place. Near Tillamook Bay, about thirty miles south of the mouth of the as yet unnamed Columbia River, Captain Gray's personal servant, a black man, was killed by the local natives. Gray gave the area the name of Murderers' Harbor, and sailed on. Later in August the *Washington* successively passed Destruction Island, Cape Flattery, and the Strait of Juan de Fuca (largely obscured by fog).

When the ship arrived at Barkley Sound, very few furs were obtained, as the industrious Meares had recently secured them all. At Clayoquot Sound, which the Americans called Hancock Harbor, luck was not much better. In Haswell's words:

> Sunday the 31 the weather was exceeding pleasant earley in the morning a great maney of the inhabitants came of

bringing with them an abundance of skins but greatly to our mortification there was nothing in our vessell except muskets would perchace one of them but that was an article of commerce we were not supplied with having scarce armes enought for our defence copper was all there cry and we had none for them, the principle or superior chief of this tribe's name is Wickananish he visated us accompaneyed by one of his brothers completely dressed in a genteerl sute of cloths which he said Capt Mears had given him, Capt. Mears name was not the only one they mentioned for they spoke of Capt. Barkley Capt Hannah Capt Dunkin and Capt Duglas what they said of them we now knew so little of there language we could not comprehend.[15]

Later the *Washington* reached Nootka, where Meares' two ships, the *Iphigenia* and *Felice*, were already at anchor. As we saw, the former had been scouring more northerly waters and the latter those to the south. Between them they had gathered a valuable cargo of furs, but Meares found it convenient to deny this, telling the Americans that the two ships between them "had not collected fifty skins."[16] The perceptive young Haswell (he was only nineteen) was by no means deceived by this:

All the time these gentlemen were on board they fully employed themselves falsicating and rehursing vague and improvable tales relative to the coast of the vast danger attending its nagivation of the monsterous savage disposition of its inhabitants adding it would be maddness in us so week as we were to stay a winter among them. . . .The fact was they wished to frighten us off the coast that they alone might menopolise the trade but the debth of there design could be easily fathemed.[17]

By this time the *North West America* was almost completed, and on September 20 it was launched.[18] Not many days later the *Columbia* appeared. Her crew was not in good shape, as "they had been so unfortunate as to loose two of there people with scurvy and most of the rest of the crew were in an advanced state of that malignant distemper."[19] Thus there were now five ships at

Nootka, while two others, the *Prince of Wales* and the *Princess Royal*, had only recently left. It was increasingly evident that Friendly Cove, unknown a dozen years before, was fast becoming a magnet for enterprising traders from the four corners of the globe.

It seems possible, indeed, that still another American vessel was on the northwest coast, if not at Nootka, some time in 1788. This was the *Eleanora*, a New York brig commanded by Simon Metcalfe. Perhaps this ship, and not the *Washington* and *Columbia*, deserves the proud title of "first American ship on the northwest coast." Details, however, are scanty, and rest upon a single source, John Boit's *Journal of a Voyage round the globe*.

As we shall see later, Metcalfe made a voyage in 1789 to the northwest coast with two ships, the *Fair American* and the *Eleanora*, the former commanded by his son. While at Hawaii Boit was told by a well-informed white resident of the islands that:

> It appeared that Captain Metcalfe had purchased this small vessel [the *Fair American*] at Macao after his arrival at that port in the *Eleanora* from the N W Coast and did there fit her with the snow for the coast again and gave the command of her to his eldest son.[20]

This would imply that Metcalfe had made a voyage to the northwest coast in the *Eleanora* in 1788. If so, he must have arrived there somewhat prior to Kendrick and Gray. However, it seems unlikely that the New York brig was at Friendly Cove in that season, as some account of the early days of the fur trade would almost certainly have mentioned the fact.[21] We do know that the subsequent careers of both these ships were destined to be dramatic, but as to the exact time or place of the first appearance of the elder Metcalfe on the northwest coast, it is still not possible to speak with certainty.

The *Eleanora* will not figure further in our story at present, and in the meantime we will bring our account of the *Columbia* and the *Washington* down to the close of 1788.

John Kendrick, commander of the first fur-trading expedition from Boston to the northwest coast, seems to have been an indecisive man of uncertain temper. Various incidents on the voyage to Nootka had testified to both these defects, and his conduct during the next few months was to show an inability to make the most of his opportunities. His first move, though, was promising enough, for it was a smooth blend of Christian charity and Machiavellian opportunism. He gave Meares some assistance in repairing his ships, in hopes that they would then quit the area. No doubt he was relieved to see the *Felice* set sail for Hawaii in September 1788, followed a few weeks later by the *Iphigenia* and the newly completed *North West America*. The Americans were now free to pursue the fur trade undisturbed, but as it was late in the year, they decided to winter at Nootka and make an early start in the spring.

Thus, as 1788 drew to its close, the evidence suggested strongly that 1789 would be a busy year on the northwest coast. Three ships under the general direction of John Meares were wintering at Hawaii, and, as we shall see, a fourth would soon be bought in the Far East for the same interests; all these could be expected at Nootka as soon as the new season opened. The first two ships from Boston to appear in these waters were already in the position to make the most of their opportunities, while a third American ship, the *Eleanora*, had apparently been on the northwest coast in 1788 and might be expected to return there in 1789.

This, however, was not to be an exclusively Anglo-Saxon year. As we saw, Spain had for some time been curious as to what was going on in the waters north of her Mexican and Californian provinces, and in the previous fifteen years had sent several expeditions to find out. Now, aware that Russia was extending her sphere of influence ever farther south from Alaska, that English adventurers had made several successful fur-trading voyages to the northwest coast, and that the young republic of the United States was beginning to take an interest in the same area, Spain resolved on a decisive step: the permanent occupation and fortification of Nootka as an outpost of the Spanish empire. This, it was confidently expected, would establish *de facto* what was already in her eyes *de jure* – that the Pacific was a Spanish ocean, and that its coasts, at least as far north as Prince William Sound, were hers, and hers alone, to occupy and enjoy.

Yet not all human ambitions are destined to find fulfilment, and 1789 was to be a year in which some, at least, would meet with a decisive setback. The balance of international power was about to tip, and just as the next twelve months in France would see the end of the old regime, so in this remote part of the world the mist of long-held illusions would begin to dissipate before the new realities of power.

CHAPTER EIGHT

Year of Crisis, Year of Destiny

"plunging half Europe
into war
to recover a wooden hut . . . "

It was now nearly three centuries since Christopher Columbus had discovered a new world for Spain. In the years that followed this discovery, her empire had become, and remained, the world's largest. Comprising all of South America except Brazil, it controlled most of the Caribbean area, had established a thriving and sophisticated society in Mexico, and in the late eighteenth century was founding new outposts on the California coast.

This was remarkable; but the pretensions of the Spanish crown were even greater. In effect Spain asserted that the entire eastern shore of the Pacific, certainly as far north as Prince William Sound, was Spanish territory, and that Spain had the sole right to its "commerce, navigation and fishery."[1]

In support of this claim, several arguments were put forward. In 1493 the Pope had declared – and amended the following year – the division of the New World between Portugal and Spain. The former of these two children of the Holy Church was to have all land east of a line drawn 370 leagues west of the Cape Verde Islands, and the latter all land west of it.[2] Moreover, had not Balboa in 1513, after remaining for a moment "silent, upon a peak in Darien," descended to the shore of the great ocean, waded boldly out into it, and taken possession of not only its waters but every shore they might wash – for Spain? Since then, the entire shore of South America, from the Strait of Magellan (first discovered by another servant of the Spanish crown) to Panama, had been brought under Spanish control, and was now ruled by governors and civil servants sent out from Madrid. Mexico also had its viceroys, and in the late eighteenth century they were preparing to extend the rule of their royal masters a considerable way up the California coast. While Captain Cook was exploring far southern latitudes in 1769 for Britain, Spain was establishing new posts at San Diego and Monterey. In 1776, the year that the Great Navigator set out on his last expedition, the best harbor on the Pacific coast was occupied by a land and sea expedition from Mexico and named after Saint Francis.

Nor was this all. As we saw, long before Cook was born, Spanish captains had made several daring voyages of discovery far up the Pacific coast. As early as 1542 Cabrillo had sailed to a point on the coast somewhere between 42° and 44°, an area also reached by Ferrelo in 1543 and Vizcaino in 1602-3.[3] Then had come a long pause, but in 1774 Juan Perez had sailed as far north as 54° and on his return entered a harbor which may have been Nootka Sound. Although he did not land and take possession of the area for Spain, he did a little trading with the natives and brought back the first description of them.

The following year, an expedition led by Hezeta and Quadra had landed in what is now the state of Washington and taken formal possession of the area for Spain. The daring Quadra had later gone on alone to reach a point about 58°N, and had taken possession of land at two other locations. In 1779 Arteaga and Quadra had gone as far north as Prince William Sound. Thus, by sailing the entire distance from Mexico to Alaska, landing at several places and taking possession according to the rigidly prescribed formulas, Spain had, in her own eyes, established (or confirmed) her right to consider the entire Pacific coast a part of her far-flung empire. In May 1780 the King of Spain gave orders that there were to be no more such voyages at present.[4]

Several motives lay behind these expeditions. There was the desire to locate the northwest passage, if it existed, and thus control an important entrance into the Pacific; there was the urge to convert the heathen to Christianity; and there was a hope that good ports might be found for the ships that came regularly across the Pacific from Manila.

There was also a growing uneasiness regarding the activities and intentions of Russia. This, indeed, had been a powerful factor in the Spanish decision to establish new posts in California.[5] No Russians had been encountered on any of the three expeditions of the 1770s, but throughout this period news of the explorations eastward from Siberia, which had begun with Bering, kept filtering into the general consciousness of the world. The Russians, then as now, had no enthusiasm for sharing their discoveries with others, and rival powers were forced to piece together the picture by whatever means they could.

As early as 1761, the new Spanish minister at St. Petersburg had been told to gather information regarding Russian discoveries in the north Pacific.[6] From 1772 onward a steady stream of despatches was sent to Madrid from the Spanish embassy in the Russian capital, warning that the Russians were advancing eastward into North America and down its nothwest coast. By 1773, the Spanish were aware that the Russians had settlements in the Aleutians,[7] by 1775 a good map of the Aleutian-Alaska area had been sent to Madrid, and the general extent of Russian penetration of this region became known to Spanish officials. In 1778 Cook had anchored for a time at Unalaska in the Aleutian chain, and the publication of his voyages in 1784 disclosed more information regarding Russian activities in that area.

All this created misgiving in far-seeing Spanish eyes. It was apparent that the barbarous Slavs bestrode the narrow Bering Strait like a colossus, and were steadily moving southward along the coast of North America. Indeed, as Spanish sailors had already reached 61°N, the two spheres of influence had, in theory, intersected.[8] Passivity or response were the alternatives, and in the last upsurge of Spanish national energy before its long decline, response was the choice. Spain decided that ships should be sent north to make contact with the Russians, or at least to gather as much information as possible regarding their intentions, whereupon further appropriate action might be taken.

Madrid accordingly issued orders in January 1787 and again in July that two ships be sent northward to determine exactly what rival powers might be doing on the northernmost shores of the Spanish ocean. The ships, the *Princesa* and the *San Carlos* (the latter sometimes called the *Filipino* as it had been built in the Philippines), were outfitted at San Blas and sailed from there under Esteban Martinez and Lopez de Haro on March 8, 1788. Proceeding directly to Alaskan waters, they anchored near Montague Island in May. Shortly afterward, they went on to Prince William Sound, and on June 1, at about 60°N, the chaplain said mass and a cross was planted at a place named "Puerto de Flores" after the Viceroy of New Spain.[9]

The Spaniards noted a few signs of earlier visitors. On a nearby island they found an abandoned log house, no doubt the winter shelter of some hardy Russian; on another occasion, twelve canoes of Indians paddled out to Haro's ship and gave him two documents, one in Russian dated 1784, and the other in English, dated 1787.

About July 1 the long-boat of the *San Carlos* went ashore at the Russian colony of Three Saints Bay and brought back to the ships four Russians, including the local commandant, Delarof. He was inclined to be communicative, telling his visitors that he had been there since late 1787, while some of the other eighty men at the post had been in this lonely place since 1784. He told Haro that Russia had six settlements along the northern coast, with six ships at their disposal, and controlled the coast as far south as 52°. According to Delarof, men and supplies to occupy Nootka were expected to arrive at Three Saints Bay in 1789.[10]

This was most important news, and when the two Spanish ships went on to Unalaska in the Aleutian chain, it was confirmed by Zaikof, the local governor. He explained that the purpose of the impending Russian move was to forestall English traders, who were known to be reaping a rich harvest of furs from the Indians of that area. Martinez was also informed that two Russian ships were already en route to form a settlement at Nootka, while two more were being built at Okhotsk for the same purpose.[11]

Surprisingly, Martinez now boldly asserted the rights of Spain in this far northern area. On the northern shore of Unalaska, not far from where the Russians were clearly so well entrenched, he buried a bottle and took formal possession of the area for Spain. A few days later, he repeated this ceremony on a small nearby island.[12] On August 18 both ships turned back to San Blas, the *San Carlos* arriving there on October 22 and the *Princesa* (which spent some time in Monterey) on December 5.

The same day, Martinez wrote to Viceroy Flores, informing him of the Russian plans to occupy Nootka, and urging that Spain forestall them by establishing her own permanent post there without delay. He told Flores that,

> according to what is learned from the work of Cook and from what I saw on my first expedition to that place (which I made in 1774), it possesses qualifications which adapt it to that purpose. By accomplishing this we shall gain possession of the coast from Nootka to the port of San Francisco, a distance of 317 leagues, and authority over a multitude of native tribes.[13]

Before the month and year were out, Flores had decided on immediate action. Not waiting for approval from Madrid, this resolute and active arm of an empire dying at its heart gave instructions to Martinez to prepare and lead an expedition to Nootka. He outlined not only its purpose but also the actions which Martinez was to take in the event of various contingencies.

The purpose of the expedition was easily defined. It was "no other, as I have indicated, than the anticipation of the Russians in taking possession of the port of San Lorenzo or Nootka."[14] Yet Flores' attention was not engaged exclusively by the Russians. He was aware that both Britain and the United States had, in recent years, brazenly sent ships through the Spanish ocean to the northwest coast, and he felt not merely resentful at such impudence but suspicious as to what this might portend. He gave Martinez some advice as to how to deal with any such interlopers at Nootka:

> If Russian or English vessels should arrive, you will receive their commanders with the politeness and kind treatment which the existing peace demands; but you will show the just ground for our establishment at Nootka, the superior right which we have for continuing such establishments on the whole coast, and the measures which our superior government is taking to carry this out, such as sending by land

expeditions of troops, colonists, and missionaries, to attract and convert the Indians to the religion and mild dominion of our august sovereign.

All this you ought to explain with prudent firmness, but without being led into harsh expressions which may give serious offence and cause a rupture, but if, in spite of the great efforts, the foreigners should attempt to use force, you will repel it to the extent that they employ it, endeavoring to prevent as far as possible their intercourse and commerce with the natives.[15]

Flores, aware of the British convict settlement recently established at Botany Bay, and suspecting that it, too, formed part of some global conspiracy against his nation,[16] supplied Martinez with useful arguments to try on the English:

> To the English you will demonstrate clearly and with established proofs that our discoveries anticipated those of Captain Cook, since he reached Nootka, according to his own statement, in March of the year 1778, where he purchased (as he relates in Chapter I, Book 4, page 45 of his work) the two silver spoons which the Indians stole from yourself in 1774.[17]

Flores also pointed out to Martinez that Cook had been ordered by his own government to avoid Spanish possessions, and that by steering clear of California the British captain had tacitly conceded Spain's right to exclude foreign ships from its ports. Her rights at Nootka, Flores believed, were equally valid – both, after all, had first been visited by expeditions from San Blas – and Martinez was expected to hold firmly to this line in any dealings that he might have with British captains.

Flores also knew that two American ships had sailed from Boston in the fall of 1787, had stopped at the Spanish possession of Juan Fernandez Island, and then gone on to the northwest coast, where they presumably still were.[18] This suggested yet another threat to Spanish supremacy in the Pacific, and Flores commented to his superiors in Madrid:

> We ought not to be surprised that the English colonies of America, being now an independent republic, should carry

139

out the design of finding a safe port on the Pacific and of attempting to sustain it by crossing the immense country of the continent above our possessions of Texas, New Mexico and California.[19]

Flores instructed Martinez on the attitude that he was to adopt toward the insolent New Englanders:

> In case you are able to encounter this Bostonian frigate or the small boat which accompanied her, but was separated in the storm, this will give you governmental authority to take such measures as you may be able and such as appear proper, giving them to understand, as all other foreigners, that our settlements are being extended to beyond Prince William's Sound, of which we have already taken formal possession, as well as of the adjacent islands, viz., in 1779.[20]

It will be observed that there was a certain amount of ambiguity in these instructions. Spain was only to use force against Russian or British ships if they used it first, yet it was not at all clear just how Spain was to prevent these nations from enjoying "intercourse and commerce with the natives" without taking some sort of physical action, or at least employing the threat of it. The viceroy seems to have hoped that "prudent firmness" would be sufficient to deter rivals. He did envision that at some point this might have to be escalated into "brinkmanship," but he did not, perhaps, reflect where this in turn might lead. In the case of a meeting with the American ships, the instructions which he gave Martinez were notably milder. They did not mention the use of force, yet by their vagueness they left the way open for it. Measures "such as appear proper" might cover almost anything.

For all this the viceroy is not perhaps to be blamed; he could not have foreseen the manifold consequences which would flow from his actions. As 1788 gave way to 1789, and preparations went forward in San Blas for the triumphant and permanent establishment of Spanish power two thousand miles to the north, few watching the situation from either Mexico or Madrid can have felt much uneasiness. Surely before the summer was out, the ripening fruit of Nootka would have dropped peacefully into their hands.

Spain, then, had both asserted her claims and was preparing to take decisive action to support them. However, Britons in general and enterprising British fur-traders in particular saw the world in very different terms. Purported divisions of the globe by the Pope aroused no automatic response in Protestant hearts, and Englishmen were not much interested in how far Balboa had waded into the Pacific off Panama in 1513. They tended to believe, especially when it was convenient to do so, that land belonged not to those who merely discovered it, but to those who occupied and used it. Their countrymen had already made considerable advances in developing the fur trade of the northwest coast, and had built both a house and a ship at Nootka. Moreover, a detailed record of Captain Cook's earlier visit to that area had been published for all to read, whereas the Spanish had kept their activities to themselves. So as far as most of the English-speaking world knew, it was the Great Navigator who had first sailed into Nootka Sound.

Looking at Spanish claims in the light of these varied considerations, most Britons would have said that they had the greater right to Nootka, and one who now proposed to act on this reassuring assumption was John Meares. Long since recovered from his tribulations in Prince William Sound in 1787, well satisfied with his voyage to Nootka and his shipbuilding operations there in 1788, he now planned a successful return to his old friends Maquinna and Wickananish, and the establishment of a permanent trading post somewhere in their realms.

This time his venture was to be on an expanded scale, with no fewer than four ships taking part. First, Meares joined forces with the group headed by the Etches brothers, and they formed a new company, variously called the Associated Merchants of London and India, the United Company of British merchants trading to the northwest coast, and the South Sea Company of London.[21] As James Colnett, one of the captains employed by this company, explained in an account which he later compiled of his activities in 1789,

> It was thought advisable by both parties to form a junction of trade under the British flag, each flattering himself from the knowledge acquired by their commanders of the coast,

dispositions of the natives, and articles coveted by them in trade, would soon expel all other adventurers, and enable us to make returns adequate to expenses of outfit which none of our former voyages had done, which was chiefly occasioned by want of knowledge of ports and harbours, which obstacle was now got over, but still a disadvantage to strangers as it remained a secret with ourselves.[22]

John Meares, as the moving spirit behind the enterprise, had no doubt of its outcome. In a directive to Captain Douglas of the *Iphigenia*, near the close of the 1788 season, he had explained:

The knowledge we have now obtained of the coast of America, of the periodical winds and seasons, gives us the advantage of all competitors. The year 1789 must be viewed by both of us as the most productive of any we may expect. Having these views before us, our exertions must be doubled to effectually sweep the coast before any ship from Europe can arrive.[23]

The *Prince of Wales*, which had done so well in 1788 under Capt. James Colnett, was returning to England, so the company replaced it with another ship, the *Argonaut*, which was built in Calcutta, and put Colnett in charge of her. Toward the end of the 1788 season Meares had given Colnett detailed instructions regarding his part in the grand design for 1789. Having sailed the *Argonaut* from the Far East to Nootka, he was to avoid trouble with the natives, make treaties with their chiefs, and build a "solid establishment, and not one that is to be abandoned at pleasure."[24] It was to be named Fort Pitt (for there was no harm in keeping on the right side of politicians in office), and it was to be put in the charge of Robert Duffin, who had explored the Strait of Juan de Fuca for Meares in 1788. This settlement would draw the natives to trade, and be a convenient place to build more ships. Eventually, similar outposts of the fur trade would be established at other suitable places along the coast. In other words, this time the British were coming to stay.

Even the areas which the various ships were to scour for furs in 1789 had been decided in 1788. Douglas in the *Iphigenia*, which had spent the winter of 1788-89 in Hawaii, was instructed to return to the northwest coast and explore northern waters, especially "the great island" (i.e., the Queen Charlotte group) where Dixon in 1787 had got 600 skins in a very short time. The *Iphigenia* was to go as far north as Prince William Sound, but not to Cook's River farther west, as "it is now so totally possessed by Russians the proceeding there would be only waste of the most valuable time."[25]

Robert Funter in the *North West America*, which also wintered at Hawaii, was to proceed to the northwest coast in the spring of 1789 and thoroughly cover the area between 43°30' and 50°N, although he could also trade as far north as 54°. Funter was made to feel, however, that even in the distant Queen Charlottes his generalissimo's eye was upon him. There was to be no trading by his officers or crew on their own account. Regarding a Mr. Shephardson given him as an assistant, he was cautioned that, "He is very young and very heedless. Make some allowances but keep him strictly to his duty and leave the vessel as little as possible in his charge."[26]

In business dealings with the natives, there was also, Funter was reminded, a right and a wrong way of doing things:

> I desire you will husband your articles of trade as much as possible and made the natives sensible of their value and as you will in all probability have to do with natives and tribes that hitherto have had no knowledge of Europeans you will take advantage of their ignorance to keep the price of your merchandise up.[27]

Nor did this exhaust Meares' instructions to the captain of the *North West America*. He was to keep a log book, make charts, record all receipts and expenditures, collect samples of minerals, and study the voyages of Captain Cook, of which he was given a copy.

At the end of the trading season, in August 1789, the *Iphigenia* and the *North West America* were to meet at Nootka, where Meares himself in the *Felice* (having traded in the waters from Nootka southward) planned to rendezvous soon afterward.[28] If Meares found none of his associates at Nootka by November 21, he would go on to Hawaii and stay there until the end of 1789. If there was still no sign of them by this time, he would "conclude that some fatal accident had happened and make the best of my way to China."

Fur was not to be the sole object of the expedition. Douglas was to keep a lookout for the northwest passage (but not waste invaluable time in actually searching for it); on his way homeward from America he was to visit Copper Island near the coast of Asia; even here the next move had been decided by Meares a year in advance:

> If the copper ore is in huge masses, you must blow them up with gunpowder and lade on board as much as you can with safety to your ship; also of sandalwood or any other sweet scented wood that you can find.[29]

As to what flags the *North West America* and the *Iphigenia* were to sail under, in this, as in so many things, Meares was prepared to be flexible. The enterprise behind their voyages was entirely British, but a Portuguese merchant of Macao, Juan Cavalho, was made a nominal partner in the firm so that, as Meares later phrased it in his famous "Memorial," the ships would "be allowed to navigate under or claim any advantages granted to the Portuguese flag." Among the advantages listed by Meares was the avoidance of high Chinese port charges. He no doubt saw others as well, for when the two ships reached Nootka they were both flying Portuguese flags, though they can hardly have expected to meet many Chinese officials at Friendly Cove.[30]

There was, in fact, another important reason why Meares was disinclined to fly the flag of his own nation, though he prudently refrained from mentioning it when it came time to compose his *Voyages* and his "Memorial." He had not obtained, as British merchantmen were obliged to do, licenses for the ships from the East India Company of the South Sea Company. If he could pass off their voyages as a purely Portuguese venture, he would be in less legal danger. Yet apparently even this did not exhaust the subterfuges which this Machiavelli of the maritime fur trade was prepared to envision. In the fall of 1788, while writing to Captain Funter, he ordered him "on no account to hoist any colours until such time as your employers give you orders for this purpose, except on taking possession of any newly discovered land; you will then do it, with the usual formalities, for the crown of Great Britain."[31] By contrast, in the spring of 1789 Meares told Captain Douglas that he would be informed in a message from the Far East, by way of Captain Colnett, which flag he was to use in northwestern waters: "You will then receive orders relative to the colours you are to hoist, which will be those of the United Company of merchants trading under the sanction of the S. Sea and Hbl. East India Company's charters."[32] There is no clear evidence that the company flag was ever used, but in dealing with this master of many disguises one can never be quite sure. A historian who claimed to have unravelled all the facts of the matter might really have done no more than enroll himself in the lengthy list of this shrewd manipulator's dupes.

At all event, the stage was now set for an important series of events; the only problem was that of agreeing on a single dramatist. The directors of Spanish national policy saw 1789 as the year in which they would decisively forestall Russian expansionism and establish themselves firmly, formally, and permanently on the northwest coast. In their view, this was already, both morally and legally, a Spanish possession. The British government, by contrast, had never conceded this claim, though it would likely have admitted that some sort of case could be made for it; the fact that Cook had refrained from taking possession at Nootka was perhaps significant. Individual British adventurers, however, took the brisk and convenient view that they were entitled to set up a trading post on the northwest coast at any point not under actual Russian or Spanish occupation, and this Meares and his friends now proposed to do.

Russia had no publicly announced policy, preferring secrecy in all things, but was extending her influence ever farther down the northwest coast. Apparently, like the Spanish and British, she envisioned the establishment of a permanent commercial outpost at Nootka.[33] The most recent arrivals on the coast, the Americans, had no plans for annexing any part of it to the United States. They merely assumed the right to trade wherever looked promising between California and Alaska. However, they can scarcely have avoided recalling that until very recently their country had been engaged in a long and desperate struggle with Britain, and this fact might have made them regard rivals or enemies of Britain with a sympathetic eye.

All these nations in one way or another would play a part in the drama about to begin. In addition, there would be an unlikely fifth player – the long-suffering masses of France, whose sudden lunge at freedom in the summer of 1789 would upset the balance of world politics for a generation, and cause major reassessments of policy in the chancelleries of Europe.

The opening move in the unfolding drama perhaps came on February 17, when the *Princesa* and the *San Carlos* left the harbor of San Blas and headed north, to establish once and for all the rights of their royal master in Madrid. The *Princesa*, under Martinez, carried 106 men, including 15 soldiers for the garrison of the proposed fort, while the *San Carlos*, under Lopez de Haro, carried 89 men, including 16 soldiers. Most of the men, apart from a few Spanish officers, were natives of California. Their instructions included gaining the good will of the natives and converting them to Christianity, erecting buildings and fortifications at Nootka, and exploring the coast between 50° and 55°. A third vessel, a packet boat with the engaging name of *Aranzazu*, would follow them a few weeks later.

While they were still making their way up the Pacific coast, the *Washington*, which had lain all winter at Nootka, made a short voyage in the opposite direction. It left Nootka on March 16 and proceeded to Clayoquot, forty miles to the south, there to spend ten days trading and hunting. Then, sailing past Barkley Sound and Nitinat, the ship entered the Strait of Juan de Fuca to a distance of about fifteen miles. By April 9 Captain Gray was back at Clayoquot and paying a friendly visit to Wickananish.

Here one of his officers found himself witnessing, indeed, almost participating in, one of the most dramatic aspects of Nootka life:

> About noon I was surprized by hearing a very sudden and loud shout allmost everyboddy runing from the village to their canoes I was soon eased from my suspence by my friend Hanna who told me Wickananish had struck a whale and that all the villagers were going to his assistance. I was curious to see them kill the large fish with such simple impliments and went in a canoe accompaneyd by Mr Treat to be spectators. On our arrival at the place I found the whale

with sixteen bladders fastened to him with harpoons; the whale was laying at this time unmolested waiting the return of the chief who was in pursute of another but immediately on his return he gave the order for the attack. His mandate was answered by a low but universal acclamation. The next brother to the chief invited me into his canoe. This I rediely complied with. We were paddled up to the fish with great speed and he gave him a deadly pearce and the enormious creature instantly expired. They fastened a number of bois on the fish and took it in tow to the village.[34]

A similar trip to the region of Cape Flattery also went smoothly, but this time when the ship returned to Nootka, on April 22, Gray found Captain Douglas in the *Iphigenia*, which had left Hawaii on March 18 and arrived at Nootka about April 19. A few days later Captain Funter, who had left Hawaii with the *North West America* at the same time as the *Iphigenia*, was also safely anchored at Nootka.

In late April two other players in the cast left distant China: the *Princess Royal*, commanded by Thomas Hudson, and the *Argonaut*, under James Colnett. The *Argonaut* brought with her the frame of a ship for completion at Nootka; she also had on board twenty-nine Chinese, who, Meares tells us, "intended to become settlers on the American coast."[35]

As spring passed into summer, three of the four ships already on the northwest coast busied themselves collecting furs. For reasons known only to Captain Kendrick, the *Columbia* remained inert at Nootka, but the *Washington*, *North West America*, and *Iphigenia* came and went on trading voyages.

Kendrick was not entirely idle in this period. He built a house at Moweena (the inlet of Nootka Sound where he usually anchored, several miles from Friendly Cove) and called it Fort Washington. Two years later, when again in the area, he secured from Maquinna a deed for the land on which it stood. This document was eventually lost.

It was Gray who first became aware that a third nation would soon be represented at Friendly Cove. He left Nootka on May 2, and the following day he met the *Princesa*, plainly on the point of arriving. The two captains had a friendly conversation,

147

and Martinez bestowed upon Gray "preasants of brandy, wine, hams, sugar and in short everything he thought would be acceptable."[36]

He also gave the American an account of his actions and plans that was at wide variance from the truth. He asserted that his ship, with two others, had been outfitted at Cadiz for voyages of exploration, that while in Mexico he had lost most of his Spanish seamen, and had then been forced to replace them with Californians. He had next, he told Gray, gone to Bering Strait, but had lost contact with his companions in a gale.[37]

The Americans seem to have taken this story at face value. Probably more puzzling in their eyes was the assertion of Martinez that he intended to capture the English vessel (i.e., the *Iphigenia*) then at Nootka, declaring that "it would make him a good prize."[38]

As a sturdy American isolationist, Gray doubtless saw no reason to take part in the disputes of European imperialists, and, as one whose country had only recently emerged from a war with Great Britain, he was unlikely to worry unduly about the fate of rival British traders. So he went ahead with his own plans for a trading voyage to northern waters. Contrary winds held him in the vicinity of Nootka for several days, and during this time he sighted a second Spanish ship, the *San Carlos*, but bad weather prevented any communication between the two ships.

Assuming, no doubt, that the Pacific Ocean and even Friendly Cove were wide enough for both Spaniards and Americans, Gray went north to the Queen Charlottes in search of furs. Unaware that this group of islands had already been named, and believing it to be a single island 170 miles long, he called it Washington Island in honor of the leader of the revolution who, a few weeks before, had taken the oath of office as first president of the United States. Here Gray found natives with an agreeably unsophisticated scale of values, one group giving him two hundred sea-otter skins for the same number of iron chisels.[39] Later a native brought to the ship "a pece of paper that informed us that the North West American schooner had been there May the 24th last."[40]

All this was promising enough, and on June 17 Gray again

anchored at Nootka, well satisfied with his efforts.[41] He found that several important developments had taken place in his absence. The two Spanish ships which he had seen earlier were now at Nootka, the *Princesa* having arrived on May 6 and the *San Carlos* on May 13. Moreover, the Spanish had already made considerable progress in fortifying nearby Hog Island, calling their fort San Miguel. They also showed other unmistakable signs that they had much more in mind than a trading voyage from California or a voyage of exploration from Cadiz. Relations between the two nationalities were friendly, however, and the Americans presented Martinez with two brilliantly decorated cloaks originally made in Hawaii, with which he was much pleased. Yet the captains from Boston seem to have felt a little uneasiness about the general situation at Nootka, for they anchored at Moweena, several miles from Friendly Cove.

One of the signs that serious developments which might lead to international complications were afoot was the temporary seizure of the *Iphigenia* by Martinez. At first, the Spaniard had treated Captain Douglas with courtesy. On his first night in port he was invited to dine on the *Princesa*; later the two captains dined with Kendrick on the *Columbia*, and on another occasion Douglas was host to Kendrick and Martinez. The Spaniard even promised to give Douglas some supplies so that he might be on his way. He did, however, make it clear to him that he had been trespassing in Spanish waters.

Not long afterward, Martinez visited the Indian village, and here (according to his own account) he renewed old acquaintances and gathered ammunition for future disputations with intrusive Britishers:

> While I was in Macuina's house, he showed me the shells which I had given him in 1774 when I came to this port with the frigate *Santiago* ... which corroborated all that I had said to the Englishman at mess. Maquinna also told me that the Indian who had robbed me of the two silver spoons (which incident Captain Cook mentions in his work) had died some time before.
>
> Likewise I learned from the English that the Indian

149

whom I hurt when I threw the shells off the ship was a brother of this Maquinna. Both men recognized me and said that when I was here before in 1774 they were then mere boys.[42]

So far, Martinez had done very little to obey his instructions to exclude foreigners from Nootka. With the arrival of Haro in the *San Carlos* on May 13, he seems to have had a change of heart. Perhaps he now felt in a stronger position, or he may have feared that he had not carried out the orders of the viceroy. He was aware that the commandant at Juan Fernandez Island, who had given a little assistance to John Kendrick, had later been dismissed from his post for doing so, and was no doubt anxious to avoid a like fate. Accordingly, on May 14 he summoned Douglas and his Portuguese "co-captain" Don Francisco José Viana, a native of Lisbon, to the *Princesa* with a view to examining their papers.

It did not take long to arouse the suspicions of the Spaniard. The vessel's instructions were in Portuguese, but most of the crew were British, and although the ship's papers listed Viana as the commander and Douglas as the supercargo, it seemed likely that Douglas was the real captain. Neither Martinez nor Douglas could understand Portuguese very well. The Spaniard, nevertheless, believed that the instructions envisioned the capturing of any Russian, English, or Spanish vessels that were encountered and taking them back to China, where they might be condemned before Portuguese courts at Macao and their crews punished as pirates.[43]

Douglas protested that, so far as he knew, the instructions dealt only with measures to be taken in case the *Iphigenia* was attacked. Martinez was unconvinced, and announced that the British ship and those on board her were his prisoners.

The British captain was indignant, and he rejected the argument that Nootka was a Spanish port. Privately, he suspected that the Americans had instigated the affair, and some suspicion must remain that this was so, but in the face of superior force, he had to submit.[44]

For nearly two weeks the Britons were prisoners on the Spanish ships. Then Martinez had yet another change of heart, apparently feeling on reflection that he might have misunderstood the Portuguese instructions. He may also have realized that he lacked the forces both to take the *Iphigenia* back to San Blas with a prize crew and also to fortify Nootka and defend it against a possible Slavic assault.

Accordingly, he released his prisoners and restored them to their ship. First, however, he made Douglas and Viana sign a bond on behalf of the alleged owner of the *Iphigenia*, Juan Cavalho. The terms stated that Cavalho's company would turn over to Spanish authorities the value of the ship and its cargo if the viceroy in Mexico later decided that because the ship had entered Nootka without a Spanish passport it had been a lawful prize.[45]

Martinez also ordered Douglas to write a letter to Captain Funter of the *North West America* (then away on a trading voyage), instructing him to sell his ship to the Spanish at a price to be determined by the American commanders – another example of Spanish-American co-operation in this period. Douglas wrote a letter, but not in the terms which Martinez, who understood no English, had laid down. He merely told Funter to act as seemed to him best. Martinez, however, was satisfied, and on May 26 the *Iphigenia* was restored to its British operators, who, moved no doubt by patriotic fervor, again raised the Portuguese flag.

At the end of May the *Iphigenia* was escorted out of the harbor and its commanders warned not to return. Douglas later claimed that he had been badly treated by the Spanish, that nearly everything of value, including trade goods, had been stolen by them from his ship, and that he had been sold only a small quantity of provisions at too high a price.[46] There are, however, differing opinions as to this. It is undeniable that on the night before the *Iphigenia* left Nootka, both Douglas and some American officers dined amicably aboard the *Princesa*.[47] Moreover, instead of sailing direct from Nootka to Macao, the *Iphigenia*, once out of sight of the Spanish fort, made a successful trading voyage northward along the coast, collecting more than 700 pelts before turning west across the Pacific.[48] This would scarcely have been possible for a ship stripped bare by the Spanish.

In the meanwhile, Martinez had embarked on another project. He was constructing a fort, which was to be named after

151

St. Michael, on a hill overlooking the harbor. Emplacements were laboriously built for the guns, which had been brought from Mexico. In his diary for June 8 he wrote of having beams cut from the forests and dragged to the spot "where I have determined to build a large house to serve as winter quarters." In a later entry (July 14) he spoke of "the house in which we are to spend the winter." All this, we should note, (despite the mysterious words in the viceroy's instructions about only making a "pretended" occupation of Nootka) suggests strongly that Martinez had every intention of remaining for a considerable time in the area.

On June 9 the *North West America* under Captain Funter returned to Nootka and was promptly seized by Martinez. Before long the ship, which was in very poor shape (Martinez later claimed that it had been abandoned) had been refitted and then rechristened *Santa Gertrudis la Magna*, after the patron saint of sailors. A few days later, under José Narváez, with David Coolidge, second mate of the *Washington*, as his assistant (another interesting example of Spanish-American co-operation) the ship made a successful trading voyage to the Strait of Juan de Fuca, securing 75 skins. Captain Funter and his men were put on board the *Columbia*, which was to sail soon for China. The skins which the *North West America* had collected were transferred to the *Princess Royal*, which had arrived at Nootka on June 14. Martinez kept back twelve of the best pelts, presumably by way of satisfying some debt which he believed was owing to him or his government.

Indeed, it soon began to appear to Martinez that considerably more might be owing to him than he had first reckoned, for when the *Princess Royal* arrived from China she brought news of the bankruptcy of Cavalho. The bond which Douglas and Viana had signed as payment for supplies was now perhaps worthless.

Clearly, troubles were mounting for the Spanish commander, far from Mexico or Madrid and the chance of consultation with his superiors. Sent northward to repel a Russian expedition believed to be planning the addition of Nootka to the realms of the tsar, he had found instead a British and an American vessel anchored there. Now other British ships, some supplied with highly suspicious papers, were beginning to arrive. He was under orders to exclude all foreigners from either the possession of Nootka or the trade with its inhabitants, yet the forces at his disposal to do so were by no means overwhelming.

While pondering this problem, Martinez decided to strengthen at least his legal position by taking formal possession of Nootka for Spain. By this time the fort was completed and had a garrison with a battery of ten cannons. Three buildings had been erected – a workshop, a bakery, and a dormitory. The "fort" built by Meares in the previous year had almost certainly disappeared, for there is no reference to it in the Spanish accounts, or, indeed, in those of anyone else. Thus there was now, to all appearance, a permanent Spanish establishment at Nootka, and no other nation could demonstrate anything comparable.

It was apparently a propitious moment. On June 24, with elaborate ceremonies conducted by the Spanish commanders and the six missionaries from Mexico, formal possession of Nootka was taken. Representatives of three nations were present, and afterward those of the two Anglo-Saxon powers drank the health of the King of Spain.[49] This monarch's ancestors had bequeathed him a great empire – in fact, the world's largest. Now it became even greater, as before the eyes of other white men and the impassive gaze of those of darker skin, wider still and wider had its bounds been set.[50]

The True Faith was also extending its sway. The six priests were busy expounding the gospel to the natives, and before long one had accepted its message to the point of consenting to be baptized. He was only a child, but he manfully accepted the new appellation of "Estevan Lorenzo Francisco Severo Martinez y Flores." Martinez carefully explained to the viceroy (for a man has to think of future promotions) that Nootka now had a resident named after the first citizen of New Spain.[51]

There remained the problem of the instrusive foreign ships, by Martinez evidently felt that he could not yet make a decisive move. The *Princess Royal*, under Captain Hudson and flying the British flag, had arrived at Nootka on June 14. On its first night in port the Spanish commandant had spent the night aboard her, as had Kendrick and Captain Funter, late of the *North West America*. What they had to say to each other we shall never know, but apparently a spirit of good will prevailed. The next day, to the accompaniment of a salute from the Spanish fort, the *Princess Royal* was towed to a good anchorage in the sound. Later Hudson, Martinez, and Kendrick repaired to the *Columbia*, some six miles away, where they spent several hours.

By this time the Spaniard felt that he should make at least an exploratory move. The next day he sent a polite note to Hudson, inquiring why he had anchored in a Spanish port. The British captain explained that his ship was in poor shape, but that if he could receive some assistance he would leave Nootka. This was satisfactory to Martinez. Certainly there was no evidence of ill will on either side, for at the banquet that accompanied the ceremony of taking possession of the port for Spain, Hudson, like the other non-Spaniards, was an honored guest.

By the end of June the Briton was ready to depart. Martinez supplied him with a letter requesting other Spanish ships to leave him unmolested, and on July 1 the launches of the American ships towed the *Princess Royal* out of Nootka Sound. Soon she was lost from sight – as Martinez hoped, forever.

Yet hardly had she slipped into the distance than another British ship arrived. This was the *Argonaut* under Captain Colnett, who had crossed the wide Pacific from Macao with orders from Meares and his associates to construct at Nootka "a solid establishment, and not one that is to be abandoned at pleasure." This, of course, was exactly what Martinez believed that he had just done. The problems of the Spanish were beginning to escalate, and the dangers of a serious confrontation to increase.

From this point on, the problems of the historian also escalate, for there has long been conflicting testimony regarding developments at Nootka in the next few weeks. All those who participated in or witnessed these events have long since descended into the silent grave, and we have only the records which they left behind. Affected by interest, colored by partisanship, distorted by emotion – such they undoubtedly are, but it is not always easy to determine the exact places where these all too human failings exert their influence. We must thread our way as best we can.[52]

We know that not long after the *Argonaut* arrived, by Colnett's reckoning, on the evening of July 3 (July 2 according to

Martinez), the Spanish commander came out to the British ship and was amicably received. Yet almost at once it became apparent that irreconcilable differences existed between them. According to Martinez, he lost no time in asking Colnett what his intentions were:

> In the conversation which I had with him, he said that he came as governor of this port, to establish a factory for collecting sea-otter skins, in the name of the company to which his ship belonged. He also said that he was entrusted to prevent other nations from taking part in this fur-trade both in this port and the other harbours of the coast, and moreover, that he brought orders from his sovereign, the King of England, to take possession of the port of Nootka and its coast, to fortify it and make an establishment. For this latter purpose he brought a number of Chinese of all occupations.[53]

In most respects this is an accurate account. There is no doubt that Colnett came to Nootka prepared to build a permanent trading post, as his instructions were to do so; it seems much less certain, indeed very unlikely, that he brought any "orders from his sovereign, the King of England."

The *Argonaut* was towed into port by the Spanish launches. There the ship was secured by two hawsers, one attached to the *San Carlos*, and one, interestingly enough, to the *Columbia*.[54] Colnett later declared that he was in effect tricked into entering the harbor, that Martinez told him he was short of supplies and that if he would provide the Spanish with some, he would then be allowed to leave whenever he wished.[55] There is some reason to believe that Colnett's statements were correct,[56] although Martinez is completely silent on this matter. He merely records that the *Argonaut* was towed into port, and then details a long argument which he had with Colnett about the ownership of Nootka Sound. Perez and Cook naturally figured prominently in the conversation, Martinez asserting the the local natives would back up his statement as to who had entered Nootka first. The Spaniard declared that Colnett "recognized that the reasons which I had given him were well founded," but Colnett has nothing to say about this interesting historical discussion or the conclusions which arose from it.

Both captains agree, however, that on the day following this conversation, (July 4 by Colnett's reckoning, July 3 by that of Martinez) a violent quarrel broke out between them on board the *Princesa*.[57] Colnett's account, which is in the form of a long footnote in a book written nine years later on quite another subject, is at least dramatic:

> On my coming into his cabin, he said he wished to see my papers; on my presenting them to him, he just glanced his eyes over them, and although he did not understand a word of the language in which they were written, declared they were forged, and threw them disdainfully on the table, saying at the same time, I should not sail until he pleased. On my making some remonstrances at his breach of faith, and his forgetfulness of that word and honour which he had pledged to me, he arose in an apparent anger, and went out.
>
> I now saw, but too late, the duplicity of this Spaniard, and was conversing with the interpreter on the subject, when having my back towards the cabin door, I by chance cast my eyes on a looking-glass, and saw an armed party rushing in behind me. I instantly put my hand to my hanger, but before I had time to place myself in a posture of defence, a violent blow brought me to the ground. I was then ordered into the stocks, and closely confined; after which, they seized my ship and cargo, imprisoned my officers, and put my men in irons. They sent their boats likewise to sea and seized the sloop *Princess Royal*, and brought her into port, for trading on the coast.
>
> It may not be amiss to observe that the Spaniards consider it contrary to treaty, and are extremely jealous, if any European power trades in those seas, but this cannot justify Don Martinez, who, not content with securing me and my people, carried me from ship to ship, like a criminal, rove a halter to the yard-arm, and frequently threatened me with instant death, by hanging me as a pirate.[58]

Martinez naturally has a somewhat different tale to tell. According to him, Colnett refused to let him see one of the documents which he requested; the British captain "did not wish to let go of the paper, or even allow me to make a copy of it, so that

I could make myself acquainted with its contents." Moreover, Colnett

> accompanied this talk by placing his hand two or three times on his sword which he wore at his belt, as if to threaten me in my own cabin. He also added in a loud voice the evil-sounding and insulting words "God damned Spaniard". I had so far acted with prudence, trying to mollify him by all means possible, so that he should calm himself, and without further attempting to evade, produce for me the papers that I had asked for.[59]

Neither man would back down, tempers flared, and whether violence was employed, as Colnett asserts, or not, Martinez finally took decisive action:

> In order to avoid the shedding of blood, I decided to arrest him in my own cabin, declaring him a prisoner of war, together with all his officers, crew and ship, to be sent later to the Department of San Blas and there disposed of by his Excellency the Viceroy of New Spain.[60]

Regardless of what actually took place in the Spanish captain's cabin, it is not hard to see the difficulty of his position. He feared that if he let the British leave Nootka, they would merely build a fort at some other convenient place on the coast. When this became well established and the authorities in Mexico and Madrid heard about it, he, Martinez, would be charged with neglecting the instructions which he had been given by the viceroy in Mexico City: to "prevent as far as possible their intercourse and commerce with the natives." There is some evidence, even so, that Martinez thought of letting Colnett depart peaceably, but that the other Spanish officers brought pressure to bear on him to take a harder line.[61]

At all events, a decisive rupture in relations had now occurred, and it might reasonably be expected that things would go from bad to worse. It is somewhat bewildering to learn that the next day, after the *Columbia* had fired a salvo of thirteen guns to celebrate the thirteenth anniversary of July 4, 1776, Captain Kendrick (according to Martinez) invited not merely the Spanish but the British officers to "a splendid banquet . . . in the course of which toasts were drunk to the health of our august sovereign, Don Carlos III (whom God protect)."[62] This did not, however hamper the Spaniard from having the "artillery, powder, ammunition, and the tackle of the packet *Argonaut*" brought aboard his own ship.

The next day the *Santa Gertrudis la Magna* (as the captured *North West America* had been renamed) returned from a voyage in the course of which the crew had not only collected a fair number of furs but also confirmed the existence and location of the Strait of Juan de Fuca.[63] Colnett, meanwhile, was still a prisoner. His captors examined his ship and found it unfit for a voyage to Mexico, so carpenters were put to work repairing it, as well as providing space for the Spanish to "place the imprisoned officers, with every assurance of cleanliness and security." Martinez noted in his diary of July 7 that "the space in the ship for this purpose was very small," which to some extent confirms Colnett's later allegations that the conditions under which he was transferred to San Blas were "too shocking to relate."[64]

Before work on the *Argonaut* was finished, a fresh complication had arisen, as the mental health of Colnett broke down under the stress of events. As Martinez recorded on July 11,

> At daybreak this morning, I was informed by pilot Don José Tobar, who is entrusted with the command of the packet for its voyage to San Blas, that Captain Colnett, from the effects of despair or madness, had thrown himself into the water through one of the port-holes or windows of his cabin. However, on hearing the noise which he made when he struck the water, he was discovered from the quarter-deck, and was picked up by the packet's launch, which went to him at once. When it reached him, he was half drowned, but they turned him on his stomach and relieved him of much of the water which he had swallowed. I immediately ordered that he be shut up in a stateroom to prevent him from suffering harm in this way.[65]

The next day, the almost equally unpredictable Martinez once more exchanged his role of jailer for that of host, and "gave the officers who are my prisoners a splendid banquet." Whether

Colnett was in a condition to participate is not recorded, but in the circumstances it seems unlikely.

In the late afternoon of the same day, Martinez had another problem to cope with: the lookout at the fort reported the sighting of a ship. The vessel was none other than the *Princess Royal*, which Martinez believed he had seen the last of ten days before, when Captain Hudson had promised to take his ship without delay to Macao. This time, however, the Spaniard did not hesitate; with the capture of the *North West America* he had embarked on a line of action from which he could hardly retreat. The *Princess Royal*, her officers and crew, were all soon prisoners of the Spanish.

At this point the crisis claimed its first victim. This was not a white man, but Callicum, kinsman of Chief Maquinna. He evidently took the side of the British, for he abused their captors in his native tongue. When his words were interpreted, he paid for them with his life, being immediately shot by the Spanish.[66]

The next day the *Argonaut* was ready for sea. Under Spanish officers it began the long journey to San Blas, carrying as prisoners Colnett, who had by now recovered his mental composure, and his men. Near the end of the month the *Princess Royal*, under a Spanish captain (Narváez) and carrying Captain Hudson and his men as prisoners, also set sail for Mexico. It was accompanied by the *San Carlos* under Lopez de Haro, whom Martinez, despairing of the arrival of the *Aranzazu*, was sending south for supplies.

During the remainder of the summer, the American ships were unmolested, and indeed relations between them and the Spanish were remarkably – some would say suspiciously – cordial. Despite the clear instructions given to Martinez to prevent other nations from trading with the natives, the *Washington* did some trading along the coast. Martinez entrusted a rather confused explanation of his policy to his diary:

> The sloop *Washington* continued on her way, not on a voyage of discovery as her commander said, but in pursuit of the fur trade, which is the principal object of all the people who come to this coast. I could have taken this sloop and the frigate *Columbia*, but I had no orders to that purpose, and my situation did not permit me to do it. I treated this enemy as

a friend, entrusting to him 137 furs to be sold on my account in Canton.[67]

During the summer of 1789 Martinez was far from idle; he was building gun emplacements for his fort, and constructing a second one, which he named San Rafael.[68] It also appears that he built a ship, though the exact details of the matter have long been in dispute. As we saw, he had captured and refitted the *North West America* and then rechristened her the *Santa Gertrudis la Magna*. Later he decided "to build a schooner of about sixty English feet in length, that should not draw more than six or seven feet."[69] This last detail implies strongly that it was merely intended for exploring local inlets. However, late in July he abandoned this plan and, dismantling the uncompleted vessel, "ordered the construction of another vessel that would be able to undertake any voyage." In early August he noted that "the carpenters and wood-cutters continue working up the timber for the construction of the schooner *Santa Gertrudis*," and it was apparently under this name that it was launched in the autumn. Exactly why Martinez should have given two ships the same name is part of the puzzle, and has suggested to some that the original *North West America* was also dismantled and incorporated in the new vessel. Others, however, have suggested that it was the newer ship which was dismantled while still incomplete and the material used to enlarge the original *North West America*.[70]

Suddenly into the midst of all this activity came the *Aranzazu*, arriving on July 29. Martinez was gratified that fresh materials and supplies would now be available for the fort – and then astonished to hear that the ship brought orders from the viceroy that Nootka was to be abandoned at the end of the season!

It is not to be wondered at that Martinez was amazed by these instructions, especially as the order was dated February 25, which was only eight days after the *Princesa* and *San Carlos* had left San Blas. It has been suggested that two considerations (or reconsiderations) were involved. Perhaps the authorities in Mexico had concluded that there were not enough supply ships on the Pacific coast to service Nootka as well as the recently established posts at Monterey and San Francisco, and that the most expendable of these was the most northerly. Moreover, it may have been reckoned that as formal possession had been taken at Nootka, and the Spanish had erected buildings there and lived in them for some time, the port was now beyond doubt an outpost of the Spanish empire.[71]

Thus the authorities in Mexico may not have felt that they were taking an irretrievable backward step. Spain's vigorous assertions of her claims during the diplomatic quarrel between Madrid and London in the following year, and her reoccupation of Nootka at that time, both show that the orders now received by Martinez were merely tactics, not grand strategy.

Yet the energetic commandant of Nootka was undoubtedly dismayed. Not only had his own career apparently received a setback, but, as he saw it, so had the fortunes of his nation. He was well aware of the key position of Nootka in a rapidly expanding industry, and was later to outline to his superiors a plan for what has been termed "a great triangular system encompassing the entire Pacific ocean" in which Hawaii would also play an important part.[72] But orders were orders, and Martinez sent word back to Haro via the *Aranzazu* that he would wait for the *San Carlos* until the end of October, and then, if she had not yet arrived, he himself would come south in the *Princesa*. He also sent a letter to the viceroy expressing regret at the turn of events:

> I can only say to your Excellency that in my opinion this is very regrettable in light of the fact that this coast is visited with frequency by the English, Portuguese, Boston men and Russians.[73]

Toward the end of the summer, Martinez dismantled his two forts, removed their cannon, and placed the buildings in charge of Maquinna, telling him that he would return the following year. He also buried a large quantity of bricks which he had brought with him, presumably so that they would be available for building material at a later time. Also, he erected a cross bearing the dates 1774 and 1789, and buried some documents in a bottle. He repeated this procedure at Tahsis near the head of the sound.

Yet his problems were still not over. In mid-October the American ship *Fair American*, with a crew of four under Thomas

Humphrey Metcalfe (aged eighteen), entered Nootka. Martinez had left the *Columbia* and *Washington* alone, and indeed accorded their activities his friendly co-operation, but in a sudden reversal of policy he now captured the new arrival.

A few days later, Martinez recorded in his diary for October 20, the new *Santa Gertrudis* was launched and put in charge of Don Jose Verdia. In a curious but perhaps significant gesture, Martinez planted a field of wheat, nailed to a tree a sign informing Haro that he had abandoned Nootka by order of the viceroy, and on the last day of October he set sail for San Blas in the *Princesa*, carrying the twenty-nine Chinese brought to Nootka by the *Argonaut*. Even as he left the harbor, accompanied by the *Santa Gertrudis* and the captured *Fair American* (now under the command of John Kendrick, junior, who had left the service of his father and his country to join the Spanish), the brig *Eleanora*, under Simon Metcalfe, father of the *Fair American's* captain, hove in sight. Martinez raised the Spanish flag and fired a shot, but the elder Metcalfe realized that something was amiss and, eluding capture, sailed rapidly for Hawaii.[74] Martinez did not go in pursuit, but set his course for San Blas, which he reached in early December, finding the *Santa Gertrudis* already at anchor there. The *Fair American* joined the *San Carlos* at Monterey.

Thus by the end of 1789 most of the actors in the Nootka drama were far from Friendly Cove. The *Iphigenia*, the *Columbia*, and the *Washington* were in the Far East,[75] as were Captain Funter and the crew of the *North West America*, albeit without their ship. The *Argonaut* and the *Princess Royal* were under Spanish control, along with one United States ship, the *Fair American*. Captain Colnett and his men, who had set out in the spring to found a permanent outpost of British power at Nootka, were prisoners, and so were their Oriental companions who had earlier planned to become the northwest's first Chinese settlers.

Martinez, who had made the long journey up the coast from San Blas to Nootka in the spring, was now back where he had started from, while his fort was dismantled and its garrison removed. He also found that the new viceroy, Revilla Gigedo, who had succeeded Flores, was apparently unaware that his predecessor had ordered the evacuation of Nootka.[76] In the long summer days Nootka had been a crowded place; now, as the winter storms swept over Friendly Cove, only the dark eyes of Maquinna and his people were left to brood over the strange deeds of the white tribes from across the sea.

Yet in fact a second act in the Nootka drama was about to begin. With the arrival of the American ships in the Far East and the Spanish with their prisoners at San Blas late in 1789, news of the events of the previous summer began reaching the outside world. Colnett wrote letters to the Spanish authorities in Mexico, and later to the British ambassador in Madrid, outlining his grievances and claiming, probably with some justice, that his ship had been plundered. Near the end of 1789 he was transferred to a town called Tepic in the interior of Mexico (perhaps so that he should learn as little as possible about Spanish naval strength), where he was at liberty to walk about. Indeed, before many months had passed, he was informing the British ambassador in Madrid that despite his illegal imprisonment,

> since my first arrival in New Spain, myself, officers and crew have been treated with all humanity and kindness and every attention paid them; in the day have liberty to go where they please.[77]

By this time, however, there had been a great change in the scale of events. What had once seemed a minor incident, involving a handful of hot-tempered men at the world's end, had now escalated into an international crisis of the first order. Somewhat surprisingly, considering the alarming developments just across the channel, the British government decided to take a hard line. They demanded from Spain the release of the ships and men, plus recompense for their imprisonment, and refused to concede or even discuss Spanish claims to any part of the northwest coast until this had been achieved.

The Spanish government was at first genuinely incredulous at this attitude, believing that their own claims at Nootka, and their actions there during the previous summer, were scarcely open to question. Before long, however, incredulity had been replaced by anger and then dismay. Notes flew back and forth between London and Madrid, the Spanish appealed to France for support, but only sympathetic noises were forthcoming from a country caught up in its greatest social upheaval in centuries.

At the height of the crisis, in the spring of 1790, two events took place. The *Princess Royal*, renamed the *Princesa Real*, had left San Blas in February, and the Spanish, under Francisco Eliza, reoccupied Nootka. At this time John Meares, orbiting easily across continents and oceans, made a dramatic splashdown in London. Soon his famous "Memorial," detailing and often embellishing his grievances, was presented to the House of Commons. Both its language and its accompanying financial estimates were inflated, but its emotional impact was considerable. Outraged M.P.'s, who might not previously have heard of Nootka, were soon voting large sums for armaments, and it seemed as if war with Spain might be close.[78]

An outcome so greatly disproportionate to its cause would suggest that deeper tides were moving beneath the surface. Prime Minister Pitt may have believed that eventually Britain would find herself at war with revolutionary France, and was using the Nootka crisis as an excuse to increase British armaments and test the national temper. He may also have realized that when Britain lost most of her American colonies she had lost prestige as well, and he may have calculated that forcing Spain to accept a diplomatic defeat would help to restore it. Again, he may have been anxious to establish a firm beachhead of British power on the northwest coast, with a view to expanding it later, and felt that this was a propitious moment to begin the process. British merchants who had become aware of the possibilities of the fur trade could doubtless be counted on for support against would-be Spanish monopolists.

In any case, the trident of power, proudly brandished since the days of Columbus, was starting to slip from the Spanish grasp, and the government in Madrid was aware of it. Spain lacked the resources to challenge the upstart heretics of the north, and with a heavy heart finally decided to accept the only alternative to war.

The new viceroy had already released the *Fair American* on his own initiative early in 1790. Even before the final decision of Madrid was known he had decided that although Martinez had not done wrong in seizing the *Argonaut*, Colnett and his ship should also be allowed to go their way. The cost of supporting so many prisoners was likely a major factor, and was another sign that although the Spanish empire still occupied a vast area on the map – the greater part of two continents – the lifeblood of money was no longer coursing freely through its veins.

On July 9, 1790, Colnett left San Blas in the *Argonaut* for Nootka, where he hoped to recover the *Princess Royal*, which the Spanish had also decided to restore to her owners. When he arrived at Nootka the new commandant, Francisco Eliza, told him that though the *Princess Royal* had been there earlier, exploring the Strait of Juan de Fuca under a Spanish captain, she had now gone back to San Blas. Nothing daunted, Colnett spent five months, between October 1790 and March 1791, trading on the northwest coast, and secured about 1,100 skins. He then left for Hawaii, where he met (but did not take possession of, as some writers have asserted)[79] the *Princess Royal* under Manuel Quimper. Leaving Hawaii, he arrived at Macao on May 30, 1791, where he found the *Eleanora* at anchor. In August he was joined by the *Princess Royal*, which was now in such poor shape that the East India Company refused to receive her, accepting in lieu a small cash payment. Soon afterward, Colnett became the first Briton since 1673 to attempt to open trade with Japan, but without success. He then sold some of his furs in northern China and the rest in England, the latter fetching £9,760.[80]

About this time an agreement was reached between Spain and Britain that removed the danger of a European war. On October 28, 1790, the two powers signed the "Nootka Convention," which defined the rights of their governments and citizens at Nootka and elsewhere on the eastern shore of the Pacific.[81] Among its most important features were that British subjects were to have restored to them the buildings and land at Nootka of which they had been dispossessed, and that they were to receive reparations for acts of violence committed against them. Citizens of either country might henceforth sail or fish in the Pacific Ocean, or land at places as yet unoccupied in order to trade with the natives, and Nootka would be open to traders of either nation. All this was a considerable recession from the claim that the Pacific was a Spanish lake.[82]

One of the main beneficiaries of the treaty was John Meares, who in his "Memorial" had detailed his psychic and financial wounds and asked $653,433 to salve them. Eventually he received $210,000, which was about what he deserved, and even, perhaps, about what he hoped for. He then receded from the focus of world attention into the shadows of obscurity, which seems, in some ways, a pity. Undaunted by dangers, unfettered by principles, remaining upon the larger stage of history he might well have garnered every honor but honor.

Peace returned to Nootka, and before long so did the fur-traders of several nations. Nootka was once more under Spanish control, but as the actual ownership of various other parts of the northwest coast was still undecided, it was apparent that further political adjustments might lie ahead. For the moment, however, no one felt disposed to interfere with a situation which was reasonably agreeable to all, and which, to the powers of Europe, was far overshadowed by the deepening crisis in France.

CHAPTER NINE

Retrospect

It

was now
fifty years since

the *St. Peter* and *St. Paul* had sailed eastward from Kamchatka
and reached the coast of North America. Since then, many others had come to these waters: the Spanish from their dominions
to the south; Cook from across the wide wastes of the Pacific; independent adventurers from the Far East; and ships from New
England via the Horn. Little by little, they had transformed
what was once but a blank space on the map into part of the general consciousness of mankind, and by 1790 a fairly accurate picture was available of the northwest coast and its resources.

In some respects, the mists of ignorance had not yet been
dissipated. It was still not realized – though a few had guessed at
it – that Nootka was on an island, and that at many places the
actual mainland of North America had not yet been reached or
explored. For example, while the western entrance of the as yet
unnamed Gulf of Georgia, the Strait of Juan de Fuca, had been
located by Charles Barkley and penetrated for part of its length
by subordinates of John Meares, the waters from Puget Sound to
Johnstone Strait were still uncharted. The summer of 1790 would
see the first moves in this direction by the Spanish, and a few
more years would bring Capt. George Vancouver to complete the
task with an accuracy which time has scarcely diminished.

The parcelling out of the coast among the great powers was also under way, although the final outcome of this process was still obscure. France seemed unlikely to participate in the ultimate division. Her ships had touched these shores, and even at one point gone through the formula of "taking possession," but not many now believed that ceremonies were an acceptable substitute for occupation. Few Frenchmen at this time saw themselves as potential colonists, especially now that their homeland was undergoing a social convulsion.

Russia, by contrast, was firmly established in Alaska, and was steadily extending her influence southward. Already she had a network of trading posts, well garrisoned and regularly supplied, in the northwest corner of the continent. Spain, advancing from the opposite direction, had what were intended as permanent outposts in California, and, despite the events of 1789, still occupied Nootka, more than a thousand miles to the north. As a result of the "Nootka crisis" and the "Convention" which brought it to a peaceful conclusion, she had receded somewhat from her claims of exclusive trading rights along the whole Pacific coast as far as Prince William Sound, but she still maintained that due to prior discovery, most of this coast was as much her possession as that of Chile or Mexico.

Yet there had already been signs that this claim was unlikely to survive a determined challenge. Although many of the limbs of the Spanish empire were still vigorous, the pulse at its core, after a late burst of energy, was beginning to falter. The advancing tide of her power, now at the flood, had reached the northwest coast but had not submerged it. There was an autumnal hint in the air that it might be here, under the dark eyes of the savage whale-hunters of Nootka, that this once majestic "pomp of waters" would begin its long, melancholy and unreversed "retreating, to the breath/Of the night-wind, down the vast edges drear/And naked shingles of the world."[1]

If this should prove true, then the trident of power might soon be grasped by other hands. Already the two branches of the Anglo-Saxon race were active on this coast. Britain had successfully challenged the most extreme claims of Spain, and its ships had made several profitable trading voyages to these waters. The United States, though thousands of miles still separated its western borders from the Pacific coast, had done the same. Its seamen were daring, its merchants watchful for opportunities, and a few of its citizens already envisioned the day when the new-born republic would stretch from one ocean to the other. Perhaps the final struggle for the northwest coast might be not between Spain and Russia, but between these two children of a common mother. No one, however, could as yet peer so far into the mists of time.

The political future of the coast might not yet be clear, but its economic possibilities were apparent. It was rich in a resource valued wherever wealth pursued distinction or vanity sought adornment, and as yet the supply seemed undiminished. Fur was perhaps not all that these deep fiords might yield; already its huge trees had been used for shipbuilding, and spars made from them had been carried to the Orient. There was a chance, too, that rare minerals lay hidden at their roots, and attempts had already been made to find them.

The area was also fast becoming part of the larger network of international trade. Cheap novelties from old or new England had already become treasures to the subjects of Maquinna and Wickananish; mandarins in Peking gave themselves added dignity with the aid of the sea-otters of Nootka; while the tea of China and the sandalwood of Hawaii were carried on long journeys on ships which had earlier anchored in Friendly Cove. Efforts had even been made, but so far without success, to draw Japan into this new order of things.

Under the stress of these new developments, the era of commercial monopoly was drawing to a close. The East India Company and the South Sea Company could no longer dictate to Americans, and they could hardly hope to maintain even their hold over Britons for much longer. The nineteenth century, high noon of private enterprise, had not yet dawned, but already the eastern skies were fretted by lines foretelling a new economic day.

The empire of knowledge had also been expanded. Men skilled in the burgeoning sciences were beginning to reduce a vast array of new facts to order and regularity, and the flora and fauna of Nootka would soon be familiar to the cultivated classes of Europe. Anthropology, too, was laying its foundations, and detailed studies of the Indian way of life had already been compiled and read with attention. These would sometimes be more accurate, indeed, than those produced in our own day. Too often the latter, under the stress of a grotesque new mythology in which the noble red man and the wicked white man would form the most prominent figures, have contrived to convert savagery and sluttishness into simplicity, and dissolve constant tribal warfare into a pastoral idyll. This was not a mode of intellectual operations with any appeal to the earliest observers at Nootka.

Yet it is beyond doubt that contact with western culture would soon have a drastic effect on age-old native ways. New goods and new customs had appeared in bewildering profusion, and in the resulting conflict of values the old order was beginning to dissolve into a chaos which even two centuries would not suffice to reassemble.[2]

In some ways, though, this was not new. The river of time makes ever for new channels, breaking its banks when it chooses, taking orders from no man. The source of the great tide of change which now beat against Nootka's shores lay hidden deep in the years – perhaps as far back as the days which saw the first Portuguese ships creep cautiously down the coast of Africa. Then, Prince Henry the Navigator had watched the waves endlessly breaking, breaking endlessly against the rock-shod foot of Europe, and had resolved to learn what lay beyond the sunset. Now, Maquinna and Wickananish, standing at the world's end amid the sunset isles, saw the same waves lapping at their feet, and wondered what they might portend.

Notes

[CHAPTER ONE]

The Space Race Begins

1. An excellent illustrated account of the history of exploration is Leonard Outhwaite's *Unrolling the Map*, rev. ed. (New York: Reynal and Hitchcock, 1938). It includes early voyages down the African coast by Phoenicians and Carthaginians (for which the evidence though not conclusive, is by no means to be ignored) and Alexander the Great's expedition to India.

2. For some account of these travellers, see W.C. Abbott, *The Expansion of Europe*, 2 vols. (London, 1919), and J.H. Parry, *The Age of Reconnaissance* (London: Wiedenfeld and Nicholson, 1963). Also *Outhwaite*, op. cit.

3. See Tryggvi J. Oleson, *Early Voyages and Northern Approaches* (Toronto: McClelland and Stewart, 1963), and Geoffrey Ashe and others, *The Quest for America* (New York and London: Praeger Publishers, 1971).

4. See H.R. Wagner, "The creation of rights of sovereignty through symbolic acts," *Pacific Historical Review*, Dec. 1938.

5. See R.P. Bishop, "Drake's course in the North Pacific," *B.C. Historical Quarterly*, July 1939. Also H.H. Bancroft, *History of the Northwest Coast 1543-1800* (San Francisco, 1890), I, 139-45. Bancroft thinks Drake got to about 43°.

6. *Encyclopaedia Britannica*, eleventh edition, 1911.

7. In 1673 the British ship *Return* arrived at Nagasaki in the hope of opening trade, but without success.

8. The first Roosevelt, Claes Martenszen van Rosenvelt, arved from Holland in the 1640s. New Amsterdam then had a population of 800. See Joseph Lash, *Eleanor and Franklin* (New York: Norton and Co., 1971), Preface.

9. Adam Smith, in his celebrated *The Wealth of Nations* (1776) declared, "The discovery of America and that of a passage to the East Indies by the Cape of Good Hope are the two greatest and most important events recorded in the history of mankind." This statement had an added interest in that it reveals the unconscious replacement since the Middle Ages in the minds of many thinkers of Religious Man by Economic Man.

[CHAPTER TWO]
Eastward From Asia

1. For an account of this great expansion of Russian power, see H.H. Bancroft, *History of Alaska* (San Francisco, 1886), chapter two.

2. See Ian Grey, *The Romanovs: the Rise and Fall of a Dynasty* (New York: Doubleday, 1970), pp.78-128.

3. F.A. Golder in his authoritative *Russian Expansion on the Pacific 1641-1850* (Cleveland, 1914; reprint, Gloucester, Mass.: P. Smith, 1960), pp. 67-95 considers Deshnev's account, though authentic, too ambiguous to be considered proof that he sailed through Bering Strait.

4. Golder, op. cit., p. 130.

5. F.A. Golder, *Bering's Voyages* (New York: American Geographical Society, 1922), I, 21-4. Also Hulley, *Alaska Past and Present* (Portland, 1970), p. 55.

6. Steller's journal; quoted in Golder, *Bering's Voyages* (New York: American Geographical Society, 1925), II, 34.

7. The name Shumagin is now given to an entire group of islands in the Aleutian chain, and this particular island is now called Nagai.

8. Sven Waxell, trans. M.A. Michael, *The American Expedition* (London: William Hodge and Company, 1952), pp. 122-23.
9. Golder, *Bering's Voyages*, I, 209. The entries are not by Bering, who was now too ill to perform even this task.
10. Bancroft, *History of Alaska*, pp. 89-90.
11. The place of the landings was probably in Lisianski Strait. The fate of the lost men has never been determined, but Spanish explorers later found some blond Alaskans in the area, who may have been descendants of the men left behind by the *St. Paul*. See J.R. Masterson and Helen Brower, *Bering's Successors 1745-1780* (Seattle: University of Washington Press, 1948), p. 49. The material in this book first appeared in the *Pacific Northwest Quarterly* for January and April 1947.
12. There is an excellent map of the voyages of the two ships at the end of Vol. I of Golder's *Bering's Voyages*.
13. Bancroft, *History of Alaska*, p. 100. For this whole period, see S.R. Tompkins, "After Bering: mapping the North Pacific," *B.C. Historical Quarterly*, January 1955.
14. Bancroft, op. cit., pp. 111-12.
15. In 1775, over 46,000 beaver skins and 7,000 otter skins, originally trapped in central and eastern Canada, found their way to Kiakhta by this route. See Bancroft, op. cit., p. 242. Many furs from Nootka were sold at the same place toward the end of the century. For a description of Kiakhta, see Hector Chevigny, *The Great Alaskan Venture 1741-1867* (New York: Viking Press, 1965), p. 44.
16. This was paralleled on our own continent by the steady movement of fur traders ever farther west toward untapped sources of supply, and the elimination of small traders by the North West Company and the Hudson's Bay Company, which in turn eventually merged into a virtual monopoly.
17. William Coxe, *Account of the Russian Discoveries between Asia and America*, 3rd ed. (1787; facsimile reprint, New York: Argonaut Press, 1966), p. 220.

    The Rev. William Coxe visited Russia in 1778 as a tutor to a young English nobleman. While there he collected numerous MSS of the Russian discoveries in the North Pacific to that time, publishing them in London in 1780.

This was the earliest authentic account in English of the major Russian discoveries of this period, and it soon went into several editions.

18. Coxe, op. cit., pp. 214-15. For an account of the similar effect on the Songhees Indians of the gold rush of 1858 in B.C., see my *Victoria: the Fort* (Mitchell Press, 1968), p. 155.

19. Bancroft, *History of Alaska*, p. 230.

20. Readers are reminded that the Russians still used the Julian calender, which at this time differed by eleven days from the Gregorian calender used by most other white nations. The Russians did not adopt the latter until after the Revolution.

⟦CHAPTER THREE⟧
Northward from California

1. For some accounts of these voyages, see H.R. Wagner, *Spanish Voyages to the Northwest Coast of America in the Sixteenth Century* (San Francisco: California Historical Society, 1929); J.B. Brebner, *The Explorers of North America 1492-1806* (London, 1933); W.M. Mathes, *Vizcaino and Spanish Exploration in the Pacific Ocean 1580-1630* (San Francisco: California Historical Society, 1968); C.E. Chapman, *The Founding of Spanish California* (New York: Macmillan Co., 1916); and *A History of California: the Spanish Period* (New York: Macmillan Co., 1925).

2. See Iris H. Wilson, "Spanish scientists in the Pacific Northwest 1790-1792" in *Reflections of Western Historians*, ed. J.A. Carroll (U. of Arizona Press, 1969); also her "Scientists in New Spain: the 18th century expeditions," *Journal of the West*, July 1962.

3. The most detailed account of San Blas in this period is Michael Thurman's *The Naval Department of San Blas* (Glendale, Calif.: A.H. Clark Company, 1967).

4. See "The instructions of Viceroy Bucareli to Ensign Juan Perez," trans. Manuel P. Servin, *California Historical Society*

Quarterly, Sept. 1961, pp. 237-48. All quotations in this series are from this source.

5. A reproduction of the 1773 map may be found in Chapman, *The Founding of Spanish California*, facing page 224.

6. It was also occasionally known as the *Nueva Galicia*. This ship was 82 feet long, 225 tons, and well armed.

7. See Herbert E. Bolton, *Fray Juan Crespi, Missionary Explorer on the Pacific Coast 1769-1774* (Berkeley: U. of California Press, 1927).

8. An article by C.I. Archer in *B.C. Studies* for summer 1973 states that "Perez landed at the Queen Charlotte Islands on July 18, 1774," but the journals do not support this statement.

9. Father Pena's account; from Donald C. Cutter, *The California Coast* (Norman: U. of Oklahoma Press, 1969), pp. 159-61. This is a bilingual version, and includes Father Crespi's account, as well as other interesting documents dealing with the period of Spanish control of Mexico. For probable identification of locations in this area, see H.H. Bancroft *History of the Northwest Coast* (San Francisco, 1884) I, 153-54.

10. Cutter, op. cit., p. 237.

11. Ibid.

12. It had been shown that Perez generally made slight errors in his calculations of latitude. See Thurman, *Naval Department of San Blas*, p. 135, and H.R. Wagner, *Cartography of the Northwest Coast of America to the Year 1800* (Berkeley: U. of California Press, 1937), I, 173. Perez believed that he had reached 55°, but later and more accurate calculations have revised this figure.

13. H.R. Wagner in an article in the *California Historical Society Quarterly* for Sept. 1930 (p. 204) wrote, "The *Santiago* certainly did not enter Nootka Sound but I am convinced anchored off the entrance." In his *Spanish Explorations in the Strait of Juan de Fuca*, Wagner states flatly that "there is no evidence that he ever entered Nootka Sound or what was afterward known as the port of Nootka." Scholefield and Howay in their *British Columbia from the Earliest Times to the Present* (Vancouver, 1914) say, "Nothing in the journals mentioned can possibly be construed as evidence that

Nootka Sound was ever seen, much less entered." Wagner in his *Cartography* (I, 173) wrote, "the latitude assigned (i.e. 49°30′) is almost correct for the sound, but in view of the errors in the observations farther north a strong presumption exists that in reality the *Santiago* was much farther south." An American, Robert Haswell, at Nootka in 1789, wrote in his log for March 16 that "Nootka Sound was discovered by Captain Cook March the 30 1778, on his passag to the northen hemisphere of this ocean, but from the natives we lern their was a ship anchored at the enterance of the sound forty months before Captain Cook's arrival. From the description they must have been Spaniards but the natives say their boats weir not out duering their tarey" (F.W. Howay, ed., *Voyages of the Columbia to the Northwest Coast 1787-1790 and 1790-1793*, Massachusetts, 1941, pp. 58-9.) Warren Cook in *Flood Tide of Empire* (Yale U. Press, 1973, p. 63) says, "Although Perez is assumed to have been just outside, the first European to enter the cove would be Captain James Cook in 1778."

14. It is believed that this is the oldest place name in B.C., apart from some, such as Musqueam, which still retain their original Indian names. There is some dispute as to whether it was named after St. Stephen or Esteban Martinez, navigating officer of the *Santiago*. Father Crespi tells us that it was named "out of regard for the second navigating officer" (Cutter, *The California Coast*, p. 257); Cook, *Flood Tide of Empire*, p. 67, says the name was given by Perez, "thus honoring the second officer's personal saint."

15. The ship cut its cable in order to escape quickly, and thus lost its anchor. If this should ever be recovered, it would establish the exact location of the *Santiago* at that time.

16. Cutter, *The California Coast*, p. 179.

17. See Robert F. Heizer, "The introduction of Monterey shells to the Indians of the northwest coast," *Pacific Northwest Quarterly*, Oct. 1940, pp. 399-402.

18. Maurelle's account of the voyage may be found in *Miscellanies by the Honourable Daines Barrington*, London, 1781. An English translation of Father Campa Cos' account (edited by John Galvin and containing an excellent map) may

be found in *Journal of explorations northward along the coast from Monterey in the year 1775*, San Francisco: John Howell Books, 1964; a translation of Father Sierra's account appears in the *California Historical Quarterly* for Sept. 1930. An unpublished translation of Quadra's account of his voyages, "Expeditions in the years 1775 and 1779 toward the west coast of North America," is in the Provincial Archives, Victoria, B.C.

19. Account of Father Campa Cos.
20. Quadra's account.
21. Father Sierra's account. When Vancouver's expedition was in these waters, the surgeon and botanist, Archibald Menzies, found the cross still there on May 2, 1793.
22. Account of Father Campa Cos.
23. Father Sierra's account.
24. It is impossible to determine from the various accounts whether a cross was erected at this time, or exactly what ceremonies were performed.
25. Father Sierra's account.
26. Quadra's account.
27. See Chapman, *The Foundation of Spanish California*, p. 243.
28. Father Sierra's account.
29. Father Sierra's account.
30. This quotation and those following are from the unpublished translation of Quadra's account.

〖CHAPTER FOUR〗
Britain at Nootka

1. The ship was actually christened the *Endeavour Bark*, to distinguish her from a warship already called *Endeavour*, but is generally known as the *Endeavour*.
2. The passage between them is now called Cook's Strait.
3. See J.C. Beaglehole, *The Voyage of the Endeavour 1768-1771*, (Cambridge, 1955), pp. 204 and 243.
4. Ibid., pp. 312 and 385.

5. When the *Endeavour* was grounded on the Great Barrier Reef, Cook ordered that 50 tons of material, including the ship's cannon, should be heaved overboard to lighten the ship. The cannon were located and recovered in 1969. See *National Geographic* for September 1971.

6. Australia was first circumnavigated by Capt. Matthew Flinders, R.N., in 1803, and soon afterward this name replaced the old one of New Holland. The first convict settlement in Australia was made in 1788 and the first settlement of free men in 1793.

7. In 1714 Parliament had offered £20,000 for the invention of a truly accurate chronometer. John Harrison made four between 1727 and 1760 (the last still preserved at Greenwich) and received the reward.

8. The cottage built by Cook's parents at Great Ayton, Yorkshire, in 1775 was removed in 1934 to Melbourne, Australia, where it is a noted historical exhibit.

9. Furneaux arrived in England in July 1774, thus becoming the first man to circumnavigate the globe in an easterly direction.

10. A comprehensive list of all the attempts to find the northwest passage by sea may be found in Ernest Dodge, *Northwest by Sea* (New York, 1961).

11. Cook's instructions are printed in J.C. Beaglehole, *The Voyage of the Resolution and Discovery 1776-1780* (Cambridge, 1967), p. ccxxi.

12. See Chapman, *The Founding of Spanish California*, pp. 376-79.

13. H.R. Wagner in his *Cartography*, I, 183, says, "Just why he was directed to reach the coast at 45° is not clear, but probably this was supposed to indicate the northern limit of 'New Albion,' to which the British kept up a kind of shadowy claim." The claim was based on the voyage of Drake, and Cook in his account refers to the coast which he reached in March 1778 as "New Albion."

14. There is a Bligh Island in both Nootka Sound and Prince William Sound. The former was named by Captain Richards of H.M.S. *Hecate* in 1862 and the latter by Capt. George Vancouver in 1794.

15. Cook says that "some account of the Spaniards having vis-

ited this coast was published before I left England" (Beagle-hole, op. cit., I, 321). The reference is probably to an article in the *London Annual Register* for June 28, 1776. See Green-how, *History of Oregon and California* (Boston, 1844) p. 124, and Wagner, *Cartography*, p. 184.

16. The Union Jack still forms part of the Hawaiian, if not the Canadian, flag. It is possible that white men saw these is-lands before Cook, perhaps as early as 1542. See J.J. Jarves, *History of the Hawaiian Islands* (Honolulu, 1872), pp. 48-9.

17. Wagner (*Cartography*, p. 185) says that it is named after a pope of that name, but Beaglehole (op. cit., I, 290) says, "This cape must have been named after St. Gregory of Nyssa, a father of the Greek church, whose feast, according to the English calendar, is on 12 March."

18. Beaglehole, op. cit., II, 263.

19. James Cook and James King, *A Voyage to the Pacific Ocean* 3 vols. (London, 1784), II, 263.

20. Ibid., p. 264.

21. Cape Cook was named by Capt. George Richards of H.M.S. *Plumper* in 1860.

22. Bancroft (*History of the Northwest Coast*, pp. 155 and 170) does not agree. Neither does Captain Walbran, who points out that the chaplains accompanying Perez describe the land around their anchorage as low and rising gently, whereas in fact at Nootka the mountains are very close to the water. He concludes that "the Spaniards did not know anything of what is now known as Nootka Sound until Cook's discovery of it in 1778 was given to the world." (Walbran, *British Co-lumbia Coast Names*, pp. 174 and 361.)

23. For a discussion of the origin and meaning of the name "Nootka," see J.M. Moziño, *Noticias de Nutka* (Toronto: McClelland and Stewart, 1970), p. 67n. It would appear that the native name for the area was Yuquat. There does not seem to be any reference to Friendly Cove in Cook's ac-count, though many writers assert that he is responsible for naming it.

24. When Captain Vancouver entered Burrard Inlet in 1792, he was preceded by natives strewing feathers on the water: "as your great explorer Vancouver progressed through the First

Narrows, our people threw in greeting before him clouds of snow white feathers which rose, wafted in the air aimlessly about, then fell like flurries of snow to the water's surface and rested there like white rose petals scattered before a bride." J.S. Matthews, *Conversations with Khahtsahlano* (Vancouver, 1955), p. 184.

25. Cook and King, *A Voyage to the Pacific Ocean*, II, 270-71.

    John Rickman, in his *Journal of Captain Cook's Last Voyage to the Pacific Ocean* (London, 1781), p. 242, says, "that they eat the flesh of their enemies we had some reason to suppose, by observing a human head in one of their canoes, and arms and limbs in another."

    Ledyard goes even further: "Like all uncivilized men they are hospitable, and the first boat that visited us in the cove brought us what no doubt they thought the greatest possible regalia, and offered it to us to eat; this was a human arm roasted. I have heard it remarked that human flesh is the most delicious and therefore tasted a bit, and so did many others without swallowing the meat or the juices, but either my conscience or my taste rendered it very odious to me." *Journal of Captain Cook's last voyage* (1783; facsimile reprint, Chicago: Quadrangle Books, 1963), p. 73.

26. The natives seem on occasion to have overcome the aversion to beads reported by Captain Cook; Lt. King later reported that "six of the finest skins purchased by us were got for a dozen large green glass beads."

27. Cook and King, *Voyage*, II, 282. These two spoons were later to figure in international diplomacy, being adduced by the Spanish during the "Nootka crisis" as evidence that their first visit to this area was prior to that of Cook, and that Nootka was thus rightly a Spanish possession. The relevant passage in King's journal (Beaglehole, op. cit., II, 1401) is: "In one of these we were surprized at seeing a couple of silver table spoons hanging down a man's neck. They were evidently not English make; the man pointed to us that they came from the southward, as did his boat, but we could learn nothing farther. . . ."

    Clerke's journal (Beaglehole, op. cit. II, 1329) tells us that "On Monday the 20th of April a party of strangers came into the cove, and having got leave of our landlords to open their market, they sold among other matters two silver table spoons. I think they are of Spanish manufacture, for if I am not much mistaken I saw once on board a Spanish vessel at Rio Janeiro [sic] some spoons made much in the same form with these."

James Burney in his *A Chronological History of North-eastern Voyages of Discovery* (London, 1819), p. 214, says, "On the 20th, two old-fashioned silver tablespoons, which we supposed to have been Spanish, were purchased of the Americans alongside the *Resolution* for a pewter wash-hand bason [sic]. These things, as well as iron and brass which we saw among them, it must be concluded they procured by their intercourse with other tribes, for it is satisfactorily ascertained and corroborated by their being perfectly unacquainted with firearms, that the people of Nootka had not, previous to our visit, had direct communication with Europeans."

28. Cook and King, *Voyage*, II, 291.

29. Ibid., pp. 301-03.

By contrast with Cook, John Ledyard described the natives as "rather above the middle stature, copper-coloured and of an athletic make." (*Journal of Captain Cook's Last Voyage*, p. 71).

30. Cook and King, *Voyage*, II, 310.

31. Ibid., pp. 314-316.

32. Ibid., p. 318.

There seems some dispute as to what domestic animals the Indians had. Cook (*Voyage*, II, 294) tells us that "hogs, dogs and goats have not as yet found their way to this place"; however, John Ledyard (*Journal*, p. 70) recorded that the Indians did have dogs.

33. Cook and King, *Voyage*, II, 318-19.

34. Rickman (*Journal*, p. 245) tells us that "their canoes were of an uncommon length, many of them from 30 to 40 yards long, made of the main body of one of their enormous trees," but this is probably an exaggeration.

35. For an account of Indian beliefs about the universe and explanations of these images, see Charles Hill-Tout, *British*

North America: The Far West, the Home of the Salish and Dene (London, 1907), Ch. IX.

36. Samwell's journal is printed in full in Beaglehole, op. cit. This excerpt may be found in Vol. 2, p. 1095. It scarcely bears out the statement in the official account (Cook and King, *Voyage*, II, 319) that "the women were always properly clothed and behaved with the utmost propriety." Yet John Meares, at Nootka in 1788, said of the local females that "in their character they are reserved and chaste, and examples of loose and immodest conduct were very rare among them." (*Voyages made in the years 1788 and 1789 from China to the North West Coast of America*, London, 1790, p. 251.)

37. Cook and King, *Voyage*, II, 296.

38. Ibid., pp. 286-7.

39. Ibid., p, 286. The chief referred to may have been the celebrated Maquinna, but Cook in his account does not mention any Indian by name.

40. See, for example, Ledyard, *Journal*, p. 70.

41. Rickman, *Journal*, p. 246. Some of the early writers seem to have used the words "beaver" and "otter" interchangeably. Judge Howay, in his article "The earliest pages of the history of British Columbia," *B.C. Historical Association, First Annual Report* (Victoria, 1924), p. 20, in quoting at some length (though not identifying) Dixon's *Voyage Round the World* (London, 1789), p. 201, twice changes the word "beaver" to "sea-otter," as well as making other alterations from the original – not generally considered the correct thing to do without notice to the reader.

42. Wagner, *Cartography*, p. 185, evidently does not agree that Cook's actions at Kaye Island constituted taking possession, for he says that "he did not take possession at Nootka Sound nor in fact at any place before he reached the end of Cook's Inlet." It is difficult to agree with this view, as Cook's accounts of his actions at Kaye Island and Point Possession are almost identical. (See Beaglehole, op. cit., pp. 341 and 368.)

43. See Beaglehole, op. cit., I, 399.

44. Cook and King, *Voyage*, II, 509.

45. Of Cook's six children, two boys and a girl died in infancy, two sons died at sea, and one son died while at Cambridge.

His direct line is therefore extinct. His last surviving ship-mate may have died as recently as May 1966; this was a tortoise he is said to have presented to a Tonga chief in 1777. See Beaglehole, op. cit., I, civ.

46. Cook and King, *Voyage*, III, 369.
47. Ibid., p. 370.
48. Ibid., 431.
49. Ibid., 437. Ledyard, *Journal*, p. 70, tells us that while the expedition was on the northwest coast, its members purchased "about 1500 beaver, beside other skins, but took none but the best, having no thoughts at that time of using them to any other advantage than converting them to the purposes of cloathing, but it afterwards happened that skins which did not cost the purchaser sixpence sterling sold in China for 100 dollars. Neither did we purchase a quarter part of the beaver and other furr skins we might have done, and most certainly should have done had we known of meeting the opportunity of disposing of them to such an astonishing profit."

    Greenhow, *History of Oregon and California*, p. 158, says that only one previous ship – a Russian one in 1770 – had brought furs direct to Canton from where they were secured.
50. "Cook saw no part of the west coast of North America, south of Mount San Jacinto or Edgecumb, which had not been previously seen by Perez, Bodega (Quadra) or Heceta; and after passing that point he was, as he frequently admits, aided and in a measure guided by the accounts of the Russian voyages. The observations of the English were, however, infinitely more minute and more important in their results than those of any or all of the other navigators who had preceded them in the exploration of the North Pacific." (Greenhow, op. cit., p. 158.)

⟦CHAPTER FIVE⟧
The First of the Fur-Traders

1. The official logs of the voyage were edited and combined into a single narrative by Dr. John Douglas, Canon of Windsor and later Bishop of Salisbury. Details of this process are given in J.C. Beaglehole, *The Voyage of the Resolution and Discovery*, Preface.

2. "By virtue of the South Sea monopoly no British subject could trade west of Cape Horn except by its permission, and by virtue of the East India Company's monopoly no British subject could trade east of Cape of Good Hope without its permission. Thus their combined effect was to close the whole Pacific Ocean to the British trader except he paid for the privilege." F.W. Howay, "The earliest pages of the history of British Columbia," p. 19.

3. See Nathaniel Portlock, *Voyage Round the World* (London, 1789), p. 3, and George Dixon, *Voyage Round the World* (London, 1789), p. xx.

4. See Greenhow, *History of Oregon and California*, p. 162. Also Bancroft, *History of the Northwest Coast*, p. 351.

5. Portlock, op. cit., p. 3, says that Hanna had only 20 men. Bancroft, op. cit. p. 173, perhaps following him, says the same. John Meares in his "Observations on the probable existence of a North West Passage" (*Voyages*, London, 1790, xli-xlvi) says Hanna's crew "scarcely amounted to thirty persons."

6. Cook and King, *Voyage*, II, 358.

7. Margaret Ormsby, *British Columbia: A History* (Macmillan Co., 1958), p. 13.

8. This and the two following quotations are from Hanna's "Journal of a voyage from Macao toward King George's Sound in the Sea Otter, Captain Hanna commander." This MS. (now in the Provincial Archives, Victoria) was discovered by his son among the papers of Capt. Charles Barkley after his death. See F.W. Howay, "Letters concerning voyages of British vessels to the northwest coast of America 1787-1809," *Oregon Historical Quarterly*, Sept. 1938.

9. From an unsigned article entitled "New Fur Trade" in the London *World* for Oct. 6 and 13, 1788. Reprinted as a chapbook by the White Knight Press of San Francisco, 1941. It is not clear why H.W. Bradley in "The Hawaiian Islands and the Pacific Fur Trade 1785-1813," *Pacific Northwest Quarterly*, July 1939, p. 275, should say, "there is no evidence that Captain James Hanna, reputed to have been the first to exploit the Trans-Pacific fur trade, ever saw the Hawaiian Islands."

   The Spanish captain Esteban Martinez, at Nootka in 1789, had an alarming story about Hanna: "Captain Hana [*sic*] went to the villages located at the northeast branch of the entrance where he killed more than fifty Indians, and not satisfied with this, one day when Macuina (the principal chief of the village of this port where we are now) went aboard to visit him, having seated himself by the binnacle, the hands of the afore-mentioned Captain spread some gunpowder under his seat, telling Macuina that that was a ceremony made to honour the chiefs. Macuina assumed that the gunpowder was dark sand, but afterwards he felt its effect because one of the Englishmen set off the fuse and poor Macuina was thrown into the air with his bottom burned and he still has the scars." *Coleccion de Diarios y Relaciones para la historia de las viajes y descumbrimientes*, (Madrid, 1964), VI, 125. The translation was kindly made for me by Professor R.M. Flores of the University of Victoria.

10. For further details of Hanna's two voyages, see *Letter and memorandum from Capt. George Dixon to Sir Joseph Banks regarding the fur trade on the northwest coast A.D. 1789*. Reprinted by the White Knight Press, San Francisco, 1941; Strange's Memorandum on the fur trade from N.W. America, India Office Records, Home Series Miscellaneous, Vol. 494, p. 431, transcript in Provincial Archives, Victoria; John Meares, *Voyages Made in the Years 1788 and 1789*, pp. li, lii; George Dixon, *A Voyage Round the World*, 2nd ed., pp. 315-17; his *Remarks on the Voyages of John Meares, Esq.*, (London, 1790), p. 12; H.H. Bancroft, *History of the Northwest Coast*, I, 174. Bancroft says Hanna's pelts fetched $20,600, but this seems to be an error.

It is not known whether Hanna obtained a licence from the East India Company to trade in Pacific waters; if he did not, it is likely that he sailed under Portuguese colors.

11. Dixon, *A Voyage Round the World*, p. 316. The ships, as we shall see, were the *Captain Cook* and the *Experiment*. Dixon, op. cit., p. 232, tells us that Hanna offered to take off John Mackay, surgeon to these two ships, who had volunteered to spend a year at Nootka, and that "he refused, alleging that he began to relish dried fish and whale oil, was satisfied with his way of life, and perfectly contented to stay till next year."

12. A photograph of Hanna's chart may be found in Scholefield and Howay, *British Columbia from Earliest Times*, I, 122.

13. As these islands were later for a time called Lanz Islands (see Walbran, *British Columbia Coast Names*, p. 447), I think it possible that the name derives from a Mr. Lanz, the owner of the *Lark*, lost in the northern Pacific in 1786. Support for this view is given by the fact that Hanna gave part of the group the name of another far eastern merchant interested in the fur trade.

14. At this time Ahousat was on Vargas Island, but is now on Flores Island. See Howay, *Voyages of the Columbia to the Northwest Coast*, p. 67. The name signifies that the port has an unobstructed view of the ocean.

15. See the various references in Howay, op. cit. Also Meares, *Voyages*, 1790, p. 136.

16. Dixon, *Voyage Round the World*, p. 317.

17. Meares, *Voyages*, p. lii. Hanna Rocks in Queen Charlotte Sound were probably named by Capt. Daniel Pender of the *Beaver* about 1865 (see Walbran, op. cit., p. 228).

18. When the Spanish authorities in the Philippines heard of Hanna's voyages, they considered the development of trade between California (then rich in sea-otters) and China, a source of quicksilver; but very little was done about the matter. There was, however, for many years some trade between California, where the natives collected furs for the friars, and the Philippines. See Chapman, *The Founding of Spanish California*, p. 419, and Bancroft, *History of California*, pp. 438-41; also Adele Ogden, *The California Sea Otter Trade 1784-1848* (Berkeley, 1941).

19. For more details of Strange's life see John Hosie, "James Charles Stuart Strange and his expedition to the northwest coast of America in 1786," *Fourth report of the B.C. Historical Association*, 1929, p. 44; Louisa Mure (Strange's niece), *Recollections of By-gone Days* (privately printed, 1883), and A. Ayyar, *An Adventurous Madras Civilian, James Strange* (Calcutta: Gov't. of India Press, 1929). An account of Dundas' career is given in his obituary in the London *Times* of Feb. 20, 1904.

20. James Strange, *Journal & Narrative of the Commercial Expedition from Bombay to the North West Coast of America* (Madras: Government Record Office, 1928), p. 1.

21. See letter from James Strange, Minutes of Council, Bombay Castle, Sept. 23, 1785. Transcript in Provincial Archives, Victoria.

22. These instructions may most conveniently be found in the *B.C. Historical Quarterly* for Oct. 1941, but are also printed in India Office Records, Home Series Miscellaneous, Vol. 494, pp. 422-27 (transcript in Provincial Archives, Victoria).

23. Sea horse teeth apparently referred to walrus tusks.

24. James Strange, *Journal & Narrative*. The next several quotations are also from this source.

    Arrack is a liquor distilled in the East Indies from rice and coconut juice. A lazaretto (from Lazarus in the New Testament) is a sick-bay.

25. See India Office Records, Home Series Miscellaneous, Vol. 494, p. 423. Bancroft, *History of the Northwest Coast*, p. 177, speaks of the ships as "sailing under the flag of the East India Company," but this seems to be an error.

26. It is not clear just how this cove received its name. Meares, *Voyages*, p. liv, says that Strange named it, but Strange himself in his *Journal & Narrative*, p. 59, tells how he explored several of the bays of Nootka Sound, "and among the number was that bay mentioned by Captain Cook under the name of Friendly Harbour." The author has not found any reference to either Friendly Harbour or Friendly Cove in Cook's account.

27. Strange, *Journal & Narrative*, p. 27. Apparent confirmation of cannibalism may be found in *Letter from W. Hunter regarding voyage of the vessels "Captain Cook" and "Experiment" to the north-*

west coast in the fur trade, A.D. 1786. Reprinted as a chapbook by the White Knight Press, San Francisco, 1940. Hunter says, "They are excellent curers, for some of our gentlemen carried some heads with them, which keep perfectly dried."

28. Strange, *Journal & Narrative*, pp. 26-7.

29. Bancroft, *History of the Northwest Coast*, p. 177, says, "They reached Nootka in June, obtaining six hundred sea-otter skins, though not so many as they had hoped for, because the natives had promised to keep their furs for Hanna, who arrived in August."

31. See *Letter from W. Hunter...* Hunter served on board the *Experiment*. See also Meares, *Voyages*, p. 132. Meares, like most early writers, calls the famous chief Maquilla.

30. Dixon in *A Voyage Round the World*, p. 232, says that "being very ill of a purple fever he was left behind for the recovery of his health, at the request of Mr. Strange, the supercargo to both vessels." Dixon also tells us that Mackay later "had made frequent incursions into the interior parts of the country about King George's Sound, and did not think any part of it was the continent of America, but a chain of detached islands (ibid., p. 233).

32. Captain Walbran, *British Columbia Coast Names*, p. 447, says that "on Vancouver's chart, published in 1798, they are named Scott's Islands, from their situation off Cape Scott." However, Strange's *Journal & Narrative* (p. 28) says that "these being our first discovery during the expedition, it naturally followed that I should give them a name whereby they may hereafter be known. I accordingly named them after the patron of this expedition, my most respected friend Mr. David Scott." Strange does not mention Cape Scott in his account, or show it on the chart he constructed, so it seems likely that it received its name later. Several names in this area commemorate this expedition – Experiment Bight, Lowrie Bay, Guise Bay, and Strange Rock.

Judge Howay in his *Voyages of the Columbia*, p. 86, says that Cape Scott, "like the Scott Islands, was named by the Strange expedition in 1786," but does not give a reference for his statement. For some time, American captains called this cape Cape Ingraham, after Joseph Ingraham, second mate of the *Columbia*, on this coast in 1788 and 1789, and later captain of the *Hope*, on this coast in 1791.

33. Captain Vancouver, *Voyage of Discovery to the North Pacific Ocean* (1798), I, 369, states that Queen Charlotte's Sound was named after the wife of King George III by S. Wedgborough, commander of the *Experiment*, in August 1786. Perhaps this officer was in temporary command of the ship.

The Queen Charlotte Islands were named by George Dixon after his ship in July 1787 (Dixon, *A Voyage Round the World*, p. 224).

34. Not to be confused with Hanna's two ships of the same name.

35. Strange, *Journal & Narrative*, p. 38. The two subsequent quotations are from the same source.

36. Dixon, *A Voyage Round the World*, p. 318.

37. Ayyar, *An Adventurous Madras Civilian*, p. 7. R.C. Etches, writing to Sir Joseph Banks in 1788, also suggested using convicts to settle the northwest coast. See his letter printed in the *B.C. Historical Quarterly* for April 1942. As is well known, the first white settlers in Australia, at Botany Bay, were convicts transported from England.

38. Hosie, "James Charles Stuart Strange," p. 54.

39. Meares, *Voyages*, p. 132.

40. Details of this voyage may be found in Meares, *Voyages. . .1788 and 1789*. (The next several quotations are from this source, and the page references are given in the text.)

41. This is Meares' account (*Voyages*, p. xxviii). Captain Portlock (*A Voyage Round the World*, p. 238) speaks of "an Indian girl that an officer belonging to the *Nootka* had purchased on their first arrival in the Sound. The girl made her escape from the *Nootka* towards the latter part of the winter, and probably gave the Indians an account of her weak and defenceless situation. . . ." Captain Dixon (*A Voyage Round the World*, p. 158) says of the Indians that "one of them, it seems, had been on board the *Nootka* several weeks."

42. John Nicol, *The Life and Adventures of John Nicol, Mariner* (1822; reprinted New York: Farrar and Rinehart, 1936), pp. 97-8. Nicol was a cooper on board the *King George* which rescued Meares in May 1787.

43. F.W. Howay, *The Dixon-Meares Controversy* (Toronto: Ryerson, 1929).
44. Ibid., p. 11.
45. Full details of the agreement may be found in India Office Records, Home Series Miscellaneous, Vol. 494, pp. 369-82; transcript in Provincial Archives, Victoria. Also in F.W. Howay, *The Journal of Captain James Colnett* (Toronto: The Champlain Society, 1940), Appendix I.
46. For detailed accounts of the voyage see Portlock, *A Voyage Round the World*; and Dixon, *A Voyage Round the World*.
47. Meares, *Voyages*, p. xxvii.
48. Ibid., p. xxxi. Some have asserted (Ormsby, *British Columbia: A History*, p. 14) that Meares broke his promise not to trade further on the northwest coast, but Judge Howay (*Dixon-Meares Controversy*, p. 11) says, "whether he kept his bond or not cannot be ascertained, for in his account of his subsequent movements, he gives no data whereby his course and conduct can be exactly followed."
49. Dixon, *A Voyage Round the World*, p. 319. See also India Office Records, Home Series Miscellaneous, Vol. 494, pp. 431 and 434. Transcript in Provincial Archives, Victoria.

    By this time sea-otter pelts were beginning to arrive on the Chinese market from California, being gathered there by the natives under the supervision of the friars and then shipped to Manila. The first shipment arrived in Manila in July 1787, and had the effect of further depressing the price of pelts in the Far East. See Adele Ogden, "The Californias in Spain's Pacific Otter Trade 1775-1795," *Pacific Historical Review*, 1932, p. 456.
50. There is some dispute as to who should be given credit for the discovery of the Queen Charlotte Islands. Meares in his *Voyages* (p. liii) divides the credit: "After remaining some time at Nootka Sound, they [i.e., Laurie and Guise] explored other parts of the coast and arrived in Snug Corner Cove in Prince William's Sound. In this progress they indisputably discovered that land to which Mr. Dixon gave the name of Charlotte's Isles, which he did merely from conjectural opinion, as they were never proved to be such until Captain Douglas in the *Iphigenia* sailed through the channel

which separates them from what was then supposed to be the American continent. Mr. Strange also first found the bay called Friendly Cove, which received its present name from that gentleman."

Some of these statements are open to question. It seems certain (see Bancroft, *Northwest Coast*, p. 183) that Captain Duncan sailed through the strait between the Queen Charlottes and the mainland in the *Princess Royal* before Douglas.

Dixon, in his *Remarks on the Voyages of John Meares*, p. 15, takes issue with Meares on some other points: "That captains Lowrie and Guise saw the southern parts of Queen Charlotte's Islands in 1786 I do not dispute, and I hope you will admit that both Captain Portlock and myself fell in with these islands in company the same year, near Hippah Island; but if this is to be called a discovery, I am inclined to think the Spaniards may claim a right to it; for it appears by the general chart to Captain Cook's last voyage that they must have seen this land in the year 1775, and I dare venture to say knew as much of it then as either captains Lowrie, Guise, Portlock or myself did in 1786. . ." Possibly the first European to see these islands was a Franciscan friar aboard the *Santiago*, who caught a glimpse of them on July 17, 1774.

51.   This was the *Princess Royal*; it is hard to explain why Dixon was unable to recall her name. See Portlock, *A Voyage Round the World*, p. 307.

52.   Ibid., p. 382. Judge Howay, in his notes to four letters from R.C. Etches to Sir Joseph Banks, printed in the *B.C. Historical Quarterly* for April 1942 (p. 130) says of Dixon's voyage to the Queen Charlottes that "his total trade at those islands amounted to 1,821 sea-otter skins, worth in China about $5,500," but this value must be a misprint. Dixon in his *Remarks on the Voyages of John Meares*, p. 11, says that the two ships between them secured 2,552 sea-otter skins, and that the cargoes "fetched 54,857 Spanish dollars at the Chinese market."

53.   Dixon, in a letter written Oct. 20, 1789, suggested that the best place for a settlement would be the northern end of the Queen Charlotte Islands; see *British Columbia Historical*

Quarterly, July 1950, p. 169. In another letter printed in the same article, he speaks of a ship called *The Fly*, which he says secured 400 sea-otter skins on the northwest coast in 1787. However, no other reference to such a ship has ever been found, and some of the other statistics he gives in this letter are quite unreliable.

54. Portlock, *Voyage Round the World*, p. 295.

55. Martin Sauer, ed., *An Account of a Geographical and Astronomical Expedition to the Northern Parts of Russia* (London, 1802), p. 281.

56. Capt. J.F. de la Pérouse, *A Voyage Round the World*, 3rd ed. (London, 1807), III, 365, suggests that the *Lark* was lost while returning from America: "The return of this vessel was expected at Kamtschatka; but Captain Peters in the meantime had made a voyage to the northwest coast of America, with a view no doubt to procure furs; and it was not till his return that at a very small distance from the harbours of St. Peter and St. Paul he lost both his ship and his life." La Pérouse says that the *Lark* was owned by "Mr. Lanz, an English merchant."

57. Bancroft, *History of the Northwest Coast*, p. 184. It is not clear from what source La Pérouse was likely to have obtained his information. Greenhow (*History of Oregon and California*, p. 183) says that La Pérouse while in Chile promised Spanish officials that he would inform the viceroy of Mexico what he learned in northern waters of Russian activities.

58. La Pérouse, *A Voyage Round the World*, III, 300. The next several quotations are from the same source, and the page references are given in the text.

59. Dixon, in his *Voyage Round the World* (p. 320) ways 600 skins; but the official French account (III, 373) says "we have purchased on the coast of North America nearly a thousand otter skins; but they were chiefly in fragments and almost rotten." James Strange in his Memorandum on the fur trade from N.W. America, says that the pelts fetched $9,000, while the French account (III, 373) says "the skins were sold for 10,000 dollars and the amount divided among the crews."

60. Vol. III, pp. 319-20. M. de Lamanon had evidently forgotten the incident of the scientists' stolen clothes.
61. C.C. Hulley, *Alaska, Past and Present*, 3rd ed. (Portland: 1970), p. 96, says that "in 1826 Capt. Peter Dillon, a Britisher, found the wreckage of La Pérouse's ships on reefs of an inlet north of the New Hebrides." See also Greenhow, *History of Oregon and California*, p. 164.

⟦CHAPTER SIX⟧
The Young Honeymooners and Others

1. Mrs. Barkley in her "Reminiscences" (written in 1836; unpublished MS in the Provincial Archives, B.C.) calls it Louden; Captain Colnett refers to it as Lowden. See W.K. Lamb's article, "The mystery of Mrs. Barkley's diary," in the *B.C. Historical Quarterly* for January 1942.
2. Mrs. Barkley in her "Reminiscences" says, "he being in his 26th year and I in my 17th."
3. Mrs. Barkley would seem to have overcome her aversion to the second mate, for when her husband was too ill to attend parties on shore, she was "chaparooned by Mr. M[oore], the second mate, who being a Leutinant in the King's service cut a dash, with his sword at his side & his naval uniform. . . ." Mrs. Barkley's spelling, one might note, is uniformly individualistic.
4. Meares in his *Voyages* (p. lv) incorrectly says that the ship arrived at Nootka in August.
5. J.T. Walbran, "The Cruise of the Imperial Eagle," Victoria *Colonist*, March 3, 1901.
6. This account of the Barkleys is based on Mrs. Barkley's "Reminiscences"; a talk by Capt. J.T. Walbran given to the Natural History Society of B.C., printed in the Victoria *Colonist* for March 3, 1901; and Dixon, *A Voyage Round the World*, pp. 231-33.

The statements of Meares in his *Voyages*, pp. lv and 124, contain some inaccuracies. The preface to Dr. C.F. New-combe's *The First circumnavigation of Vancouver Island* (Victoria: B.C. Archives Memoir No. 1, 1914) is useful, but Captain Barkley's "Journal of the proceedings on board the Lou-doun" (MS. in Provincial Archives, Victoria) is not illumi-nating. W.K. Lamb, "The mystery of Mrs. Barkley's Di-ary," *B.C. Historical Quarterly*, January 1942, combines the above sources.

Mrs. Barkley kept a diary during her voyage to the northwest coast. Captain Walbran read it and copied out some passages from it, but the diary itself was lost in a fire at Westholme, V.I. on Nov. 22, 1909, which also claimed the life of Capt. Edward Barkley, R.N., grandson of the Bark-leys. He is buried in St. Paul's churchyard, Quamichan, V.I.; Captain Walbran attended the funeral.

Mackay's account of his year at Nootka has been lost. This seems a pity, as Meares, who read it, declared, "the pe-rusal of this gentleman's journal would shock any mind tinc-tured with humanity" (*Voyages*, p. 132).

7. The authority for this statement is Captain Walbran, who derived the information from Mrs. Barkley's diary. See Wal-bran, *British Columbia Coast Names*, p. 39.

8. Transcript made by Captain Walbran; now in Provincial Archives, Victoria.

9. Captain Walbran believed strongly in his claims, and was prepared to give his reasons. See his *British Columbia Coast Names*, p. 274. Bancroft devotes over ten pages (70-81) of his *History of the Northwest Coast* to discussing the question.

10. It lies in 47°41′N, off the western coast of Jefferson County, state of Washington. It will be recalled that Quadra lost a party of men in the same vicinity on July 14, 1775; he gave the island the name of Isla de Dolores (Island of Sorrows). Further details of the fate of Barkley's men may be found in the entry for Dec. 8, 1795, of the ship *Ruby*. See the article by T.C. Elliott in the *Oregon Historical Quarterly* for Sept. 1927.

11. Portlock, *Voyage Round the World*, p. 368. Portlock calls the ship *Lowden* and its captain Berkley.

12. Lamb, op. cit., p. 45.

13. Captain Walbran says she died in 1843, but 1845 is correct (see Lamb, op. cit., p. 47).
14. Meares, *Voyages*, p. 200.
15. Dixon, *Voyage Round the World*, p. 230. Staten's Land is just east of the Strait of Magellan.
16. Ibid., p. 228.
17. More details of the activities of these two ships in 1787 may be found in Howay, *The Journal of Captain James Colnett*, p. xx, and C.F. Newcombe, ed., *Menzies' Journal of Vancouver's Voyage* (Victoria: Archives of B.C. Memoir No. 5, 1923), p. xiii.
18. George Dixon, *Further Remarks on the Voyages of John Meares, Esq.*, (London, 1791), p. 29.
19. Bird Island is situated about 120 miles northwest of the Hawaiian group. Vancouver visited it in March 1794. It is about one mile square and covered with what Vancouver called "vast flocks of the feathered tribe."
20. James Strange, Memorandum on the fur trade, India Office Records, Home Series Miscellaneous, p. 436.
21. For fuller accounts of the *Princess Royal*, see Ralph Kuykendall, "James Colnett and the *Princess Royal*," *Oregon Historical Quarterly*, March 1924, and F.W. Howay, "Captain Colnett and the *Princess Royal*," *Oregon Historical Quarterly*, March 1925.
22. Meares, *Voyages*, p. 25. The following several quotations are from the same source, and the page references are usually given in the text.
23. The Spanish usually called him Macuina.
24. This assertion by Meares, that he bought a piece of land from the natives at this time, may be found in both his *Voyages* (p. 114) and his later "Memorial" to the House of Commons. It was a matter of some importance, bearing on whether British possession or occupation of any part of Nootka Sound was prior to that of Spain. However, evidence about the transaction is conflicting. William Graham, who arrived at Nootka on the *Felice* in May 1788, later deposed that "he saw Mr. Meares deliver some articles of merchandize to Maquilla, the sovereign prince of the said sound, which he then understood and believed were given in

a consideration for an establishment on shore." (This deposition is printed in the appendix of Meares' *Voyages*, and was among the documents attached to his "Memorial.") Vancouver was later told by Robert Duffin that Meares had bought "the whole of the land that forms Friendly Cove, Nootka Sound, in His Britannic Majesty's name, for eight or ten sheets of copper and some trifling articles." *Voyage of Discovery to the North Pacific Ocean*, (1798), I, 405. By contrast, Meares in his *Voyages* (p. 114) says he purchased some land for a pair of pistols and some gifts to the local high-born ladies.

On the other hand, the American officers Gray and Ingraham informed Quadra in 1792 that "as to the land Mr. Meares says he purchased of Maquinna or any other chief, we cannot say further than we never heard of any, although we remained among these people nine months and could converse with them perfectly well. Besides this, we have asked Maquinna and other chiefs, since our late arrival, if Captain Meares ever purchased any land in Nootka Sound; they answered No; that Captain Kendrick was the only man to whom they had ever sold any land." Bancroft, *History of the Northwest Coast*, p. 196.

Despite all this, the "Nootka Convention" of 1790, which ended the crisis between Spain and Britain by stipulating that land and buildings of which British subjects had been dispossessed in 1789 should be restored to them, tacitly implied that Meares had owned both at Nootka. The fact that in 1792 Quadra offered to turn over to Vancouver, as representing Britain, the land on which Meares' hut had stood shows that the Spanish also felt there was some substance in his claims; Vancouver, however, asserted that all of Friendly Cove should be recognized as British, which implies that he accepted the claims of Meares and Duffin to have purchased this whole general area from the natives.

25. Howay, *Voyages of the Columbia*, p. 48. This was apparently the first building erected by white men, with native labor, on Vancouver Island. It was still standing on October 1, 1788, for when a salute was fired by the American ships to celebrate the first anniversary of their departure from Bos-

ton, it was answered by "Captain Funter at the house on-shore" (Howay, *Columbia*, p. 53). It seems to have been dismantled soon afterward by Captain Douglas of the *Iphigenia*, who kept some of the material and gave the rest to Captain Kendrick, who used it as firewood on his ship. Meares in his "Memorial" does not mention dismantling the house, no doubt preferring to give his readers the impression that it was still standing; his second-in-command, Robert Duffin, told Vancouver in 1792 that "on Mr. Mears' [*sic*] departure, the house &c was left in good condition, and he enjoined Maquinna to take care of them until his (Mr. Mears's) return or else some of his associates on the coast again." E.S. Meany, ed., *A New Vancouver Journal on the Discovery of Puget Sound* (Seattle, 1915), p. 29. However Gray and Ingraham reported to Quadra in the same year that though they had seen a house or hut on their arrival at Nootka in 1788, it had disappeared by 1789 (Greenhow, *History of Oregon and California*, p. 415). The journal of the *Iphigenia* for May 22, 1789, mentions erecting a tent to put empty casks in which suggests that there was no other convenient shelter available at that time. The Spanish journals for 1789 do not mention seeing any buildings when their ships arrived at Nootka in that year.

As late as 1818, a French traveller visiting Nootka enquired about this famous building. "The result of my enquiry was, that Meares' house had been built with the permission of Macuina, but that there had not been any act of cession or treaty between them. . . . Such was the subject of the quarrel which was on the point of kindling a war between the three great maritime powers in 1790, and for which France alone fitted out forty-five ships of the line." C. De Roquefeuil, *A Voyage Round the World between the Years 1816 and 1819* (London, 1823), p. 97.

26. On Dec. 8, 1795, some natives came on board the *Ruby* and provided further grisly details of the fate of Barkley's men. See *Oregon Historical Quarterly*, Sept. 1927, p. 270.

27. The Indians had no written language, but Maquinna had apparently grasped the significance of Mackay's literary efforts.

28. The chief's name is now generally spelled Wickaninnish; his village was about forty miles south of Friendly Cove.

29. At the farewell banquet to Sir James Douglas in Victoria in 1864, only the male guests sat down to eat; the ladies merely "looked on." (New Westminster *British Columbian*, March 12, 1864.)

30. See Howay and Scholefield, *British Columbia from the Earliest Times to the Present*, I, 24. The story was first published in 1625 by Samuel Purchas, and was based on information supplied by Michael Lok, a reputable merchant trading in the eastern Mediterranean.

31. Meares, *Voyages*, p. 171.

32. See Walbran, *British Columbia Coast Names*, p. 39.

33. A vivid account of this lively battle may be found in Meares, *Voyages*, 1790 edition, appendix IV.

34. See "Observations on the probable existence of a North West Passage," printed in the introduction to Meares' *Voyages*, p. lv. Meares was a firm believer in the passage; in this interesting essay he points out that Cook had not explored the coast between 47° and 48°, or between 50° and 56°, and had possibly not touched the mainland at hardly any point, since it was quite likely that "the whole coast hitherto seen is part of a lengthened chain of detached islands."

35. Meares, *Voyages*, p. 179.

36. Dixon, *Further Remarks on the Voyages of John Meares, Esq.*, pp. 14 and 46, estimated, after studying Duffin's account, that he had penetrated the strait to about eleven leagues. Greenhow, *History of Oregon and California*, p. 176, suggests it was as little as ten miles. The strait is about fourteen miles wide.

37. Meares' instructions to Duffin are printed in the appendix to his *Voyages*.

38. Meares, *Voyages*, p. 173.

39. Meares, *Voyages*, p. 219.

40. Meares in his *Voyages*, p. 116, says that the *North West America* was 40 or 50 tons; in his "Memorial" he estimated it as "about 40 tons." Robert Haswell of the American ship *Columbia*, who saw the launching, estimated it at "about 30 tons." (Howay, *Voyages of the Columbia*, p. 48.)

41. According to Meares (*Voyages*, p. 220), the British flag was flown both on the new ship and over the fort on this occasion. This seems quite likely, though his great enemy Dixon tried to cast doubt on the matter, declaring in his *Further Remarks on the Voyages of John Meares, Esq.* (p. 24; see also p. 34) that he had been informed by Captain Duncan that Meares had "a small vessel on the stocks at Nootka, where, he told me, he had a fort, guns mounted, and Portuguese colours flying." However, William Graham, who came to Nootka on the *Felice* in 1788, made a deposition before a British magistrate in 1790 "that he saw said vessel launched in said harbour under British colours and navigated under the British flag" (deposition printed in appendix to Meares' *Voyages*).

    It is noteworthy that throughout both his *Voyages* and his "Memorial" Meares consistently refrains from ever telling us what flags the *Felice* and *Iphigenia* flew in 1788; however, his statement that he had obtained the right to fly the Portuguese flag suggests that he actually did so, and certainly the *Iphigenia* flew that flag in 1789, as is made plain from all the accounts of those at Nootka in that year.

42. Meares, *Voyages*, p. 225. For an echo of this statement, see my *James Douglas: Servant of Two Empires* (Vancouver, 1969) p. 178.

43. It may be found in Meares *Voyages*, pp. 226-271; readers will also find interesting Robert Haswell's account in Howay, *Voyages of the Columbia*, pp. 58-66.

44. This was confirmed by a friar at Nootka in 1789, who reported that "Macuina used to eat the children of his enemies who had the misfortune of becoming his slaves." See Tomas Bartrioli, "The Spanish Establishment at Nootka Sound, 1789-1792," M.A. thesis, U.B.C., 1960, pp. 326-7.

45. Meares, *Voyages*, p. 216.

46. Dixon in his *Further Remarks*, p. 67, asserts that Meares secured 750 skins, worth $38,000.

47. Meares, *Voyages*, p. 316. John Etches was the brother of R.C. Etches, and was supercargo on the *Prince of Wales*.

48. See Greenhow, *History of Oregon and California*, p. 415. The hut was standing as late as Oct. 1, 1788, as a salute was fired on that date from "the house on shore." (Haswell's log in

Howay, *Voyages of the Columbia*, p. 53.) Yet it was certainly gone by the spring of 1789, as there is no mention of it in any journal kept at Nootka at that time.

⟦CHAPTER SEVEN⟧
Stars and Stripes on the Northwest Coast

1. Judge Howay, "The earliest pages of the history of British Columbia," *B.C. Historical Association, First Annual Report* (Victoria, 1924), p. 20, estimated that Britain regained her supremacy in the northwest fur trade about 1834 – the year, incidentally, that marked the end of the East India Company's monopolistic rights and the triumph of the economic philosophy of free enterprise. I have ventured in my *S.S. Beaver: The Ship that Saved the West* (Vancouver: Mitchell Press, 1970) to suggest that the victory was sealed by the arrival of this little ship on the Pacific coast in 1836.

2. G.R. Elliott, "Empire and Enterprise in the North Pacific 1785-1825," PhD thesis, U. of Toronto, 1957, p. 30.

3. Ibid., p. 44.

4. Ibid., p. 45. See also C.L. Ver Steeg, "Financing and outfitting the first United States ship to China," *Pacific Historical Review*, Feb. 1953, and R.A. Rydell, *Cape Horn to the Pacific* (U. of California Press, 1952), p. 24.

5. Elliott, op. cit., p. 45.

6. It is possible that John Ledyard had some influence on these early voyages from New England to the northwest coast. F.G. Young in "Spain and England's quarrel over the Oregon country," *Oregon Historical Quarterly*, March 1920, p. 16, says, "John Ledyard, an American, who had been a sailor with Cook's expedition, was particularly active in canvassing the matter, and was probably largely instrumental in getting the company of Boston merchants to despatch so promptly the *Columbia* and *Washington* under Kendrick and Gray."

7. Efforts were later made to have Queen Charlotte Sound known as Pintard Sound, but this venture into creeping republicanism failed to take. See F.W. Howay, *Voyages of the Columbia to the Northwest Coast 1787-1790 and 1790-1793* (Boston: Massachusetts Historical Society, 1941), p. 87.

8. Meares in his *Voyages* (p. 219) lists the *Columbia* as 300 tons – yet another example of his many inaccuracies. Bancroft in his *History of the Northwest Coast* gives it as 220 tons.

9. For more details of the Kendricks, see F.W. Howay, "John Kendrick and his sons," *Oregon Historical Quarterly*, Dec. 1922.

10. See Howay, *Colnett*, p. 155, and Greenhow, *History of Oregon and California*, pp. 179-81.

11. H.H. Bancroft, *History of California* (San Francisco, 1884), p. 445. It will be observed that these instructions contain some inaccuracies – General Washington had no connection with the voyage, and the Russians had no posts on the southern American coast (though they did establish one, Fort Ross, not far north of San Francisco, in 1812). As we shall see, Martinez, Spanish commandant at Nootka in 1789, was given rather milder instructions as to how to deal with Kendrick and Gray if they arrived there.

12. Greenhow, *History of Oregon and California*, p. 184.

13. Howay, *Voyages of the Columbia*, p. 34.

14. Ibid., p. 35.

15. Ibid., p. 44.

16. Dixon in his *Further Remarks*, p. 67, estimates that Meares had actually secured 750 skins.

17. Howay, op. cit., p. 49.

18. Haswell (Howay, p. 50) gives the date as September 19, and Meares (*Voyages*, p. 220) as September 20. The discrepancy is probably due to the fact that Meares had crossed what is now the international date line en route to Nootka, while the Boston ships had not.

19. Howay, op. cit., p. 27.

20. John Boit, *The Journal of a Voyage Round the Globe 1795-1796*, p. 6. (Photostat in Provincial Archives, Victoria.)

21. For more on Metcalfe and his sons, see F.W. Howay, "Captain Simon Metcalfe and the brig Eleanora," *Washington Historical Quarterly*, April 1925. It is possible that Metcalfe

was the first to take sandalwood from Hawaii to China; see H.W. Bradley, "The Hawaiian Islands and the Pacific Fur Trade 1785-1813," *Pacific Northwest Quarterly*, July 1939, p. 286.

⟦CHAPTER EIGHT⟧
Year of Crisis, Year of Destiny

1. See F.W. Howay, *The Journal of Captain James Colnett*, p. xxii. By a Spanish royal ordinance of 1692, any foreign vessels found on the west coast of the Americas could be seized, "seeing that no other nation had, or ought to have, any territories to reach which its vessels should pass around Cape Horn or through Magellan's Straits." (Greenhow, *History of Oregon and California*, p. 184). The treaty of Paris (1763) had prohibited British ships from trading in Spanish domains in the new world.

2. The original line was fixed by the Pope on May 4, 1493, as 100 leagues west of the Cape Verde Islands. This division gave the entire new world to Spain, while Africa and India went to Portugal. The revision of line by the treaty of Tordesillas on June 7, 1494, had the effect of giving Brazil to Portugal.

3. See H.R. Wagner, *Spanish Voyages to the Northwest Coast of America in the 16th Century*.

4. Bancroft, *History of the Northwest Coast*, I, 173.

5. "It was just such fears of Russian expansion from bases in Kamchatka which led to the opening of the Mexican Naval Department of San Blas in 1767, and to the occupation of San Diego, Monterey and San Francisco. The pretext was that the Philippine ships needed additional bases, but the real reason was to place some limits upon Russian expansion." C.I. Archer, "The transient presence: a re-appraisal of Spanish attitudes toward the northwest coast in the 18th century," *B.C. Studies*, UBC, summer 1973, p. 4.

6. See Stuart Thompkins and Max Moorhead, "Russia's approach to America," *B.C. Historical Quarterly*, July 1949, p. 233.
7. Chapman, *The Founding of Spanish California*, p. 232.
8. Ibid., p. 240. Chapman says that Chirikof was at 55°41′ in 1741 and Perez at 55°40′ in 1774.
9. I have followed in this account H.R. Wagner, *The Cartography of the Northwest Coast*. It differs slightly from the older accounts in Greenhow, *History of Oregon and California*, pp. 183ff., and Bancroft, *History of Alaska*, pp. 270ff.
10. C.C. Hulley, *Alaska, Past and Present*, 3rd ed. (Portland, 1970), p. 97.

    Delarof is said to have told Haro that Russian ships often visited Nootka for furs. As there is no reason to suppose that they did so, either the Russian was boasting or the Spanish made up the story in order to impress their superiors in Mexico and Madrid with the necessity for prompt action in securing a fair share of the fur trade for Spain.
11. Greenhow, op. cit., p. 186. The ships that had recently left Kodiak were likely an expedition which at this time went along the Alaskan coast as far east as Mt. St. Elias, while those being built at Okhotsk were probably intended for the expedition under Joseph Billings, which in 1790 went from Okhotsk to Unalaska, Kodiak, Prince William Sound, and then back to Petropavlovsk. See Martin Sauer, ed., *An Account of a Geographical and Astronomical Expedition to the Northern Parts of Russia*.

    Captain Douglas recorded in his journal of the *Iphigenia* (entry for May 24/25, 1789, printed in appendix to Meares *Voyages*) that Martinez had been informed by a Russian official at Unalaska "that he expected three vessels from Kamtschatka with a number of men; that on their arrival at Oonalashka, he was to take command and conduct them to Nootka Sound, where they were to form a settlement; that he expected to arrive at Nootka by the middle of July or 1st of August 1789; that two Russian frigates were to sail from Petersburgh by the way of Cape Horn and join them in Nootka Sound with stores and other necessaries that they might want."

12. This was no doubt the sort of action which prompted Green-how to declare, "The Spaniards, the British, the Russians and the French had, indeed, landed at many places on those coasts, where they had displayed flags, performed ceremonies, and erected monuments, by way of taking possession – as it was termed – of the adjacent territories for their respective sovereigns; but such acts are, and were then, generally considered as empty pageants, securing no real rights to those by whom, or in whose name, they were performed." (*History of Oregon and California*, p. 187.) This, however, is a nineteenth century American view; few European foreign offices in the eighteenth century would have concurred in it, at least publicly. Yet they were certainly coming round to it; W.R. Manning, "The Nootka Sound Controversy," *Annual Report of the American Historical Association for 1904* (Washington, 1905), p. 310, says that by 1789 "it had long been conceded by other nations that discovery alone, or even discovery with formal acts of taking possession, can not give a valid title. It is essential that some effort be made to use the land discovered and to develop its resources; and before the claim is fully established, actual and continued possession must be taken." See in this connection H.R. Wagner, "Creation of rights of sovereignty through symbolic acts," *Pacific Historical Review*, Dec. 1938.

    Many pamphlets on the Nootka crisis appeared in London in 1790, and they mostly took the line that discovery "is a species of claim too absurd to be depended upon in these days." See Lennox Mills, "The real significance of the Nootka Sound incident," *Canadian Historical Review*, June 1925, p. 115. This did not, however, prevent the British from basing their claim to Nootka on the visit of Captain Cook, who made no effort to develop the resources of the area.

13. Martinez to Flores, Dec. 5, 1788; quoted in Manning, op. cit., p. 300. It will be observed that Martinez was in no doubt as to his having been at Nootka in 1774 – a question which many scholars have since debated.

14. Flores to Martinez, Dec. 23, 1788, in Manning, op. cit., p. 300. Wagner, *Cartography*, p. 215, tries hard to make out that the Spanish expedition to Nootka in 1789 was designed to

forestall not the Russians but the British. In the light of the viceroy's statement, however, the arguments which he puts forward seem unconvincing. There is a puzzling remark in Flores' instructions that Martinez was only to "pretend" to establish a permanent Spanish base at Nootka (see W.L. Cook, *Flood Tide of Empire*, p. 131). Martinez' actions in 1789 seem hard to reconcile with this, and he seems to have been genuinely surprised and dismayed when ordered to abandon the post later.

15. Flores to Martinez, Dec. 23, 1788, in Manning, op. cit., p. 304.
16. "We see that the Russian projects and those which the English may make from Botany Bay, which they have colonized, already menace us." (Flores to Valdes, Spanish minister of Marine, Dec. 23, 1788 in Manning, op. cit., p. 302.)
17. Manning, op. cit., p. 305. It will be recalled that the spoons came from a tribe which lived not at Nootka but to the south of it.
18. In his instructions to Martinez (loc. cit.) Flores says that "by a letter from the most excellent Señor Viceroy of Peru, it is known that a frigate, which is said to belong to General Washington, sailed from Boston in September 1787 with the intention of approaching the said coasts, that a storm obliged her to stop in distress at the islands of Juan Fernandez, and that she continued her course after being relieved." Flores' information was slightly garbled; General Washington had no part in the venture; but one of the ships was the *Lady Washington*.
19. Flores to Valdes, Dec. 23, 1788, in Manning, op. cit., p. 302.
20. Ibid., p. 305. The exact dividing line between the Spanish and Russian spheres, though reckoned to be in the vicinity of Prince William Sound, was not yet precisely defined. Kendrick, in a letter to his sponsor Joseph Barrell, dated July 13, 1789, at Nootka, says of Martinez that "he has taken possession of the sound, and has orders to take possession from the Spanish settlements [i.e., in California] to Cook's River." (*Washington Historical Quarterly*, Oct. 1921, p. 253.)
21. Martinez in his diary (entry dated July 2, 1789, printed in

Howay, *Colnett*, p. 308) calls it "the Company of Free Commerce of London."

22. Howay, op. cit., p. 3. We shall see that despite the reference to the British flag, the Portuguese one was used whenever it seemed convenient.

23. Ibid., p. 33.

24. Ibid., p. 20. In these instructions to Colnett Meares does not specify the exact location of the proposed trading post; but in his "Memorial" he says that "Mr. Colnett was directed to fix his residence at Nootka Sound." This is one of the many instances in which it seems likely that the "Memorial" was touched up in order to have the greatest possible impact on its readers. It is worth noting that Meares in these instructions does not mention the hut which he had built at Nootka in 1788; there would surely have been some reference to it if it had still been standing.

It seems probable that the letter of instructions to Colnett was in fact written and signed by Daniel Beale, one of the financial backers of the company, but that when it came time to reprint a selection of documents in his "Memorial," Meares found it convenient to magnify his own importance by substituting his own name as the author. See W.L. Cook, *Flood Tide of Empire*, p. 144.

25. Howay, *Colnett*, p. 34.

26. Ibid., p. 37.

27. Loc. cit.

28. Ibid., p. 35. As we shall see, not every detail of this plan was put into effect, as Meares sold the *Felice* in the winter of 1788-89 and arranged for the purchase of the *Argonaut* for the 1789 season.

29. Loc. cit. Meares and Kendrick seem to have been the two earliest to envision an international trade in Hawaiian sandalwood; it became fully developed within about twenty years. See F.W. Howay, "Early relations between the Hawaiian Islands and the northwest coast," *The Hawaiian Islands* (Honolulu, 1930), p. 37.

30. There is no doubt that the ships were entirely British; Meares in a letter to Douglas (Howay, *Colnett*, p. 18) speaks of Cavalho as "having sold to the said Co. and lawfully

made over all his shares and concern in the *Ephigenia Nubiana* and the *America* [*sic*] and they are now to be considered entirely as English property." In his "Memorial," Meares says that "the *Iphigenia* and her cargo were actually and bona fide British property." Thus C.I. Archer's reference in *B.C. Studies*, Summer 1973, p. 12, to "A Portuguese ship called the *Efigenia Nubiana*" is not, strictly speaking, correct. However he sins in good company; according to Vancouver, (*Voyage*, I, 388), even Quadra believed "that the Ephigenia did not belong to the English."

Meares skilfully avoids mentioning in either his *Voyages* or his "Memorial" what flags these ships actually flew on their way to Nootka and after their arrival. However, confirmation that they were flying the Portuguese flag at Nootka may be found in a wide variety of sources: Howay, *Colnett*, p. 17; Haswell's log in Howay, *Voyages of the Columbia*, pp. 101 and 124; and Captain Gray's letter to one of the sponsors of the American expedition, ibid., p. 129.

31. Howay, *Colnett*, p. 38. In his "Memorial" Meares says "formality."

32. Howay, p. 18.

33. The Russians never did make any attempt to establish a post at Nootka, but this was not on account of the latitude, as in 1812 they founded a settlement, Fort Ross, not far north of San Francisco, and maintained it for about thirty years. They did, not, however, make any claim to ownership of the area by their country. See E.O. Essig, "The Russian Settlement at Ross," *California Historical Quarterly*, Sept. 1933. The Hudson's Bay Company established a post at Yerba Buena near San Francisco in 1841, arrangements for this having been made by James Douglas during a visit to California in that year. It was abandoned a few years later.

34. Haswell's log in Howay, *Voyages of the Columbia*, p. 77.

35. Meares in his *Voyages* (p. 3) says his expedition brought 50 Chinese to Nootka; in his "Memorial" he revised this to "near 70 Chinese"; Manning, no doubt following Meares, says (*Nootka Sound Controversy*, p. 289) "of the 90 men on the two ships 50 were Chinese"; but Martinez and Colnett agree there were only 29. These comprised 7 carpenters, 5

blacksmiths, 5 masons, 4 tailors, 4 shoemakers, 3 seamen and a cook. See Howay, *Colnett*, p. 15 and Martinez, diary entry for July 6, 1789, reprinted in Howay, op. cit., p. 314. All this casts some light on Meares' standards of accuracy.

The materials for a new ship (to be called the *Jason*) brought by the *Argonaut* were apparently later used by the Spanish to enlarge the *North West America* after they had seized it. Compensation was eventually paid for this in the general settlement of the Nootka crisis.

36. Haswell's log in Howay, *Voyages of the Columbia*, p. 85.

37. This story has independent confirmation; Douglas in the journal of the *Iphigenia* for May 6, 1789 (printed in the appendix to the 1790 edition of Meares' *Voyages*) says that when he first met Martinez on May 6, the Spaniard told him that he had recently been at Unalaska, Prince William Sound, and Cook's River. It has been suggested that Martinez was describing his voyage of 1788 and that this was misunderstood by the English (see H.I. Priestley, "The log of the *Princesa* by Estevan Josef Martinez," *Oregon Historical Quarterly*, March 1920, p. 22).

38. Haswell's log in Howay, *Voyages of the Columbia*, p. 85.

39. Howay, *Voyages of the Columbia*, p. 96. Bancroft is wrong when he says (*History of the Northwest Coast*, p. 207) that "at one point the unsophisticated savages gave two hundred sea-otter skins, worth about eight thousand dollars, for an old iron chisel."

40. Howay, op. cit., p. 98.

41. During this voyage Haswell had come to the same conclusion earlier reached by Meares: that "all the range of coast north of Juan de Fuca Straits, as far north as we went, is a vast chain of islands, and the entrances betwixt them may be taken for straits, gulfs, etca. but when explored it will be found the coast of the continent has not yet been seen." (Ibid., p. 99.) Haswell's suspicions were confirmed by Vancouver in the years 1792-94.

42. Martinez diary, entry for May 5. It should be noted that Cook mentions acquiring the spoons, but says nothing of any incident in which the Spanish had lost them.

43. A translation of the instructions may be found in Greenhow,

History of Oregon and California, p. 173, and in the appendix to Meares' *Voyages*. It will be noted that the reference in them to "Russian, English or Spanish vessels" implies that the *Iphigenia* was being pictured as Portuguese. The courts where officers and ships captured by the *Iphigenia* would be charged would also necessarily be the Portuguese ones at Macao, as Meares could hardly afford to have any dealings with British courts. It is not at all clear why no one could understand the instructions, as Viana was Portuguese and must have understood some English and Spanish. See W.L. Cook, *Flood Tide of Empire*, p. 153.

Another interesting point is that according to Martinez (diary May 24) the papers of the *Iphigenia* were "signed by Don Juan Carvallo of the same nation, the owner of the packet and of another called *La Feliz Aventureyra*, which had already returned to Macao." This latter ship was the *Felice*; Meares was later to claim that both ships were entirely of British ownership.

44. Douglas declared in his journal for May 14 that he had "been informed Captain Kendrick was privy to my being taken prisoner, and that it was settled when the Spanish commodore was last at Moweena." (Journal of the *Iphigenia*, printed in appendix to Meares' *Voyages*.) However, Martinez' diary does not suggest that he and Kendrick had any private consultations at Moweena in this period.

Bancroft, *History of the Northwest Coast*, p. 214, says, "The Englishman suspected that Kendrick had instigated the seizure, and I have little doubt that he did so," but does not give his reasons for believing this. However, Colnett in his journal (Howay, *Colnett*, p. 161), speaking of Martinez, says, "the American he had taken into partnership in commerce," and Martinez in his diary says of the *Washington*, "I treated this enemy as a friend." See F.W. Howay, "Captains Gray and Kendrick: the Barrell letters" (*Washington Historical Quarterly*, Oct. 1921), p. 251.

45. See Enclosure IV, attached to Meares' "Memorial"; in appendix to his *Voyages*. The bond names Francis Joseph Viana as the captain of the ship and William Douglas as its supercargo. Cavalho is named as the person "to whom belongs

said packet-boat," and the bond was witnessed by the Americans Kendrick and Ingraham.

46. See Meares' "Memorial" and Journal of the *Iphigenia* for May 30, 1789.

47. See Journal of the *Iphigenia* for June 1, 1789.

48. In his *Voyages* (pp. 361-69) Meares deals at length with this successful voyage to the Queen Charlottes; however by the time he came to pour out his manifold grievances in his "Memorial" it had (so we must assume) completely slipped his mind; he merely states that the *Iphigenia* after leaving Nootka "proceeded from thence to the Sandwich Islands."

49. They were actually drinking the health of his successor, Carlos III having died near the end of 1788. News of the accession of Carlos IV was brought from Mexico by the *Aranzazu* on July 29, Nootka probably being the last part of the Spanish empire to hear it.

50. There may have been an earlier and less formal ceremony. John B. Treat, the American furrier, wrote from Nootka in July 1789 that the Spanish "took possession here in May last." (See *Pacific Northwest Quarterly*, July 1940, p. 286.) Vancouver was informed by Quadra in 1792 that "under the orders of the Viceroy of New Spain, Martinez entered Nootka and took possession the 5th of May 1789 with visible demonstrations of joy in the Indians." (*Voyage*, I, 387). However the June 24 ceremony must have been quite out of the ordinary, since one Spanish observer declared that "the ceremonies of this function were sufficient to move the Protestants who attended it, as they themselves declared to our commander." (Tomas Bartrioli, "The Spanish Establishment at Nootka Sound, p. 268.)

51. Bartrioli, op. cit., p. 269.

52. Our main sources for these events are Martinez' diary (no full English translation of which has yet been published); letters which Colnett wrote to Spanish and British authorities while he was a prisoner in Mexico; a long footnote in a book he wrote some nine years later about quite another voyage; letters written by Robert Duffin to Meares from Nootka in the summer of 1789; and depositions of various British seamen made after their release from captivity.

There are also a few letters written by Americans from Nootka in 1789.

Interesting but less dependable is a letter written in 1792 by the Americans Gray and Ingraham to Quadra; although they were present at Nootka in 1789, their letter is apparently based on memory rather than records, as many of the dates they give are wrong.

Captain Vancouver's account of what he learned of events at Nootka in 1789, when he himself arrived there in 1792, as well as what he heard later from Colnett in England, is interesting but of course second-hand. As to the "Memorial" which Meares presented to the House of Commons in 1790, it is perhaps sufficient to note that Meares was not present at Nootka in 1789, that the "Memorial" was composed with an eye to the maximum possible effect on British public opinion, and that it is frequently at variance with his own *Voyages*. W.R. Manning's massive monograph on the Nootka controversy is the most detailed account to date, but we should bear in mind that it was written while it was still believed that Martinez' diary and Colnett's journal of the *Argonaut* (the former discovered about 1920 and the latter in 1935) were permanently lost. More recent is the highly useful *Flood Tide of Empire* by Warren L. Cook, which incorporates recent research by its author in the Spanish archives.

53. Martinez diary, entry of July 2, 1789, in Howay, *Colnett*, p. 308. The Spanish system of dates is one day behind that of the British throughout, probably a reflection of the fact that the latter had crossed what is now the International Date Line on their way to Nootka. Yet it would appear that the American ships kept to the same system as the Spanish, as their ships saluted Independence Day on what Martinez also reckoned was July 4.

54. Colnett later told Vancouver in England that Martinez "ordered the *Columbia*, an American ship, to fire into the *Argonaut* if she attempted to unmoor," but this statement may be doubted. (Vancouver, *Voyage*, III, 495.)

55. James Colnett, *Voyage to the South Atlantic* (London, 1798), p. 96n. Some have doubted that Martinez could have been

short of supplies, but it seems quite possible, as his supply ship the *Aranzazu* had not yet arrived.

56. It seems quite likely that Martinez at first intended to let Colnett depart peaceably; Robert Duffin, in a letter written from Nootka on July 12 to Meares, says that he had been told by Martinez "that he had given Colnett permission to depart, and would have assisted him all in his power but that Captain Colnett insisted on erecting a fort opposite his." Martinez had, after all, previously let the *Princess Royal* leave unmolested.

57. Martinez in his diary for July 3 says that the Spanish observed Colnett spying on the fort from a rowboat before dawn, but Colnett says nothing of this.

58. Colnett, op. cit., p. 96n. There is nothing comparable to the last few lines of this excerpt in Martinez' account, yet there is some reason to believe it to be true, as Martinez was of a hot-tempered nature, and admits in his diary for July 12 that he "gave Hudson to understand, by means of the interpreter, that if his crew offered any resistance I would have him hanged at the yard-arm, as a warning to the other prisoners in the port." This is the same day, one might note, that Martinez records that "today I gave the officers who are my prisoners a splendid dinner." The Britons at Nootka in 1789 must have found Martinez as puzzling as he was alarming.

59. Martinez diary, entry for July 3, in Howay, *Colnett*, p. 310. Colnett (Howay, op. cit., p. 59) says that there were some Americans in the cabin when he arrived, but that they left when the dispute broke out. Martinez makes no reference to any Americans being present, but it is interesting to note that a deposition made by Captain Funter and others of the *North West America* at Canton in December 1789 (printed in appendix to Meares' *Voyages*) states that when Martinez first boarded the *Argonaut* he was accompanied by Richard Howe, supercargo of the American ships.

60. Martinez diary, July 3. According to Martinez, Colnett had threatened to sail regardless, and thus force the Spanish fort to fire on his ship. This might well have caused the "shedding of blood" to which he refers.

José Mariano Moziño, the naturalist, who was at Nootka in 1792, though not in 1789, says: "Although he found himself with inferior forces, Martinez of course had to oppose the demands which the Englishman set forth. The Spaniard then commited the indiscretion of insulting him, and even of putting his hand on his sword in order to kill him. It is likely that the churlish nature of each one precipitated things up to this point, since those who sailed with both complained of them equally and condemned their uncultivated boorishness." (I.H. Wilson, trans., *Noticias de Nutka*, p. 74).

Gray and Ingraham later asserted that it was Colnett who first threatened violence (W.L. Cook, *Flood Tide of Empire*, p. 173). However, like Mozino, they were not eyewitnesses and were merely repeating what they had been told by others.

61. Robert Duffin in a letter written to Meares on July 12 (printed in appendix to Meares' *Voyages*) said that Martinez "appeared to be exceedingly sorry for what, he said, his officers compelled him to do," and that "his officers insist on his going on with what he acknowledges he too rashly and hastily began, and without deliberating what might hereafter be the consequences."

62. Martinez diary, July 4, in Howay, *Colnett*, p. 313. Carlos III had died on Dec. 14, 1788.

63. Martinez had been ordered by the viceroy to explore the coast as far north as Prince William Sound, but he seems to have done nothing about this. His interest in the Strait of Juan de Fuca was understandable, however, as he had hopes that it would prove to be connected with the Mississippi. (Bartrioli, p. 272; Martinez diary, July 5.)

64. Colnett, *Voyage to the South Atlantic*, p. 99n.

65. Colnett agrees (Howay, *Colnett*, p. 61) that events "made me distracted for five days and five nights," while Robert Duffin, in a letter written from Nootka on July 12, says, "Since our being captured, Captain Colnett had been in a high state of insanity. Sometimes he starts, at others he asks how long he has to live? Who is to be his executioner? What death is he to be put to? With all such delirious expressions,

accompanied by a number of simple actions, which induces me, and every other person who sees him, to believe his brain is turned, owing to the great charge that was under his care." (Printed in appendix to Meares' *Voyages*.)

66. Judge Howay in *Voyages of the Columbia*, p. 101, states that it was Martinez who killed Callicum, whereas in his *Journal of Captain James Colnett* (p. 317) he says that a sailor killed Callicum after Martinez' gun missed fire. Both statements are asserted by Howay to have been derived from a translation of Martinez' diary in his possession; however the latter statement is the only one supported by the diary. See also Moziño, *Noticias de Nutka*, p. 75n.

Colnett himself (Howay, *Colnett*, p. 62) says that Martinez "had cruelty enough to do anything, for he killed Caleacan [*sic*] the greatest chief at Nootka, for only telling him it was wrong to stop his friend the English." Callicum in fact ranked below Maquinna in importance.

Meares, who at one place in his *Voyages* called the Indians "filthy brutes," in another part of the same work described the dead chief as having "possessed a delicacy of mind and conduct which would have done honour to the most improved state of our civilization" (see pp. 117 and 210 of his *Voyages*). Naturally this latter remark was made with an eye to its effect on British public opinion.

There is a possibility that Callicum was actually denouncing Martinez for allowing his sailors to steal some boards from an Indian village. A French traveller who visited Maquinna in 1818 talked with a lesser chief about the affair: "Noak gave me an account of the death of Canicum [*sic*], who was killed by Martinez, whom he had bitterly reproached, calling him a robber, on account of the plundering of a hut by his people." De Roquefeuil, *A Voyage Round the World*, p. 29. See also Cook, *Flood Tide of Empire*, p. 162.

67. Quoted in F.W. Howay, "Captains Gray and Kendrick: the Barrell letters," p. 251. Douglas in his journal for May 14 says, "I enquired the cause of his not taking the Washington sloop, as he had orders from the King of Spain to take every vessel he met with on this coast. He gave me no satisfactory answer." However in his journal for May 24 Douglas re-

cords being told by Martinez that "his orders were to take
Captain Kendrick if he should fall in with him anywhere in
those seas; and mentioned it as a great secret that he would
take both him and the sloop Washington as soon as she arrived in port." It is quite possible that this was indeed Martinez' eventual intention; a warrant for the arrest of the
American ships had been issued earlier in the year by the
governor of California. (Cook, op. cit., p. 156.)

It should be noted that Martinez never received the
money due him for the furs he entrusted to Kendrick.

68. It has been suggested that San Rafael and San Miguel were
different names for the same fort, but the references to them
in Martinez' diary for May 15, August 8, 10, and 17 seem to
make it clear that they were separate strong points. See
Cook, op. cit. p. 154.

69. Martinez diary, July 29.

70. This is the opinion of Warren Cook (op. cit., p. 188). The
usually meticulous H.R. Wagner adds a confusing note
when he speaks of Martinez later arriving at San Blas with
"the *Santa Saturnina* which he had built." (*Spanish explorations
in the Strait of Juan de Fuca*, p. 12.) On p. 141 of the same work
he declares that there were three ships called *Santa Saturnina*
on the northwest coast in this period: Funter's *North West
America*, "which presumably was returned to him," "the
schooner which Martinez built in Nootka in the fall of 1789
and took back with him to San Blas," and a ship built by
Eliza at Nootka in 1790. In his *Cartography of the Northwest
Coast* (p. 219) Wagner speaks of Martinez arriving at San
Blas "with the *Princesa, the Santa Saturnina* (which it seems was
the *Santa Gertrudis,* cut in two and lengthened) and an American schooner, the *Fair American,* which he had seized just as
he was leaving Nootka." Bartrioli in his thesis "The Spanish
establishment at Nootka Sound 1789-1792," p. 383, speaks
of "The *North West America,* which Martinez had enlarged
and rechristened *Santa Saturnina.*" However I see no reason
to suppose that any ship named *Santa Saturnina* was either
built or christened at Nootka in 1789, although Thurman
(*The Naval Department of San Blas,* p. 292) seems content to go
along with Wagner on this point.

71. See C.L. Stewart, "Why the Spaniards temporarily abandoned Nootka Sound in 1789," *Canadian Historical Review*, June 1936, p. 170. It is difficult to accept the author's conclusions unreservedly, as Nootka was reoccupied by Spain in 1790 and regularly supplied from California for the next five years.

72. See C.I. Archer, "The transient presence: a re-appraisal of Spanish attitudes toward the northwest coast in the eighteenth century," *B.C. Studies*, UBC, summer 1973, p. 21. Also Howay, "Early relations between the Hawaiian Islands and the northwest coast," p. 35. H.W. Bradley in "The Hawaiian Islands and the Pacific Fur trade 1785-1813," *Pacific Northwest Quarterly*, July 1939, p. 285, agrees that Martinez correctly judged the future importance of Hawaii, as "by 1810 Honolulu had clearly emerged as the metropolis of the eastern Pacific."

73. Martinez to Flores, August 6, 1789; quoted in Stewart, op. cit., p. 171. So far as is known, no genuinely Portuguese ship had as yet visited Nootka.

74. Manning, "The Nootka Sound Controversy," p. 324, says that Martinez captured both American ships, but this is incorrect. See Howay, "Captain Simon Metcalfe and the brig Eleanora." Vancouver, *A voyage of discovery*, II, 136, says that "The *Eleanor* [*sic*] came on in the autumn of that year to the Sandwich Islands and remained principally about Owhyee during the winter." T.H. Metcalfe was killed by the natives of Hawaii in 1790; his father and younger brother Robert were killed by natives of the northwest coast in 1794.

75. The *Washington* got to China in January 1790 with $18,000 worth of skins. The *Columbia's* cargo sold for $21,400. See Howey, *Colnett*, p. 229.

76. See Stewart, op. cit., p. 169. Quadra became commandant at San Blas about this time.

77. Howay, *Colnett*, p. 320. It is interesting to compare this statement with that in his journal a few weeks later: "July 9th, 1790 at ten P.M., the day and hour of release of a twelve month and four days cruelty, robbery and oppressive treatment of the Spaniards of New Spain" (Howay, *Colnett*, p. 169). Strong evidence that the British prisoners were not

well treated is that six of them died and a seventh committed suicide in the fall of 1789. (Ibid., p. 322.)

78. That a general European war was believed possible is shown
by the fact that members of the American government debated what attitude they should adopt if it came. Jefferson
was cautiously pro-Spanish, but most of his colleagues fa-
vored neutrality. See Manning, op. cit., Chapter x.

79. E.g., Manning, op. cit., p. 359. However, see Howay, *Colnett*,
p. 233.

80. Ibid., p. xxviii.

A.S. Morton, in his *History of the Canadian West* (Nelson,
n.d.), p. 395, says: "Americans and Britons alike owe much
to Captain Colnett, whose perspicacity and obstinacy raised
the issue as to whether the Pacific coast should be as open
to traders as in the past, and who thus contributed to a final
settlement momentous to both the American Republic and
the British Empire."

81. The full text of the Nootka Convention may be found in
Greenhow, *History of Oregon and California*, pp. 476ff.

82. It was not made clear in the agreement exactly what land
and buildings the British had possessed at Nootka in 1789,
and this problem was to be examined and debated by Vancouver and Quadra and their respective governments in the
years to come. Among the subjects which they had to consider was Meares' claim to have bought land from the natives at Nootka and at another place farther to the south.

[CHAPTER NINE]
Retrospect

1. Matthew Arnold, *Dover Beach*. Spain ceded Louisiana in
1800 to France, who sold it to the U.S.A. in 1803; Florida was
ceded to the U.S.A. in 1819; Mexico and most of South America were lost as a result of native rebellions between 1810

and 1825; Cuba, the Philippines, and Puerto Rico were lost as a result of the Spanish-American war of 1898.

2. Liquor played an important part in this process. The first ship to use it as a regular article of trade was probably the French ship *La Flavie*, on the northwest coast in 1792/93. The American Robert Haswell says of the French ship, "Their next port was Nootka Sound, where they sold a considerable quantity of spirituous liquors and clothing for sea-otter skins" (Haswell's log, Howay, *Voyages of the Columbia*, p. 347). By 1800 it was in general use – the ship *Boston*, for example, carried 2,000 gallons of rum in 1803. See F.W. Howay, "The introduction of intoxicating liquors amongst the Indians of the northwest coast," *B.C. Historical Quarterly*, July 1942.

We should note, however, that the zenith of Indian art still lay ahead, and that its late flowering was doubtless aided by new tools acquired from the fur-traders.

Chronology

1492	Columbus reaches the new world.
1497	John Cabot explores the mouth of the St. Lawrence.
1498	Vasco Da Gama rounds the Cape of Good Hope and goes on to India.
1519	Cortez in Mexico. Magellan sets out with five ships to circumnavigate the world.
1522	The *Victoria*, sole survivor of Magellan expedition, becomes first ship to circumnavigate the world.
1534	Jacques Cartier explores the Bay of Chaleur.
1540	Spanish explorers see the Grand Canyon.
1579	Drake lands briefly in California.
1608	Samuel de Champlain founds Quebec.
1620	Pilgrim Fathers settle in Massachusetts.
1639	Russians reach the Pacific at Okhotsk.
1682	La Salle descends the Mississippi.
1725	First expedition under Bering.
1733	Second expedition under Bering sets out.
1741	Bering and Chirikof reach North America; death of Bering.
1771	Samuel Hearne reaches the Arctic Ocean along the Coppermine River.
1774	The *Santiago* (Juan Perez) reaches the Queen Charlottes from San Blas, later anchors near Nootka.

1775   Second Spanish expedition to the northwest coast.

The *Santiago* under Juan Perez and *Sonora* under Quadra land and take possession in Pacific northwest.

Sonora later reaches Alaskan waters.

1776   Spanish found settlement at San Francisco.

Publication of Adam Smith's *Wealth of Nations*; foreshadows era of free enterprise.

1778   The *Resolution* (James Cook) and *Discovery* (Charles Clerke) at Nootka in March and April. They later search for Northwest Passage in Alaskan waters.

1779   Death of Cook at Hawaii February 14.

Third Spanish expedition to the northwest coast; Arteaga and Quadra in Prince William Sound; they take possession at two locations.

1780   *Resolution* and *Discovery* return to British waters.

1784   Official publication of Cook's third voyage.

Russians found first settlement in the new world at Kodiak Island.

1785   James Hanna reaches Nootka in the *Sea Otter*.

1786   Hanna's second voyage.

James Strange reaches Nootka with the *Captain Cook* (Henry Laurie) and *Experiment* (John Guise).

John Mackay left at Nootka. The ships explore Prince William Sound and go on to the far east.

Sea Otter (William Tipping) and *Nootka* (John Meares) arrive on the northwest coast from India.

King George (Nathaniel Portlock) and *Queen Charlotte* (George Dixon) arrive on the northwest coast from the British isles.

La Pérouse on the northern coast in *l'Astrolabe* and *La Boussole*.

1787   Portlock and Dixon rescue Meares in Prince William Sound, later go on to the far east.

Captain Charles Barkley reaches Nootka in the *Imperial*

Eagle; John Mackay comes on board. Later Barkley discovers the Strait of Juan de Fuca.

Washington and *Columbia* leave Boston in the fall for Nootka via Cape Horn.

Prince of Wales (James Colnett) and *Princess Royal* (Charles Duncan) arrive at Nootka from the British isles.

1788   The *Felice* (John Meares) and *Iphigenia* (Captain Douglas) arrive at Nootka from the far east in May. Meares erects a building at Friendly Cove. Robert Duffin, a subordinate of Meares, enters the Strait of Juan de Fuca.

Launching of the *North West America* at Nootka in September. *Felice, Iphigenia* and *North West America* leave for Hawaii at the end of the season.

Washington (Robert Gray) and *Columbia* (John Kendrick) arrive at Nootka, later winter on the northwest coast.

Princesa (Esteban Martinez) and *San Carlos* (Lopez de Haro) sail from San Blas to Prince William Sound; they visit a Russian settlement on Kodiak island and take possession for Spain at two places in Alaskan waters.

Prince of Wales and *Princess Royal* leave for China at the end of the season.

1789   *Princesa* (Martinez) and *San Carlos* (Lopez de Haro) leave San Blas in February to take possession of Nootka.

Washington (Gray) explores the entrance to the Strait of Juan de Fuca in March; the *Columbia* (Kendrick) remains at Nootka.

Iphigenia (Douglas) and *North West America* arrive at Nootka from Hawaii in April.

Princess Royal (Thomas Hudson) and *Argonaut* (James Colnett) leave China for Nootka.

Princesa and *San Carlos* arrive at Nootka in May.

The Spanish construct Fort San Miguel. *Iphigenia* seized by Martinez, later released.

North West America returns to Nootka from trading cruise in June and is seized by Martinez, who renames her *Santa Gertrudis la Magna*.

1789 Gray and Kendrick exchange commands; Gray takes *Columbia* on to the far east, followed later by Kendrick in the *Washington.*

Martinez takes formal possession of Nootka in June.

Princess Royal (Hudson) arrives at Nootka in June, is later escorted out of port by the Spanish.

Argonaut (Colnett) arrives at Nootka from the far east in July, with orders to found a permanent British trading post. Is arrested by Martinez and his ship seized.

Princess Royal returns to Nootka; is seized by Martinez and sent to Mexico in charge of Narvaez, with Captain Hudson and his men on board as prisoners.

Colnett leaves for Mexico as a prisoner on board the *Argonaut,* now under Spanish officers.

San Carlos also goes south.

Aranzazu arrives at Nootka with orders for a Spanish withdrawal from the area.

Outbreak of the French Revolution on July 14.

Fair American enters Nootka under Thomas Metcalfe in October, is seized by Martinez.

Martinez launches *Santa Gertrudis.*

Martinez leaves for San Blas in *Princesa,* accompanied by *Santa Gertrudis* and *Fair American.*

Spanish fort at Nootka abandoned.

The *Columbia* reaches Canton late in the year.

1790 *Washington* arrives in the far east in January.

Fair American released early in the year by the Spanish, sails for Hawaii.

Word of capture of British ships reaches London; beginning of diplomatic quarrel with Spain.

Massacre of natives by *Eleanora* (Simon Metcalfe) at Hawaii in February. Attack on *Fair American* by natives of Hawaii; death of Captain Thomas Metcalfe.

Martinez leaves San Blas in February with *Concepcion, San*

Carlos and captured *Princess Royal*, now renamed *Princesa Real*.

In April, Martinez re-occupies and fortifies Nootka with Catalonian Volunteers under Pedro Alberni.

In May, Fidalgo begins exploration of Alaskan waters in *San Carlos*.

In June, Manuel Quimper explores the Strait of Juan de Fuca in the *Princesa Real*; takes possession at Sooke, Royal Roads, Neah Bay and New Dungeness; returns to San Blas in November.

In July, Colnett and his ship released by the Spanish; he leaves San Blas with Hudson for Nootka in the *Argonaut*. Later he trades on the northwest coast and then goes on to the far east.

In August, the *Columbia* reaches Boston; leaves again for Nootka in September.

In October, First Nootka Convention signed by Spain and Britain; Spain agrees to return captured ships and restore some land at Nootka to British sovereignty.

Bibliography

BOOKS

ABBOTT, W.C. *The Expansion of Europe*. London, 1919.

ARCHER, I.H., trans. *Noticias de Nutka*. Toronto: McClelland and Stewart, 1970.

ASHE, GEOFFREY, et al. *The Quest for America*. New York and London: Praeger Publishers, 1971.

AYYAR, A.V. *An Adventurous Madras Civilian, James Strange*. Calcutta, 1929.

BANCROFT, H.H. *History of the Northwest Coast 1543-1800*. 2 vols. San Francisco, 1890.

———— *History of California 1542-1800*, Vol. I. San Francisco, 1884.

———— *History of Alaska 1730-1885*. San Francisco, 1886.

BAKER, J.N. *A History of Geographical Discovery and Exploration*. London, 1937.

BEAGLEHOLE, J.C. *The Voyage of the Resolution and Discovery 1776-1780*. 2 vols. Cambridge, 1967.

BOLTON, H.E. *Fray Juan Crespi, Missionary Explorer*. Berkeley: U. of California Press, 1927.

BREBNER, J.B. *The Explorers of North America*. New York, 1933.

BURNEY, JAMES. *A Chronological History of Northeastern Voyages of Discovery*. London, 1819.

CARROLL, J.A. (ed.) *Reflections of Western Historians*. Tucson: U. of Arizona Press, 1969.

CAUGHEY, J.W. *History of the Pacific Coast*. Los Angeles, 1933.

CHAPMAN, C.E. *The Founding of Spanish California*. New York: Macmillan, 1916.

CHEVIGNY, HECTOR. *Russian America: The Great Alaskan Venture 1741-1867*. New York: Viking Press, 1965.

COLNETT, JAMES. *A Voyage to the South Atlantic*. London, 1798.

COOK, JAMES and KING, JAMES. *A Voyage to the Pacific Ocean*. 3 vols. London, 1784.

COOK, WARREN L. *Flood Tide of Empire*. Yale University Press, 1973.

CORNEY, B.G. *The Quest and Occupation of Tahiti by Emissaries of Spain during the Years 1772-1776*. London: The Hakluyt Society, 1913.

COXE, WILLIAM. *Account of the Russian Discoveries between Asia and America*. London 1780. 3rd ed.; facsimile reprint, New York: Argonaut Press, 1966.

CRONE, G.R. and KENDALL, ALAN. *The Voyages of Discovery*. New York: G.P. Putnam, 1970.

CUTTER, D.C. (ed.) *The California Coast: Documents from the Sutro Collection*. Norman: U. of Oklahoma Press, 1969.

DIXON, GEORGE. *Remarks on the Voyages of John Meares, Esq*. London, 1790.

———— *A Voyage Round the World*. London, 1789.

———— *Further Remarks on the Voyages of John Meares, Esq*. London, 1791.

FERRIS, R.G. (ed.) *The American West: an Appraisal*. Santa Fe: Museum of New Mexico Press, 1963.

GALVIN, J. (ed.) *A Journal of Explorations along the Coast from Monterey in the Year 1775*. San Francisco: John Howell Books, 1964.

GOLDER, F.A. *Russian Expansion on the Pacific 1641-1850*. Cleveland: Arthur Clark Company, 1914.

———— *Bering's Voyages*. 2 vols. New York: American Geographical Society, 1922 and 1925.

GREENHOW, ROBERT. *The History of Oregon and California*. Boston, 1844.

GREY, IAN. *The Romanovs: the Rise and Fall of a Dynasty*. New York: Doubleday, 1970.

HILL-TOUT, C. *British North America: the Far West, the Home of the Salish and Dene.* London, 1907.

HOWAY, F.W. *The Dixon-Meares Controversy.* Toronto, 1929.

—— ed. *The Journal of Captain James Colnett.* Toronto: The Champlain Society, 1940.

—— ed. *Voyages of the Columbia to the Northwest Coast 1787-1790 and 1790-1793.* Massachusetts Historical Society, 1941.

HULLEY, C.C. *Alaska Past and Present.* 3rd ed. Portland, 1970.

JARVES, J.J. *History of the Hawaiian Islands.* Honolulu, 1872.

JOHANSEN, D. and GATES, C.M. *Empire of the Columbia: a History of the Pacific Northwest.* New York: Harper, 1957.

LA PÉROUSE, J.F. *A Voyage Round the World, performed in the years 1786, 1787 and 1788.* 3 vols. London, 1807.

LAVENDER, DAVID. *Land of Giants: the Drive to the Pacific Northwest: 1750-1950.* New York: Doubleday, 1958.

LEDYARD, JOHN. *A Journal of Captain Cook's Last Voyage.* Hartford, Conn., 1783; reprint, Chicago: Quadrangle Books, 1963.

MARSHALL, J.S. and C. *Vancouver's Voyage.* Vancouver: Mitchell Press, 1967.

MASTERSON, J.R. and BROWER, HELEN. *Bering's Successors 1745-1780* San Francisco, 1968.

MATHES, W.M. *Vizcaino and Spanish Expansion in the Pacific Ocean 1580-1630.* San Francisco, 1968.

MATTHEWS, J.S., *Conversations with Khahtsahlano.* Vancouver, 1955.

MAYNE, R.C. *Four Years in British Columbia and Vancouver Island.* London, 1862.

MEARES, JOHN. *Voyages Made in the Years 1788 and 1789 from China to the N.W. Coast of America.* London, 1790.

MORISON, S.E. *The Maritime History of Massachusetts 1783-1860.* Boston, 1921.

MORTON, A.S. *A History of the Canadian West.* Nelson, n.d.

MOZIÑO, J.M. *Noticias de Nutka.* trans. I.H. Wilson. Toronto: McClelland and Stewart, 1970.

MURE, LOUISA. *Recollections of By-gone Days.* Privately printed, 1883.

NEWCOMBE, C.F. *The First Circumnavigation of Vancouver Island.* B.C. Archives Memoir No. 1, Victoria, 1914.

—— ed. *Menzies' Journal of Vancouver's Voyage.* B.C. Archives Memoir No. 5, Victoria, 1923.

ODLE, FRANCIS. *The Picture Story of World Exploration.* London: World Distributors, 1966.

OGDEN, ADELE. *The California Sea-otter Trade 1784-1848.* Berkeley, 1941.

OLESON, TRYGGVI. *Early Voyages and Northern Approaches 1000-1632.* Toronto: McClelland and Stewart, 1963.

ORMSBY, MARGARET. *British Columbia: A History.* Macmillan, 1958.

OUTHWAITE, LEONARD. *Unrolling the Map.* rev. ed. New York: Reynal and Hitchcock, 1938.

PARRY, J.H. *The Age of Reconnaissance.* London: Liedenfeld and Nicolson, 1963.

PORTLOCK, NATHANIEL. *A Voyage Round the World.* London, 1789.

RICKMAN, JOHN. *Journal of Captain Cook's Last Voyage to the Pacific Ocean.* London, 1781.

RIENITS, REX and THEA. *The Voyages of Captain Cook.* London and New York: Paul Hamlyn, 1968.

RYDELL, R.A. *Cape Horn to the Pacific.* U. of California Press, 1952.

SAUER, MARTIN (ed.) *An Account of a Geographical and Astronomical Expedition to the Northern Parts of Russia.* London, 1802.

SCHOLEFIELD, E. and HOWAY, F.W. *British Columbia from the Earliest Times to the Present.* 4 vols. Vancouver, 1914.

STRANGE, JAMES. *Journal and Narrative of the Commercial Expedition from Bombay to the Northwest Coast of America.* Madras: Government Record Office, 1928.

SYME, RONALD and FORMAN, WARNER. *The Travels of Captain Cook.* New York and Toronto McGraw Hill, 1971.

THURMAN, M.E. *The Naval Department of San Blas*. Glendale, Calif: A.H. Clark Co., 1967.

VANCOUVER, G. *A Voyage of Discovery to the North Pacific Ocean*. 3 vols. London, 1798.

VILLIERS, ALAN. *Captain Cook*. London: Hodder and Stoughton, 1967.

WAGNER, H.R. *Spanish Voyages to the Northwest Coast of America in the Sixteenth Century*. San Francisco: California Historical Society, 1929.

────── *Spanish Explorations in the Strait of Juan de Fuca*. Santa Ana, Calif: Fine Arts Press, 1933.

────── *The Cartography of the Northwest Coast of America to the Year 1800*. 2 vols. Berkeley: U. of California Press, 1937.

WALBRAN, J.T. *British Columbia Coast Names, 1592-1906*. Ottawa, 1909.

ZWEIG, STEFAN. *Conqueror of the Seas: the Story of Magellan*. New York: Viking Press, 1938.

ARTICLES

ARCHER, C.I. "The transient presence; a re-appraisal of Spanish attitudes toward the northwest coast in the eighteenth century." *B.C. Studies*, summer 1973.

BRADLEY, H.W. "The Hawaiian Islands and the Pacific fur trade 1785-1813." *Pacific Northwest Quarterly*, July 1939.

CUTTER, DONALD C. "California, training ground for Spanish naval heroes." *California Historical Society Quarterly*, June 1961.

────── "Spanish scientific exploration along the Pacific coast." *The American west–an appraisal*. Santa Fe: Museum of New Mexico Press, 1963.

BENNETT, G.V. "Early relations of the Sandwich Islands to the old Oregon territory." *Washington Historical Quarterly*, April 1913.

GOLDER, FRANK. "A survey of Alaska 1743-1799." *Washington Historical Quarterly*, April 1913.

HOSIE, JOHN. "James Charles Stuart Strange and his expedition to the northwest coast of America in 1786." *B.C. Historical Association, 4th annual report*, 1929.

HOWAY, F.W. "Early relations between the Hawaiian Islands and the northwest coast." *The Hawaiian Islands*. Honolulu, 1930.

────── "Captain Colnett and the Princess Royal." *Oregon Historical Quarterly*, March 1925.

────── "John Kendrick and his sons." *Oregon Historical Quarterly*, Dec. 1922.

────── "Captain Simon Metcalfe and the brig Eleanora." *Washington Historical Quarterly*, April, 1925.

────── "The introduction of intoxicating liquors amongst the Indians of the northwest coast." *B.C. Historical Quarterly*, July 1942.

────── "Captains Gray and Kendrick: the Barrell letters." *Washington Historical Quarterly*, Oct. 1921.

KUYKENDALL, R.S. "James Colnett and the Princess Royal." *Oregon Historical Quarterly*, March 1924.

LAMB, W.K. "The mystery of Mrs. Barkley's diary." *B.C. Historical Quarterly*, Jan. 1942.

LONGSTAFF, F.V. "Spanish naval bases and ports on the Pacific coast of Mexico 1513-1833." *B.C. Historical Quarterly*, July 1952.

MANNING, W.R. "The Nootka Sound controversy." *Annual report of the American Historical Association for 1904*. Washington, 1905.

MILLS, LENNOX. "The real significance of the Nootka Sound incident." *Canadian Historical Review*, June 1925.

OGDEN, ADELE. "The Californias in Spain's Pacific otter trade 1775-1795." *Pacific Historical Review*, 1932.

SERVIN, M.P. (trans.) "The instructions of Viceroy Bucareli to Ensign Juan Perez." *Calif. Historical Society Quarterly*, Sept. 1961.

STEWART, C.L. "Why the Spaniards temporarily abandoned Nootka Sound in 1789." *Canadian Historical Review*, June 1936.

THURMAN, M.E. "Juan Bodega y Quadra and the Spanish retreat from Nootka 1790-1794." *Reflections of Western Historians.* Tucson: U. of Arizona Press, 1969.

TOMPKINS, S.R. and MOORHEAD, M.L. "Russia's approach to America." *B.C. Historical Quarterly*, April and July 1949.

VER STEEG, C.L. "Financing and outfitting the first United States ship to China." *Pacific Historical Review*, Feb. 1953.

WAGNER, H.R. "The creation of rights of sovereignty through symbolic acts." *Pacific Historical Review*, Dec. 1938.

WALBRAN, J.T. "The cruise of the Imperial Eagle." Victoria *Colonist*, March 3, 1901.

WILSON, IRIS. "Spanish scientists in the Pacific Northwest 1790-1792." *Reflections of Western Historians.* Ed. J.A. Carroll. Tucson: U. of Arizona Press, 1969.

THESES

BARTRIOLI, TOMAS. "The Spanish establishment at Nootka Sound 1789-1792." M.A. thesis. U.B.C., 1960.

ELLIOTT, C.R. "Empire and enterprise in the North Pacific. 1785-1825." PhD thesis. U. of Toronto, 1957.

JONES, OAKAH. "The Spanish occupation of Nootka Sound 1790-1795." M.A. thesis. U. of Oklahoma, 1960.

LITTLE, MARGARET. "Early days of the maritime fur trade." M.A. thesis. U.B.C., 1934.

UNPUBLISHED MANUSCRIPTS

BARKLEY, C.W. A journal of the proceedings on board the Loudoun.

BARKLEY, MRS. FRANCES. Reminiscences.

BODEGA Y QUADRA, J.F. Expeditions in the years 1775 and 1779 toward the west coast of North America. Translation in Provincial Archives, Victoria.

HANNA, JAMES. Journal of a voyage from Macao toward King George's Sound in the Sea Otter (1785).

MARTINEZ, E. Diary, 1789. Translation in Provincial Archives.

PHELPS, WILLIAM DANE. Solid Men of Boston. Transcript in Provincial Archives. (Original in Academy of Pacific Coast History, U. of California.)

PERIODICALS

British Columbia Historical Quarterly
B.C. Studies
California Historical Society Quarterly
Journal of the West
National Geographic
Oregon Historical Quarterly
Pacific Historical Review
Pacific Northwest Quarterly
Transactions of the Royal Society of Canada
Washington Historical Quarterly

INDEX

BOOKS BY DEREK PETHICK

British Columbia Recalled
James Douglas: Servant of Two Empires
Men of British Columbia
SS Beaver: The Ship That Saved the West
Vancouver Recalled
Victoria: The Fort